VAT

A WAY OUT OF THE INDIAN TAX

MUDDLE

VAT

A WAY OUT OF THE INDIAN TAX MUDDLE

(Problems and Prospects of Adopting Value Added Tax)

**Foreword by Jaswant Singh,
Former Finance Minister of India**

Revised Edition With FAQs

Dr. G.K. Pillai

JAICO PUBLISHING HOUSE

Mumbai • Delhi • Bangalore • Kolkata
Hyderabad • Chennai • Ahmedabad • Bhopal

Published by Jaico Publishing House
121 Mahatma Gandhi Road
Mumbai - 400 023
jaicopub@vsnl.com
www.jaicobooks.com

© G.K. Pillai

VAT – A Way Out of The Indian Tax Muddle
ISBN 81-7992-160-3

First Jaico Impression: 2003
Second Edition (Revised & Updated): 2004

Printed by
Rashmi Printers
31, New Islam Mills Compound
Currey Road (E), Mumbai-400 012.
E-mail: tiwarijp@vsnl.net

CONTENTS

		Page
LIST OF TABLES		vii
LIST OF FIGURES		ix
LIST OF ANNEXURES		x
LIST OF ABBREVIATIONS		xi
FOREWORD		xiii
INTRODUCTION		xv
PROLOGUE		xxiii

Chapter

I	Vision 2100	1
II	Taxman's Horrorscope	9
III	What is so great about VAT?	17
IV	Indian Tax Imbroglio	31
V	Kelkar's Quantum Jump And Quiet Fall	53
VI	Why the world is on a VAT mode?	69
VII	The Indian forerunners	79
VIII	In the Wonderland of VAT	87
IX	Ideal VAT for India	98
	Conclusions	117

SELECTED BIBLIOGRAPHY		228
EPILOGUE		241
INDEX		251

Other books by the same author

1. An In-Depth Study of Central Excise Duties in India
2. Value Added Tax – A Model for Indian Tax Reforms
3. Mystic Awareness for the Modern Mind

List of Tables

Table	Description	Page
I	TAX- GDP RATIO	32
II	SHARE OF MODVAT CREDIT IN GROSS EXCISE REVENUE	85
III	A DECADE OF PROGRESS IN CENTRAL EXCISE REFORMS	206
IV	CHANGES IN RATES OF EXCISE DUTIES	213
V	CHANGES IN RULES OF VALUATION	214
VI	TRANSITION FROM MODVAT TO CENVAT	215
VII	CENTRAL EXCISE REVENUE FROM TOP 20 COMMODITIES	217
VIII	COMMODITIES GIVING EXCISE REVENUE OF MORE THAN Rs. 500 CRORES BUT LESS THAN Rs. 1000 CRORES	218
IX	CUSTOMS REVENUE FROM MAJOR ITEMS OF IMPORT	219
X	TOP TEN CUSTOMS COMMISSIONERATES	220
XI	COMMODITIES GIVING CUSTOMS REVENUE OF Rs. 1000 CRORES AND MORE	221
XII	GROWTH OF PERSONAL INCOME TAX BASE	222
XIII	COST OF COLLECTION OF CUSTOMS & CENTRAL EXCISE REVENUE	223
XIV	INDIA'S EXPORT OF PRINCIPAL COMMODITIES	224

XV   INCOME TAX RATE FOR UPPER MIDDLE
CLASS IN SOME ASIAN COUNTRIES   225
(INCOME AT RS.5 LAKHS PER ANNUM)

XVI   ESTIMATED EXCISE EVASION DURING
PAST 10 YEARS   226

XVII   SERVICE TAX: REVENUE & NUMBER OF
ASSESSEES   227

List of Figures

Sr No	Description	Page
1.	MODVAT CREDIT UTILIZED AS % OF GROSS REVENUE	86
2.	AN IDEAL MODEL FOR INDIRECT TAX SYSTEM	111
3.	A VAT AUDIT MODEL	113
4.	MODEL TAX STRUCTURE FOR INDIA	125
5.	VAT WORKING MODEL	204
6.	GROWTH OF CENTRAL EXCISE REVENUE	205
7.	GROWTH OF CUSTOMS REVENUE	206

List of Annexures

Annexure	Description	Page
I	THE CONSTITUTION OF INDIA : Articles relevant to taxation	127
II	INDIRECT TAXES LEVIABLE BY CENTRAL GOVERNMENT AND STATE GOVERNMENTS	133
III	EXPANSION OF EXCISE TAX BASE : A Chronological Presentation	136
IV	EXTRACTS FROM THE RECOMMENDA-TIONS OF TAX REFORMS COMMITTEE, 1992	145
V	EXTRACTS FROM THE REPORT OF THE CENTRAL EXCISE (SELF REMOVAL PROCEDURE) REVIEW COMMITTEE, 1973	157
VI	EXTRACTS FROM THE REPORT OF THE INDIRECT TAXATION ENQUIRY COMMITTEE, 1977	164
VII	EXTRACTS FROM THE REPORT OF THE TECHNICAL STUDY GROUP ON CENTRAL EXCISE TARIFF, 1985	175
VIII	REQUIREMENTS OF VAT COMPUTER SYSTEM	188
IX	SERVICE TAX BASE — A CHRONOLOGICAL OVERVIEW	192
X	EXTRACTS OF THE BUDGET SPEECHES (2003-04 AND 2004-05) RELATED TO TAX REFORMS SUGGESTED BY KTF	197

List of Abbreviations

AG	—	Accountant General
AED	—	Additional Excise Duty
BED	—	Basic Excise Duty
CVD	—	Countervailing Duty
CST	—	Central Sales Tax
CBEC	—	Central Board of Excise & Customs
CENVAT	—	Central Value Added Tax
EEC	—	European Economic Community
EU	—	European Union
EDI	—	Electronic Data Interchange
EOU	—	Export Oriented Unit
EPZ	—	Export Processing Zone
EXIM	—	Export-Import
FDI	—	Foreign Direct Investment
GDP	—	Gross Domestic Product
GST	—	General Sales Tax
GNP	—	Gross National Product
ITA	—	Information Technology Act
IPR	—	Intellectual Property Rights
KTF	—	Kelkar Task Force
MRP	—	Maximum Retail Price
MODVAT	—	Modified Value Added Tax
PSU	—	Public Sector Undertaking
PAN	—	Permanent Account Number
PLA	—	Personal Ledger Account
RBI	—	Reserve Bank of India
SRP	—	Self Removal Procedure

SSI	— Small Scale Industry
SED	— Special Excise Duty
TIN	— Tax Information Network
TDS	— Tax Deducted at Source
TBS	— Trust Based System
UN	— United Nations
VAT	— Value Added Tax
WTO	— World Trade Organisation

वित्त मंत्री
भारत
FINANCE MINISTER
INDIA

= 9 JUN 2003

FOREWORD

Dr. Pillai's book on VAT first published in 1994, was a path breaking endeavour suggesting a comprehensive model for Indian Tax reforms. It was rightly acclaimed as an excellent introduction to VAT.

In his new book on VAT, he now presents all its attractive features and gives convincing answers to a number of questions that currently agitate the general public. He has explained in detail why VAT is an effective tax instrument in 120 countries.

For the uninitiated, this book presents a wealth of information about VAT and its positive global impact. It describes the experiences of different countries in the initial stages of introduction of VAT. It enables us to face the challenges of implementation of VAT at the state level. Similarly, the Indian experience of adoption of VAT at central level presents a useful model for the states to emulate.

I am sure that this book will be a valuable addition to our tax literature. It will stimulate public debate on VAT and create an awareness that implementation of VAT is a consequence of economic progress. The transparency and neutrality of VAT can definitely give our economy a much needed push to achieve higher growth rate and mobilize additional revenue without tampering with rate structure. Not all the suggestions in this book are practical in the current political scenario, but they are definitely thought provoking. I am happy to see an authoritative work on VAT.

(Jaswant Singh)

INTRODUCTION

Anybody who is not shocked by this subject has failed to understand it.

[Niels Bohr]

In my book entitled "Value Added Tax — A Model for Indian Tax Reform", VAT was acclaimed as the finest fiscal instrument created in the post-war period. That book was published in 1994. Even today, I hold on to my opinion, as nothing better has emerged in the interregnum. Nor is there any immediate prospect of finding a more advanced system that can cure at a stroke many of the tax-induced distortions in the economy.

Even in the 21st century, we are only contemplating permutations and combinations of a comprehensive VAT acceptable to all claimants of tax proceeds. About 120 countries in the world comprising of 80 per cent of human population are enjoying the benefits of VAT regime. But in India, many hurdles delay the implementation of a national VAT although a hardening of attitudes in favour of VAT is very much perceptible. It is definitely a welcome development in the right direction.

Many states have already passed Bills to adopt VAT in their tax regimes. But the target set for the national switch over by April and June 2003 could not be achieved as many states did not complete the formalities required for the historic transition. This is the fourth time that the mutually agreed deadline could not be met by the wavering states. Of course, VAT should have been in our tax system some time in the early fifties. We are always late for the dinner. Nevertheless, let us be thankful that at last we have reached the most critical threshold of indirect tax reforms.

The Central Govt. has recently appointed a Task Force headed by Dr. Kelkar (KTF) for yet another in-depth examination of our ailing tax system. The stated objective was to give a "big push" to systemic changes that can hopefully improve taxpayer's confidence and deploy the advantages of information technology in tax administration. KTF wanted to find long-term sustainable solutions to enhance transparency, to reduce transaction costs, and to promote economic growth with better compliance. The net effect of the exercise was expected to bring about a substantial increase in the tax-GDP ratio and stimulate growth.

In the realm of direct taxes, KTF was asked to suggest measures for rationalization and simplification of tax structure by removing anomalies and improving efficiency. Other objective was to impart transparency and better voluntary compliance by offering world-class customer services. The Task Force was also told to redesign procedures for strengthening enforcement of direct tax laws. They were asked to examine how in the recent past, many successful economies increased their tax revenue to GDP ratio by simplifying the tax structure, widening the tax base and improving the quality of tax administration. They were also told to suggest progressive structural changes for facilitating faster economic growth.

I mentioned the mandate of the latest Task Force for fiscal reforms to highlight the grave concern of the Government and taxpayers about the deteriorating standards of our tax regime. It is a foregone conclusion that taxes, whether direct or indirect, has been a fertile breeding ground for corruption and economic inefficiencies. At different levels, we have inducted immense structural complexities and undesirable controls presumably for mopping up revenue for meeting the ever increasing demands of the exchequer. It is an undisputed fact that the cumulative impact of defective tax policies and practices since independence adversely affected both economic growth and tax to GDP ratio. Maybe, the alarm bells of diminishing revenue and huge fiscal deficits finally woke up the policy makers in the North Block. They would have felt the acute need for some immediate action. And as usual, no one dares to change status quo without the authority of recommendation from a committee or task force.

I fully agree with the popular resentment against the decadent tax regime. But tax system is just one spoke in the big wheel of a multi-faceted economy. It is unreasonable to put all blames on the taxman. In this context, it is relevant to recall some reliable forecasts about the implosive future of Indian economy. Very disturbing forebodings are given in a recent report prepared by the Mumbai-based Strategic Foresight Group headed by Sandeep Waslekar. They concluded that if we persisted with the present policies, the economy would simply collapse in about ten years. The report gives reasonable estimates of demand and supply constraints created by unfavourable socio-economic factors. They found that only one percent of the billion population actually benefited from globalization. The positive impact of the opening up of the economy has not yet reached the common man.

You may say that such doomsday predictions have been heard in the past from different disgruntled interests. Still the economy survived several global calamities like the Gulf war and oil price boom. But I take the report seriously as it has analyzed huge database with a macro perspective. It calls for 9 per cent GDP growth rate to avoid the eventuality of a total breakdown. The institutions in our country are in no way equipped to meet the challenges that are likely to face us in the near future. The increasing unemployment and the spiraling domestic demand for food grains and various goods and services cannot be met by any moderate growth.

We have to introduce revolutionary changes in the economic and social policies and practices that can thoroughly overhaul the existing archaic institutions. Administration will have to control corruption and increase efficiency through automation to facilitate growth. The report also outlines the urgent need for several important policy changes like speedy resolution of social conflicts, improving relations with neighboring countries and so on. Authorities in power are not likely to accept such sweeping suggestions for policy changes particularly in the current socio-economic milieu. They may not worry about the future scenario, which will follow only after at least two more general elections.

I briefly mentioned about Sandeep Waslekar's report to underline the enormity of the task involved in averting an unpleasant future. The conventional palliatives can no longer correct the accelerating all-round deterioration. The present model of development is highly skewed in favour of a few fortunate ones in the billion population. It is evident that if we persist with the current policies and practices, the apocalypse will be sooner than expected.

In this book, I am not examining any aspect of the economy other than the tax system. I know that revolutionary changes in the tax system alone cannot give us a sustainable GDP growth of the magnitude of 9 per cent. At best, a good tax system can achieve the targeted revenue without affecting the natural growth of economic activities. We all agree that direct and indirect taxes place severe constraints on economic growth. I need not reiterate the obvious, just take a look at the number of committees created since independence exclusively for prescribing a panacea for the same illness. But the patient is still sick and sinking and the entire world is aware of his state of health.

Such assertions may sound like gross exaggeration but just look at some of our recent performance indicators. In 1990, value of our exports was $ 18 billion and Chinese exports for the same period was $ 62.1 billion. In 2000, we improved it to $ 43 billion but China reached the astounding figure of $ 249 billion. Similarly, our FDI was $ 0.2 billion in 1990, which increased to $ 2.3 billion by 2000. During the same period China raised FDI from $ 3.5 billion to $ 38.4 billion. Our share of important commodities in EEC imports went down from 0.8 percent to 0.7 per cent during 1990 to 2000 but China has improved the same from 3.4 per cent to 9.2 per cent. In North American imports also, our share was stagnating at 1 per cent during the last decade, whereas China improved from 11.8 per cent to 25.3 per cent.

Our fiscal deficit gives another shock. At about 10 per cent of GDP, the combined deficit is near the peak reached in 1993-94. The total government debt now is at a cool 70 per cent of GDP that cannot be repaid in many generations. According to the latest financial indicators, the internal debts and other liabilities come to more than Rs.17 lakhs crores. About 40 per cent of non-plan revenue expenditure goes for debt servicing and subsidies eat away 17 per cent. After meeting the defense expenditure of 15 per cent, what is left is just a quarter of the gross revenue for other expenditure.

No wonder the central plan outlay and state plan assistance remains at the insignificant level of 24 per cent of total expenditure. Surprisingly our investment in future is less than the debt service liability. Out of the total spending, capital expenditure is just 16.5 per cent and 8.7 per cent of GDP goes for defense, interests and subsidies. What we heard about the future crunch cannot be ignored as a false alarm. All that these figures indicate is that our half-baked efforts to globalize the economy did not bring about any desirable levels of growth. There is absolutely no doubt that with GDP growth at 4 or 5 per cent, we cannot avert a total breakdown without a miracle.

One of the key areas where we can achieve lot of improvement in the immediate future is definitely the tax system. I admit that the endemic problems of the Indian economy particularly in the realm of tax administration are beyond the reach of the theoretical solutions evolved on the basis of western experiences. In India, we have been periodically entrusting the task of revamping tax regime to the bureaucracy and lo and behold, where do we stand? Committees after committees examined the inefficiencies of the system with the same stethoscope. The marginal reforms that they suggested for improving administration actually created more avenues for corruption and uncertainties. It is evident that the bureaucracy that has a clear stake in the status quo will never advise fundamental changes. They are too clever to forgo the divine rights.

I am not understating the need for tax reforms at this crucial juncture. We have plenty of evidences available to indicate that tax reforms can usher in unprecedented economic growth. The reforms initiated by President Reagan in the 80's by reducing the marginal income tax rates and simplifying the tax structure resulted in a perceptible improvement in economic activities. Tax induced incentives improved savings and investment and motivated better performance in all areas. With suitable changes in the monetary policy, the American economy recovered to lead other world economies in the 90's in spite of a global recession. We cannot entirely attribute economic recoveries to occasional tax cuts, but the American example is definitely thought provoking. The left may disagree, but do they have any other recipe for growth? Protecting the interests of organized labour and maintaining corpses of PSUs cannot pull us out of the doldrums. We need some fundamental change to trigger positive value addition in the economy.

In India, tax reforms have been confined mostly to cosmetic changes as the policy makers always apprehended considerable loss of revenue if any fundamental changes were attempted. From the 1990 model of marginal reforms, we find that while they substantially reduced revenue, savings and investments did not appreciate as expected. The fiscal deficit continued to rise in spite of the changes in tax rates and administrative procedures to expand the base. KTF has also been extremely careful not to deviate from the revenue neutral path. If we look back, it is evident that such cosmetic reforms have always been counterproductive. They can at best maintain the tax to GDP ratio but the growth rate will continue at the same stagnant level.

What we actually need now is to put our priorities in proper order and cut down the weeds affecting a healthy growth. The first step is to improve domestic saving and investment. To achieve this objective, there is no alternative to reducing taxes to the minimum level, whether they are direct or indirect. If the government appropriates more than 60 per cent of the value addition in the economy in the form of various taxes, there is no disposable income left for anyone to invest for growth. Even the present tax threshold does not take care of the barest subsistence requirement of a small family. Just look at the income tax rates in Singapore, Hong Kong and Taiwan, the three astounding success stories of Asia. The left should have no problem in emulating Russia, their ideological showpiece. But will they accept the flat rate of 12 per cent and let the economy grow faster?

It is distressing to note that even in the 2003-2004 budget, no positive steps were taken for rate reforms. Many of KTF's recommendations on administrative reforms had been accepted. They are timely and targeted to improve the efficiency of tax administration. But the rate structure was left untouched for fear of increasing the revenue deficit. The fact is that such half-hearted, revenue neutral reforms cannot take us out of the doldrums. We need a more daring and positive approach to tax rates. I have given a model tax structure in the conclusions and explained the pressing need for empowering the economy for better performance.

In my first book on Value Added Tax, I proposed a comprehensive VAT regime as an urgent step required for improving the efficiency of the tax system. The book was meant both for the expert and the layman. A suitable model of VAT was suggested, keeping in view the diverse and country specific constraints. The model was considered utopian, but several administrative reforms introduced in the recent past are taking us closer to that ideal. In this book, I am presenting the current scenario in our indirect tax regime and the prospects of implementing a full fledged VAT at state level to remove inefficiencies. I am also giving my views on some of the path-breaking suggestions of KTF. Once again, the basic characteristic and significant features of the pure and modified versions of VAT are reiterated to drive home its advantages over other conventional taxes.

I admit that it is extremely difficult to foretell the future of taxation. One chapter in this book exclusively deals with the challenges of E-Commerce and our state of preparedness to deal with the advent of the inevitable. The Internet is about to steal the bread and butter from many middlemen including the taxman. The E-Commerce regime will make life miserable for all of them and the consumer will enjoy the fun of making them dance to his tunes.

This book also points out certain basic rate reforms urgently required to achieve accelerated growth. The suggestions given here for tax reforms can hopefully stimulate public opinion for generating informed feedback to facilitate the smooth transition of states to the VAT regime. It has already been fully installed at the central level with the customer friendly features of CENVAT-2000. VAT will hopefully become the law of the land in all states in the very near future. The Union Cabinet has already approved a proposal to amend the constitutional provisions to allow the states to collect and appropriate the tax on certain services. Earlier, Service Tax was not included in the union list, state list or concurrent list. It is being collected by the central government using the residual powers available under Entry 97 of the Union List.

The empowered committee for enforcing VAT at the state level assumed that a complete switchover by April 2003 was an achievable target. In spite of a firm assurance of 100 per cent compensation of the probable revenue loss in the first few years of VAT operation and gradual abolition of CST, many states are still dithering without any convincing cause. Even with such hiccups, some variants of VAT will definitely prevail all over the country very soon. A fiscal Responsibility and Budget Management Bill has also received the cabinet nod for introduction in the budget session. Thankfully, a sense of fiscal responsibility has finally caught up with the managers of our economy. The heat of accountability can now melt even the red stone statues of the North Block.

In the 2004-05 budget speech, the Finance Minister has requested the states to complete the legislation work on VAT, before the end of 2004, for its introduction by April 2005. He pointed out that the experience of the state of Haryana shows that VAT would only increase the revenue, but in case of any revenue loss, suitable compensation could be considered. The Finance Minister offered the states a technical experts committee to help them move steadily towards the stage of implementation.

All views and opinions expressed in this book are my personal perceptions based on available data. They do not reflect in any manner the official point of view on such matters. I hope this book will be a useful addition to the literature on indirect taxation.

❏❏

PROLOGUE

ROAD MAPS ROLLED BACK

"Of course, money is not above God, but by God, it is not in any way less either."

[Judeo Tapes]

Is India Really Shining?

You can't miss the shimmer whether you like to see it or not. Even some of the left-wing politicians privately admit that something is shining out there. True, the glitter can be either from the metal or the fresh coat of polish applied specially for the recent elections. But whatever is the source, it shows an unprecedented upturn. Let us hope the radiance will last beyond the BPO boom.

Admittedly, after independence, we couldn't create a perfect political system to uplift the destiny of the hungry millions. Our economy has been growing leisurely by trial and error without reaching any perceptible level of prosperity even after five decades of freedom. Many early setbacks and deplorable bunglings decelerated its slow motion ascent for a decent niche in the planet. Undoubtedly, we have been learning from the numerous slip-ups to create appropriate systemic changes to achieve sustainable progress. Maybe, our belated economic reforms and the recent revamping of institutions culminated in some qualitative changes in the national scenario.

Of course, pessimists may point out the tardy rate of economic growth, undesirable levels of unemployment, increasing social tensions, and many other glaring failures in preventing calamities and bloodsheds. Some others may not like to learn from the errors of the past. They want to realise the impossible through the socialistic visions of the bygone era. It is better to let them enjoy the fantasy. The future doesn't belong to them, as Einstein puts it, "It comes soon enough".

A closer look will reveal that despite the deep social divisions, we have carefully nurtured a working democracy that empowered the common man. When we look around the neighbourhood, we find that most of them are still struggling to get out of the stranglehold of their feudal past. Our per capita income has been on the rise albeit very moderately. As Moody's admitted recently, compared to the world records, our performance may not be the best, but it is definitely above average and promising. With more than $100 billion foreign exchange in the kitty and GDP showing about 8.2% growth in the last fiscal, India is really poised to enter the elite group of developed nations.

Another promising pointer is the fact that 54% of our population is less than 25 years' old whereas the entire European Union will be slipping into post 50's very soon. Every year about two million graduates emerge from our universities and our expat population has already exceeded 25 million. In fact, the average income of the expat Indian now is about three times more than that of the resident Indian. The growth in our foreign exchange reserves is unbelievable, as we had only $1 billion in 1991, but now we are adding about $5 billion every month. The boom in the stock market has also made the investors richer by Rs.6000 million in one year.

In some sectors like the automobile industry, the growth rate is simply miraculous. We produced only 1,25,000 motor cars in 1990 whereas in the current year we are likely to export as many. As far as two wheelers are concerned, we have already become one of the biggest producers in the world. The most important fact is that every automobile produced anywhere in the world has at least one component made in India. While moving and shaking the world, India is indeed talking incessantly. The rapid rise in mobile connections is simply mind-boggling. They are likely to reach 100 million by the end of

2004. The long distance calls are now much cheaper by about 3/4th of the peak rates in past two decades.

There is a perceptible boom in the construction industry as the cost of housing finance has sharply come down from 18% to 7% in the last decade. In the field of software, we have done extremely well thanks to our early entry and linguistic advantages. By 2006, India will have about 10 software companies having more than a billion dollar turnover. Presently, our share in global software scenario is about 18%, which is likely to double in the near future.

Not only that, we will be among the top five producers of food grains, pulses, fruits, poultry, vegetable and milk. India has become a favourite destination for international tourists and the arrivals have increased by 50% in the last three months. It improved the occupancy rates of hotels from 65% in December 2002 to about 85% in 2003. With a few more healthy monsoon showers and peace on the borders and other sensitive spots, India Inc. will soon provide better quality life to its distressed citizens. We can confidently say that one more global economic power has already risen in the east.

Feel Good or Feel Dead

Some sceptics may ask, "Isn't it too early to jump with joy? Are we really shinning or is it only the reflection on a passing monsoon bubble?" The latest human development index of the UNDP places us at the unsightly127th slot although the value improved from 0.51 in 1990 to 0.59 in 2001. China has made a great upward swing in the index from 0.679 in 1995 to 0.721 in 2001.

That gives us a good measure of the prevailing quality of life in India. Then we have other national shames like a very high score of 71 in the corruption index. About 235 million people live below poverty line and almost 50% of the population suffers from illiteracy. Our share in the world trade is a measly 0.8% albeit the noise we make in WTO and other forums about free trade. We have 40 million children suffering from malnutrition. They will never become normal adults and many of them may end up as bonded labourers. The anti-globalization lobby may not probably be aware of the fact that we are only at 61st place out of 62 nations in the latest index of globalization. Another surprising fact is that only 2% of the total population in India is computer literate. Rural India is still in the strangle-hold of feudal land lords and upper castes who will resist all attempts to empower the poor and the downtrodden.

The state of the domestic economy is no better. We have again reached a combined fiscal deficit of more than 10% of GDP and we spent about 40% of the non-tax revenue for debt servicing. The huge debt burden is growing year after year despite having the highest tax incidence in the world. Every Indian is unknowingly saddled with the debt of Rs.18,138, which is the individual share in the total national burden of about Rs.19 lakhs crores. No wonder our savings and investments remain at the miserably low level of 25% of GDP.

Forget about the debt, but look at the miserable failure of the tax efforts by the Central, the States and the local governments that can mobilize only the measly revenue of 13% of GDP, whereas US, Canada, and even Brazil have tax ratios of 20%. We may not achieve the 34% level of the UK or 22% of Turkey and Australia but can we not collect a decent sum of at least 20% in tax revenue when the tax incidence of direct taxes is above 30% and that of indirect taxes is about 50%? The conclusion is inevitable that it is too early for celebration.

Super Scams

More disgraceful than some of the glaring deficiencies listed above, and the stock market and fake stamp paper rackets, are the two humiliating national shames that remain untackled. The first one is indeed the worst; just one individual holding the entire nation of one billion people to ransom. A jungle brigand has been kidnapping and killing people at will and getting away with hefty rewards for releasing hostages. Several hundred crores of rupees have been spent ostensibly to catch him. Special forces of two great states tried and failed to bring him to book and the despicable episode stands out like a sore thumb overshadowing all our achievements in other spheres. It exposes all our tall claims of good governance and reveals the abject inefficiency of all institutions concerned. Do we lack the manpower or material resources to hunt down just one sickly, old dacoit? I wonder what the real reasons are, let us not waste time on pondering over the obvious. Our place in the corruption index is an eye opener.

The second shame is much less public. Very few people are privy to it, but it has wrought immense havoc on the national economy. In fact, the huge public debt that we have amassed in the past few decades and the unbearable strain of serving it are all the indirect fall out of its extensive impact. Many people are not even aware of the immeasurable reach of its adverse effect that has spread like an incurable cancer. It is now fully official. Dr.Asim Dasgupta, the Finance Minister of West Bengal and the Chairman of the Empowered Committee of State Finance Ministers for implementing VAT in lieu of Sales Taxes, stated in his keynote addressing the CII on 17-12-03, that rampant evasion of taxes is to the tune of Rs.100,000 crores per annum.

After the usual political innuendos for the lack of support for implementing VAT, the Minister admitted that with the introduction of VAT, the great damage caused by tax evasion could be checked effectively. At least fifty percent of success rate in plugging evasion through VAT would bring in a huge bonanza to the national exchequer. He pointed out that the State of Haryana, which implemented VAT in a limited and isolated way has already started reaping the benefits. Then why not others?

It is an intriguing puzzle that defies all laws of economics and good governance. A former Chief Minister of an important State admitted while releasing the first edition of this book that the extent of Sales Tax evasion is about Rs.80,000 crores. We don't have to strain further in search of the real cause of the national allergy for VAT. The stakes being so high, the current beneficiaries are going to oppose VAT with all their money power and political clout. Who wants to kill the statutory hen that goes on laying so many golden eggs year after year? If the tax ratios are low, the government can go to the market for more borrowing. But where will they go for the bounteous income if sales tax is abolished? Since the status quo is so lucrative, very few would support the reforms that upset numerous apple carts.

Why VAT is a Must

To put it bluntly, adoption of VAT atleast now is an unavoidable consequence of even our badly delayed economic development. Of course, if we opted for VAT in the late fifties, the tax scenario would not have created such insurmountable debt impasse. We would not have been wasting precious time at this late hour lamenting about the lost opportunities to improve tax ratios and to reform tax administration. Both are at miserably low levels and if we don't wake up at least now, the debt burden will definitely break the back of the nation.

Our economic development is somewhat peculiar as compared to that of other developing nations. In the fifties, agriculture contributed to about 60% of GDP, which predictably declined to 22% now. During the same period, the share of industry rose from 15% to 27%. But the greatest surprise is the quantum jump of services that has gone up from 28% to about 50%. We simply sidestepped manufacture and entered the exalted domain of developed countries with a strong service sector.

The Chinese economy on the other hand followed a different growth track with services contributing about 33% and industry and agriculture with 51% and 16% respectively. They opted for a strong industrial base, which gave it the much-admired double digit GDP growth. However, China has not surpassed our excellent service track record. But the dominance of services also gives an unmistakable message. If we have to improve the tax ratio, the indirect tax system will have to be world class.

The central government has already accepted this axiom and adopted a full-fledged VAT at the manufacturing stage for the central excise duties. Beyond that, adopting VAT to replace the archaic sales taxes falls in the fiefdom of state governments. It is a fragmented path with lot of potholes.

Only future can tell us which route to development was better and shorter. But it is necessary to know why our service sector is on a fast track. Many people may not know that it is the much-maligned bureaucracy that is making great waves in service sector. From 93-94 onwards, public administration has grown at the rate of more than 30%. The total salary bill of the State and Central Government is presently a staggering sum of Rs.167,715 crores. A recent study has revealed that in about 7 years time, the total pension liability may exceed Rs.1,89,000 crores, which the nation will find difficult to pay. It is more than all the States' deficit and amounts to about 8% of GDP. Other notable contributions to service sector come from wholesale and retail trade (15%), Banking (6%) health, education and other community services (5.5%) transport (5.5.%) and real estate (4.5%).

Having seen the contribution of different sectors to GDP, let us find a way to mop up a fairly decent part of it as tax revenue. Agriculture being a holy cow in India, no one dares to tax it. Some inputs pay nominal taxes but about 22% of GDP from farm sector is simply untaxable. Thus we depend for revenue solely on industry, the taxman's perennial whipping horse. Its contribution to GDP is about 27% but a substantial portion of it (40%) enjoys perpetual tax holiday like agriculture. The small sector and cottage industries get hefty concessions, leaving the organized sector to bear the full burden of the Central and State Governments tax fury. No wonder while our industry limps forward like a sloth, the Chinese economy is a soaring kite. Our direct and indirect taxes at all levels bleed only the organized sector of industry giving it no space for growth.

Now let us go back to services that contribute about 51% of GDP. Some of them are now taxed lightly at 8% by the Central

Government and a few are also tapped by State Governments. The major component of services is public administration, which is taxable only at the higher levels through direct taxes. Out of the remaining services, the most significant ones are the wholesale and the retail trade (15%). They are traditionally accessed by sales tax. That is where we find the colossal evasion of about Rs.100,000 crores every year. Not only that, in different states, tax rates and practices of assessment vary widely and unreasonably. They vie with each other to offer tax holidays and deferment schemes to entice business. If we fail to close the flood gates of sales tax evasion, the tax ratio will remain stagnant and the organized industry and salary classes will go on bleeding more and more for the prosperous thieves.

Other than implementing VAT at State level, our options for tax reforms are now fully exhausted. Kelkar Committee has taken care of that. Our direct taxes are at the peak level as compared to that of neighbours and competitors. The organized industry is miserably over-taxed and we have already forfeited its growth potential for more revenue. The central VAT is working well, but the deplorable state of sales tax needs a sea change. And that change can come only with VAT which can definitely raise the tax ratio from the current 13% to a decent level of 20 or even more. Any further delay will only cause irreparable damage to the economy; the shine may not last longer than one monsoon. VAT is not only the best, it is the only choice if we want to enter the domain of developed economies.

Five Aborted Launches

Detailed road maps for implementation of VAT in lieu of sales tax were made with a great deal of consensus and fanfare. The shots for the start went out one after another, but every time the race was recalled. The story of our VAT introduction is not different from the tryst with other economic reforms. We have perfected the fine art of procrastination.

The process began with the Conference of the Finance Ministers of the states in 1998 which suggested that the central government should reduce the maximum rate of CST to 3% w.e.f.1st April, 2001 to facilitate the adoption of VAT. It is interesting to note that only four states have more than 10% share in total CST collections, which indicates very clearly that the major economic activities happen only in a few regions and the others are just consuming states. It was also suggested that the central government should compensate the state governments to the extent of 25% of the present revenue of CST at least for the first two years. The estimated amount of compensation worked out to approximately Rs.1250 crores per year. It is the stumbling block which is incompatible with VAT. With the introduction of VAT, CST will have to be zero-rated or full remission of duty should be allowed to the exporter of a commodity to other states.

The Finance Ministers' conference also suggested several enabling measures for the states to augment their revenue. On November 16, 1999 the conference of the Chief Ministers and the Finance Ministers agreed upon the floor rates of VAT to eliminate rate competition. It also brought out a reduction in the number of exempted items and arrived at a consensus to remove the plethora of sales tax incentives to industries.

There has also been a general agreement for ensuring proper documentation of inter-state sales with mandatory 'C' forms. It was also agreed that when VAT is adopted by the states, the centre should delegate the power of collecting tax on a number of localized services to the state governments. The central government will continue to tax on other services and prescribe a uniform rate for the states to collect and retain the tax. About 12 services have been identified and ear-marked for the states. The total revenue involved in the proposed transfer would be about Rs.1839 crores.

VAT is Really in Store

The basic features of the proposed VAT have been designed by the Empowered Committee after consulting all the states and the centre. They broadly envisage payment of VAT by registered dealers on the value addition of the goods when sold by them. The net tax payable by the dealer will exclude the input tax credit collected during the payment period. The payment period means the same month for VAT paid within the state on inputs/supplies for both intra-state and inter-state transactions. There is no condition that credit will be available only when the inputs are utilized or the goods are sold. The VAT liability will be self-assessed after taking permissible deductions available in that month. In case the tax credits exceed the taxes collected in a month on the sales within the state, the excess can be brought forward to the next month. Input tax credit can be carried forward till the end of the next financial year and there is also provision for refunding the excess unadjusted VAT. Tax paid on capital goods will also be eligible for credits but it will be adjusted over a maximum period of 36 equal monthly installments.

In the case of exports from the country, a provision has been made to give refund of all the taxes collected in a state immediately after the end of the financial year. For stock transfers out of the state, input tax paid in excess of 4% will be allowed, as CST at 4% collected on interstate sales is not VATable in the importing state. Adjustments of the tax incidence will be made for inter-state stock transfers but no credit will be available on the tax paid on inputs procured from other states through stock transfers or imports. In this connection, it is noteworthy that no declaration form is required for sale under VAT since there is an automatic provision for set off of input taxes. Registration will also be compulsory, only for dealers having turnover above a threshold limit, which will be decided by the state concerned. All the existing dealers of sales tax in a state will be automatically registered under the VAT Act of that state. The registration number of each dealer will be a 10 digit one for the entire country. It includes a state code, office code, specific number, Act identification code and a check digit.

Exemption from VAT will only be for a very few items which are presently not taxed. Items like petrol, diesel and ATF (aviation turbine fuel) would not be eligible for input tax credit.

All other goods including declared goods will be subject to VAT and they will be eligible for input tax credit even if they are used as fuel. The units availing deferment or remission schemes will have to pay tax on procurement of inputs and collect the tax for their sales at the usual rates. In the case of remission, it will be converted into deferment to the extent of 30% extra period and above. Deferment scheme will also apply to the firms enjoying tax holiday. Instead of deferring the sales tax liability, the VAT payment of such units will not be collected for the unexpired period subject to the ceiling of the unused portion.

Towards Unity

The greatest achievement of the empowered committee was in reaching a consensus on the VAT rates applicable uniformly all over the country. According to the proposal, only two basic rates will be there for VAT, the lower being 4% for some essential commodities, sensitive goods and basic inputs. The general VAT rate for standard goods will have a floor rate of 10%. The actual rate should not, however, exceed 12.5% although a revenue neutral rate can be fixed by a particular state. Only two exemptions are allowed on the basic rate structure. One percent rate is given for gold, silver, precious and semi-precious stones. To discourage consumption, liquor is allowed to be taxed at a higher rate starting with a floor level of 20%.

The goods that fall in the totally exempted category are natural and unprocessed products like betel leaves, earthen pots, etc. and items which are statutorily banned from taxation on sale like newspaper and national flag. Exemption is also extended to certain goods having social and cultural relevance like books, periodicals, primary education equipments, etc. The lower rate of 4% will be applicable to basic necessities like branded bread, bulk drugs, writing paper, industrial and agricultural inputs, declared goods and capital goods.

The states have also agreed to accept a common definition of capital goods. The cut off date for input tax credit has also been agreed upon and credit is uniformly allowed on purchase of all capital goods. There is also clear consensus on the fixing of threshold for VAT at Rs.5 lakhs per annum and a provision has also been made for composition of VAT for assessees having turnover upto Rs.25 lakhs per annum. The option for composition will be available on payment of a small percentage of the gross turnover. The dealers opting for composition will not be eligible for issuing tax invoices but they will be free from the documentation requirements for each transaction.

The Empowered Committee has also evolved uniform procedures for assessment. The VAT liability will be self-assessed in the returns to be filed after availing the tax credit. The forms and procedures will be kept simple and identical for all states. The assessment will be completed automatically if no notice is issued and there will be no compulsory assessment scheme at the end of the year as it is presently done in several states.

The departmental audit will check the correctness of the self-assessment and a certain percentage of the dealers will be taken up for audit on a scientific basis. It will be something like the random checking of income tax returns. Better tax compliance will invite lesser audit, but all dealers are expected to be audited at least once in 5 years. Tax evasion is likely to be less, as there is a provision for assessment of previous periods upto 5 years if any fraud is found on audit. To keep out the bias, the audit wing will be separated from the tax collection and monitoring wing. The Empowered Committee has agreed upon simultaneous restructuring and computerization of sales tax directorates in all states. The road map is clear and well laid, but it has been rolled back for reasons beyond common man's comprehension.

Why VAT is Delayed

The main objection to VAT is that it is too transparent. With full documentation of all transactions, nothing can be held back or misdeclared. Some people talk about administrative difficulties of accounting all sales and purchases. But the fact is that the truly small firms are not required to pay any VAT and the medium ones have the composition option. So it doesn't really hurt any genuine retailer or wholesaler.

VAT actually simplifies tax accounting. With fewer rates and exemptions, bookkeeping will become much easier. Some people also talk about the inflationary impact of VAT, which is far from true. If the rates are not excessive, tax cannot push up the prices. Now the rates chosen by the Empowered Committee are designed to be revenue neutral, which means VAT will have no inflationary impact.

Some left-oriented economists talk about the regressive impact of VAT but it is an incorrect view based on the presumption that all essential commodities will be taxed. As discussed earlier, many of the consumer necessities will be kept outside the purview of VAT and some are also given the low rate of 4%. But let us note that without VAT, the nation is paying a huge price. And it is evident that the beneficiaries of tax evasion are not the poor; they are the rich traders interested in sustaining poverty. The continuation of the status quo is a sure way to make them richer and keep the rest starving. If the country goes on amassing heavy public debt, the repayment burden will keep many future generations in perpetual poverty. Let us not leave such a harsh legacy to the children aspiring for a decent existence.

The announcement in the 2004-05 budget that the states will be given technical assistance and compensation for probable revenue loss in the implementation of VAT is an indication of the resolve to introduce it from 1st April, 2005.

The latest Kelkar report on fiscal responsibility also points out the immediate need to introduce an integrated VAT on goods and services, both at the central and state level. China has adopted such a modern tax system in the early 90s and any further delay in ushering in VAT would benefit only our competitors. Let us hope that an integrated VAT regime would dawn very soon.

❏❏

CHAPTER I

VISION-2100

But up there in the immensity of the cosmos, an inescapable perspective awaits us.

[Carl Sagan]

WHAT THE STARS DO NOT FORETELL

In the immediate future of a few decades, the stargazers may not find any surprising events that would change the fortunes of human kind on planet earth. Galactic tragedies like the earth eventually becoming a fireball and the upcoming collision between the Milky Way and Andromeda are still billions of years away. A repetition of Chixulub that wiped out dinosaurs may occur earlier, but it would probably not cause global extinction of life. Let us assume that in the foreseeable future of about 100 years, celestial event like an asteroid of more than 10 Km. radiuses may not fall on earth. Climatic variations may create some havoc but in all probability, taxman will survive to extract.his pound of flesh from the tremendous growth of activities in the cyber space. But his task will be an extremely different and challenging one. He may be outwitted by the masters of new technology.

Before we begin to speculate on the future of taxation, let us briefly overview the likely changes in science and technology in the next few decades. The incredible increase in computing power will shortly create advanced tools that can assist us to acquire great wealth of knowledge and new technologies. In the very near future, knowledge will become the global asset available to all, irrespective of national or linguistic barriers. Our conventional ideas about economic activities based on factors like capital and labour will be replaced by intelligent systems based on electronic data. Ultimately, knowledge will become the only relevant and genuine measure of income and wealth. Literacy will soon spread like wild fire even in the most backward regions of the world. Only rational ideas will survive the avalanche of discoveries and all the inherited ignorance of humanity will soon become historic curiosities. This is not the wish list of an incurable optimist. Cognitive events of superior kind and quality are inevitable rewards of our intense quest for more knowledge.

Another revolutionary change will be the convergence of knowledge acquired from different fields for creating an inter-disciplinary worldview. Super computers will give us the power to penetrate deeper into the mysteries of matter and life. We may even achieve the capability for re-engineering the mind. In the next few centuries', discoveries of a fundamental nature will be made in the realms of biotechnology, molecular biology, and cosmology. Many new gadgets and appliances will be created to make life much more comfortable than ever before. Here, we will confine our overview to certain technological advancements in the near future that will have a significant impact on taxation.

Residents of heaven

Before the end of this century, we are likely to succeed in planet hunting for a future migration from earth. Serious efforts are now on to find an earth-size planet with identical atmospheric conditions that can sustain life. Several satellites and space stations will be set up as launching pads for the innumerable space probes required to reach distant planets. Global co-operation will ensure that much before the expanding sun puts out life on earth forever, we will migrate to new habitable planets. When large number of people live in space stations or space colonies, it will be difficult to find taxable events or identify the taxpayers. There are possibilities of terra forming of another planet or using an asteroid as space colony. Such developments may take quite some time, but we can envisage the magnitude of the tracking problems of the taxman to reach internet trading, E-money and E-commerce. The seamless cyber space will slowly make geographical entities irrelevant for all practical purposes other than tax collection. The question is what kind of a tax can reach the ethereal abodes to collect adequate revenue for governance.

It is true that the government has sovereign powers to levy taxes on any kind of transaction whether it is physical or virtual. Since cyber transactions are going to steal the business of the future, governments cannot ignore the probable loss of tax revenue. But there are many problems in taxing E-commerce as it has no global position for the tax to reach the transaction. What kind of transactions can be taxed and which government will have the right to reach them are the most difficult legal challenges for governments. They will have to formulate universally acceptable treaties for E-taxation. The norms of taxation like neutrality, simplicity, certainty and economic efficiency can be relied on to evolve an ideal tax system for the future. Actually, E-taxation needs a very flexible and fair tax system with a mutually agreed single rate structure without exemptions. The question is will the governments accept the model E-taxation laws formulated preferably by an international agency like the United Nations? The idea of a sovereign nation will have no place in the seamless globe. The experience of the European Union can be replicated to avoid ego clashes between countries vying for the tax pie in the heaven.

Taxing the clones

Cloning, whether we agree with its ethical implications or not, has become a scientific reality. Scientists have successfully cloned animals and it is strongly rumoured that human cloning has also been attempted. The technology for cloning will undergo wonderful changes in the near future. There are several moral and legal issues related to human cloning but they will be sorted out and carbon copies of adult individuals will ultimately be found everywhere. An international law may be enacted to control indiscriminate cloning of humans and animals. Ethical considerations apart, cloning will definitely pose difficult legal problems of tax liability particularly for taxes on income and expenditure. The current laws of inheritance will be inadequate

3

to deal with the demands of the carbon copies for a part of the income and wealth of the originals. The UN may have to suggest some model legislation to tackle the problems of space residents and tax liability of clones. The more desirable option will be to abolish direct taxes and put the entire revenue burden on consumption.

Intractable sources of Energy

The imminent breakthroughs in physical sciences will give us several innovative technologies to tap clean energy resources. Known reserves of fossil fuels are likely to last only for about few decades. Solar light is the cheapest source of energy but the equipment cost for its conversion to usable forms is presently prohibitive. If silicon wafers are mass-produced shortly, we may get inexhaustible supply of solar energy. Another excellent source is seawater, which can be converted into power through controlled fusion reaction. But scientists are still struggling to overcome the problems of high temperature fusion.

The cheapest and most promising source of energy in the immediate future is fuel cells. They use hydrogen to generate power and harmless water is the only byproduct. Cost effective micro powerhouses will cater to all domestic and industrial energy needs. The proton exchange membrane cell will be available for commercial application in a few years time. Another technology called solid-oxide fuel cell is about to enter the market. An alkaline technology is also ready for commercial applications. Fuel cell powered cars have already been road-tested to sort out storage and other problems.

Before fuel cells become available for daily use, vehicles using hybrid technology and electric cars will be the common means of transportation. The tremendous impact of micro power will be felt when they replace large power plants, which presently supply all our needs. The taxman will find it difficult to reach use or source of power for collecting revenue. The products using power will become intractable when it is generated and consumed domestically. The taxman will have no idea about the

4

production and consumption of tangible goods and their sale and purchase using E-commerce and E-money.

Quantum Computing

The greatest achievement of the 21st century will be super computers of micro size. In almost two decades time, computers will become invisible as they get embedded almost everywhere. Spectacles and contact lenses may carry three-dimensional displays to create a virtual visual environment better than the real one. Blindness will be eradicated completely as electronic eyes implanted in the brain can easily replace the biological ones. Similarly, auditory gadgets for high resolution sound with three dimensional effects can be put in the ear canal or even in the jewellery.

Educational institutions will offer intensive coaching through software based robotic teachers instead of humans. Teachers can also reach several learning situations simultaneously through the state of the art audio and video equipments. Retinal and neural implants will become very common and computer controlled nerve stimulations and robotic devices will help disabled persons to function as effectively as normal humans. Tax exemptions for physically challenged persons will become the relics of the middle ages. The practice of taxing luxury consumption of audio and video products will be a part of the history of taxation.

In the field of communications, gadgets capable of high resolution three-dimensional displays projected through direct implants will replace conventional landlines and mobiles. Three-dimensional phonographic images will also be available to make users feel the physical proximity of the caller. The web, which will no more require any specific equipment support, will soon replace cable based communication systems. Business transactions will be done with simulated persons having animated personality and two-way communication equipments. They will be the personal assistants for conducting business with other automated persons. The automated office assistants will exchange appropriate knowledge structures instead of using language-based business communication. Robots using very little energy and equipped with highly developed software will perform all the household work. Computerized cars and personal flying machines will be the common household gadgets by 2100. The normal life expectancy will reach a minimum of 120 years with the use of molecular medicines and new organs grown out of stem cells.

Nano technology

Nano technology can create biological applications from the incredible developments in physical sciences. Atoms and molecules can be manipulated to create micro size molecular machines for different purposes. They will have the advantages of low cost of production and easy maintenance. Molecular machines can replicate themselves using the unlimited biological raw materials available in the environment. Robots will do all hazardous jobs that endanger human life. In medicine, molecular machines will be used to combat invading microbes and provide proper diagnosis. Even frozen bodies may be brought back to life one day by repairing or replacing the damaged cells with molecular machine.

Another innovation will be the creation of nano tubes of carbon to conduct electricity and connect parts of molecular machines. Nano tubes are hollow tubes made of carbon molecules. They are many times stronger than steel and have negligible weight. Nano technologies will totally revolutionise the computer industry. But the most formidable challenge will be the ultimate merger of machine and intelligence. The barrier between man and machine will disappear when virtual reality takes over objective reality in many real life situations. In fact, by the end of this century, intelligence will not be tied down to any particular individual or machine. It will become the freely available universal property of humanity. Software based intelligent machines will become far more efficient than neuron-based humans. The nano era will present a horrible nightmare to the taxman. He will have to search for a suitable base to tax income, consumption and service. More frightening challenge

6

will be to detect tax evasion, which may involve the use of nano technology. It will be an absorbing fight against invisible machines with incredible intelligence.

Conscious Machines

Very important developments will be seen soon in neural implants that can easily enhance our limited capacity of perception. Since neuron-based human intelligence has low memory and inferior speed of computation, it will be supplemented by implants that can reduce individual differences in intellectual abilities. Eventually, biological matter may even lose its dominance as machines gain ascendancy with quantum computing. Computers may also acquire some sort of consciousness to take over many repetitive tasks without human interventions. Already, successful attempts have been made to create machines capable of replicating conscious human functions. Initially, such machines may give only conventional responses to environmental challenges. But in course of time, we may have fully conscious machines that can take over most of the human functions and leave us free for enjoying a totally relaxed and carefree life. If the intelligent machines earn income independent of any human help, will it be liable to pay tax as a machine? It will definitely be a nerve-racking exercise for the taxman to find the taxable events and the elusive taxpayers.

If Wishes Were...

The future scenarios outlined here may look like wishful thinking when viewed from the present state of the technology. But they are not daydreams of overheated or idle brains. Nano technology and molecular medicines are in the advanced stage of development. Fuel cells are already available for application. Formal education will no longer be essential for any work as online knowledge can be accessed at any time from anywhere in the world. When knowledge becomes less expensive and more user friendly, it will create better standards of life in unimaginable ways. Steve Grand has already created "Lucy," the conscious robot capable of creating and recalling memories of learning experiences from her neural network.

The next few decades will give surprising jolts to human credibility. We have no clear idea about the possibilities of developments in cyber business. Internet does not recognize national boundaries or cultural or political barriers. We cannot even guess what kind of changes will come in bandwidths and encryption technologies. But one thing is quite certain that the free flow of information across all physical barriers will change our conventional ideas of business in commodities and services.

Presently, only about 3 per cent of the world population is capable of using the internet. But in another 20 years time probably only 3 per cent of the world population will not be online. Similarly, E-commerce has now reached only about 1 per cent of the world retail sales. I do not expect that in another 20 years the percentages will be reversed. But the current trend clearly indicates that there will be substantial shift of more than 50 per cent of traditional paper based transactions to paperless deals in cyber space. From physical goods and services, business transactions will turn to non-physical and intangible goods and services offered for sale in various websites. Internet auctions and bargain deals are already becoming more popular as firms find it an effective and economical way for offloading inventories. I have presented here only a few of the clear possibilities based on the present trend in research and development. There is unlimited scope for many more exciting events before we enter the next century.

❑❑

CHAPTER II

TAXMAN'S HORRORSCOPE

The thrill of unexpected discovery cannot help but stir the blood.

[Isaac Asimov]

There is a famous quote attributed to Benjamin Franklin about the uncertainty for everything in the world except death and taxes. It will definitely be a challenging job for the taxman to keep track of the transactions originating and culminating in the seamless cyber space. He will find it difficult to tax digital products like music, software and videos, which can be easily downloaded from the net. In the initial stages, internet sales may not be of significant volumes. The state authorities can conveniently close their eyes on stray cyber sales, but if they reach more than 50per cent of the total retail sales, taxman can no longer ignore his income loss. If it becomes too hard to collect taxes, the governments will be compelled to curtail welfare expenditure, which would be politically unwise.

Who taxes least wins?

With the acute global competition for keeping the tax burden at the lowest level to attract business, higher rates will only see the flight of capital to low taxed countries or to tax havens. Online operations can be made from anywhere and tax authorities in the country of destination may not be able to identify the origin of the business or the consumer. In cyber space, what matters is only a domain identity. It will be difficult to trace the location of a site or identity of the owner. There are also plans to introduce anonymous E-money for transactions in cyber space. If such weird things happen, the present banking system may also undergo a sea change. The tax administration will have to equip itself with suitable software to face the challenges of internet revolution.

Presently, the threat of internet invasion to physical business is not serious, as many goods cannot be digitized and distributed for sale. The mobility of individuals and firms may not be of the huge scale some people anticipate, but Europe has already made a beginning with the issue of direction that foreign companies having annual cyber sales of more than Euro 10,000 to register for VAT in at least one EU country. It is only a fond hope that online traders will offer themselves for tax registration. They may not even know what kind of tax to be paid for the deals on the web sites. Maybe, an automatic check can be flagged on the transactions concluded without tax deduction? But the question is who will be entitled for the tax revenue? Both the country of origin as well as destination will demand their pound of flesh! They may finally agree to share revenue on the basis of some global treaty.

ITA 2000

Unlike in other matters, India has taken an early initiative to exploit the advantages of information technology. The Information Technology Act, 2000 gives the government the legal authority to access to cyber transactions. The E-commerce era has already been recognized and transactions with government agencies are facilitated by making amendments in the Indian Penal Code, the Evidence Act, the Reserve Bank of India Act, etc. ITA 2000 is based on the model law for E-commerce adopted by a UN General Assembly resolution. The resolution recommended all countries to give full and favorable consideration for the model law while enacting or revising the national laws for dealing with information technology. The UN resolution wants to ensure uniformity of the laws applicable to cyber space and the use of information technology.

ITA 2000 gives elaborate definition of the terms normally used in E-commerce. It describes interalia, the functions of various cyber authorities, procedures, legal recognition of electronic record and digital signatures and so on. Surprisingly, the laws make provisions for imposing penalties for offences under ITA 2000 like causing damage to the computer systems, hacking, manipulation of computer documents and breach of privacy and similar digital offences. ITA 2000 also applies to any offence committed outside India by any person using the internet. Consequential amendments to various other Acts like RBI Act, authorizes fund transfers through electronic medium between banks or other financial institutions. The amendment to the Foreign Exchange Management Act, 1999 stipulates that the exporters of E-commerce shall furnish to the RBI or other specified authority a declaration containing material particulars of the payment received for goods or services exported.

ITA 2000 gives the government authority to deal with the developments in E-commerce in the short run. In fact, recently a Delhi court has passed the first conviction order in a fraudulent cyber transaction case. It involved the misuse of a credit card for purchase of goods online. However, it does not give scope for extending all existing tax laws to the intangible transactions on the internet. Another UN resolution may probably recommend a model law for internet taxation like what it has done for information technology. There is greater urgency now for unification of laws relating to E-commerce and physical transactions. In view of the increasing tax competition between governments to prevent flight of taxable events to tax havens, it is necessary to create a model rate structure in consultation with the UN. There will be tremendous pressure on governments to reduce taxes on consumption and profits may shift the base from commodities and services to income, real estate and tangible use of resources like water and electricity.

Tax net for E-commerce

Presently, the tentacles of taxation extend to all essential services associated with information technology. Electricity, telephones (both landline and mobile) and various other supporting infrastructures suffer from some burden of taxation. No specific tax exemption is available for E-commerce and the profit that the companies derive out of their transactions in cyber space. Just like in the conventional system, taxes are payable for all online businesses. But the problem is to verify the declared income from such activities, which may not represent the true dimensions of electronic transactions. Suppression of income from cyber activities is a simple matter of erasing or editing the data entered by the taxpayer.

The governments will have to devise new means to raise revenue from the resources moving to cyber space. Some people advise temporary respite as E-commerce is still in its early infancy. It should be allowed a healthy growth without the taxman breathing down the neck with innumerable questions about transactions. It is well advised, as hardly one per cent of the total retail transactions are now getting diverted to cyber space. They can very well wait until a sizable proportion of about 10 per cent get diverted to E-commerce. For the time being, tax authorities can afford to ignore the occasional forays of the buyer into the net more out of curiosity than necessity. They can contemplate on the facilities required for a market friendly approach to E-commerce.

More competitive tax systems can be conceived to overcome hurdles in the cyber race. The governments will have to accept the fact that in E-commerce the consumer will always be the focal point in the global competition to catch his attention. They should design foolproof methods to deal with the challenges of evaders ably supported by electronic intelligence. It is extremely difficult to trace anonymous transactions and just like the present day hackers, there may be very enterprising people specializing in tax avoidance. They may even offer tax evasion services to less informed taxpayers.

Assuming that by 2100 more than 90 per cent of the commercial transactions will be on electronic mode, we have to equip the tax system with the infrastructure necessary to raise adequate revenue. The innumerable complex issues at national and international level will have to be sorted out before a sound tax system can be made operational. Trade and business would be worried about the possibility of double taxation, which will be detrimental to the growth of E-commerce. International tax treaties, both bilateral and multilateral, would be required to prevent indiscriminate taxing of cyber transactions by governments at the origin and destination of the trade flows. Several issues relating to security, interpretations, verification and organization will have to be sorted out with the taxpayers in a mutually acceptable manner. If a government takes arbitrary decisions on the basis of available technology, the natural growth of E-commerce could be stunted very early.

Presently, all legal systems supporting the tax laws are functioning for collecting revenue from physical transactions. E-taxation will require a different approach based on the latest interpretations of tax laws and practices, made intelligible to the technocrats. The current trend is to extend the existing laws applicable to physical transactions to the cyber space with marginal modifications. The physical location of persons transacting business is no more relevant for the location of a server. The place of business cannot be fixed with reference to the location of a server in lieu of a permanent establishment for conducting business. The issues relating to place of business will have to be thrashed out in tax treaties by suitable interpretations acceptable to the trade.

An international agency will have to help in allocating income arising from cyber transactions to reduce the scope for litigations. Maybe, we will get about 5 years time to prepare a model tax structure in accordance with the United Nations guidelines. VAT is the only known system that can fully take care of the net transactions. While accepting it for the national tax regime, we have to create adequate knowledge systems to face the challenges of intangible transactions in commodities and services. The tracking method of VAT can penetrate cyber transactions more efficiently than any other taxes. In fact it offer a better alternative to the ineffective direct taxes.

From the various features of VAT that will be discussed in the next chapter, it will be evident that it has the flexibility to encompass all kinds of E-commerce. Since the base is value addition, the cascading effect of input taxation can be automatically avoided. E-commerce operators will not find any difficulty in accepting the nominal tax burden. Moreover, VAT can also operate on origin or destination principle with single or multiple rates. Computation of tax liability will be easier and the cost of collection will also be negligible. VAT can incorporate any tax rate and collection procedures required for globalization. It can make the tax system compatible with that of all trading partners and tax treaties can be entered into without any hassles of country specific amendments.

Tax evasion is one area that deserves immediate attention in the short run. Electronic transactions give opportunities to hide deals, prices, profits and income. The legal system for E-commerce will have to take care of proper enforcement of provisions including the requirement for data preservation and verification systems. The potential for evasion will be more in the use of electronic money. New software will be required for the audit to reach transactions in cyber space. A competent accounting system will have to track the flow of the money from origin to destination. Tax laws will have to accept digital identification systems and make it legally admissible evidence of discharging payment liabilities. It is also necessary to give some sort of exemption for micro level transactions involving no intermediary and very low turnover.

Borderless World

It is true that we have already completed the initial exercise for entering the E-world by enacting ITA 2000. But it is only the starting point. The debate will continue throughout the century to evolve a universally acceptable cyber tax system. We have to find solutions for resolving national and international disputes that are likely to arise in abundance in E-commerce. The USA constituted a federal advisory commission on E-commerce in as early as 1998 to examine tax issues at the national, sub-national and international levels. The report submitted by the commission failed to get the approval of the US Congress. Another study group that looked into the state issues relating to E-commerce failed to reach consensus on the various problems posed by E-commerce. They found several serious concerns at the sub-national level about the future of their sales tax base. Taxes on income may not have very serious problems like indirect taxes that depend on production and transaction of goods and services.

In a borderless world, it will be difficult to keep track of the movement of goods and services across political and geographical boundaries. Only the technical developments in the next two or three decades will tell us what kind of challenges the tax system will have to face for keeping its revenue in tune with the scale of transactions. Even in the realm of direct taxes and services, E-commerce will pose immense difficulties for verification of the actual income earned or the consideration received for the services provided. We will have to tackle the problems with updated software and a simplified tax structure. Since the sales tax revenue is likely to be much less in future, the Central Government will have to find adequate provisions to support the ever increasing fiscal needs of state governments. It is imperative to introduce value added tax at the earliest opportunity so that governments at all levels will be fully prepared for the ultimate switch over to E-commerce.

It is interesting to see some of the recommendations of KTF for modernizing direct taxes that are likely to have a bearing on cyber transactions. They suggested that the government should immediately establish a national tax information network (TIN) on a build, operate and transfer basis. They want a world class (common carrier) network system for the IT infrastructure, which should be scalable to offer easy access for tax administration and taxpayers. In fact, the network should have facilities akin to systems operating in security markets. It should establish secular and seamless logistics of tax collection through integration of primary information, record keeping, dissemination and retrieval. They expect that data mining software associated with such relational databases will bring about easy identification of non-compliance and abuses.

KTF wants 'TIN' to receive all 'TDS' returns for digitization either online, or through magnetic media or in printed format. Such digitized information could be downloaded by national computer center and regional centers of the income tax department for further processing. It should also have the capability of downloading information from the banks as and when required. Even the taxpayer should be allowed the facility to access the 'TIN' through a secure and confidential PAN based identification to ascertain tax payments credited and the status of returns and refunds. Once 'TIN' is made operational, the requirement to issue 'TDS' certificates to the payee can be dispensed with and the scheme should be extended to even the smaller taxpayers. The Task Force recommended further simplifications in tax returns and accounting system by utilizing the automated and all pervasive 'TIN'. Similar automated systems are also suggested for indirect taxes to facilitate administration and simplify the outdated tax structure.

But the question is can such belated automations take care of the surge in cyber activities? We have not yet achieved even partial digitization of physical transactions. It may take another 5 years to create all facilities to make a functional 'TIN'. Simply stated, the taxman is not bothered about the future. The complexities of the present give him ample food for thought and scope for more unpopular pursuits.

□□

CHAPTER III

WHAT IS SO GREAT ABOUT VAT?

Bureaucracy is the death of any achievement.

[Albert Einstein]

Most of us meekly accept the fact that taxation is an unavoidable human tragedy. It gets worse as your hard work for worldly achievements begin to bring in the deserving deserts. The majority meekly pays the taxman's share and prays for the best. No one can ensure that a hefty demand would not follow even after paying taxes as correctly as one could comprehend. Thank god, we no longer see the kind of tax collectors who made life miserable even for Hager the Horrible. But modified versions of the cartoon characters are still masquerading in life as modern tax collectors. They still knock at the door at odd times to seek more details of your income and expenditure. The undeniable fact of life is that a taxman can never feel happy or satisfied. And his noose and nose are great tools for unearthing hidden treasures. Just take a look at the income tax query list accompanying the scrutiny memo. You will be astonished at their atrocious manner of peeping into your personal life.

Having reconciled to the inevitable event of taxation, we have to look for the best tax instrument for its collection without too much of torture and tears. There are several conventional methods for tax collection like head counting, but most of them have already been abandoned as archaic even before the Second World War. Surprisingly, in India we still persist with obnoxious taxes like octroi that civilized countries in the world would shudder to even think of. No wonder about 120 countries in the world accepted VAT as the ultimate savior. And no one has yet come out with another system that can outshine its attractions.

For direct taxes, KTF suggested an ultramodern online system called 'TIN'. They also urged the immediate implementation of VAT by all state governments.

The greatness of VAT is that it is the most modern and scientific method for collection of taxes. In recent times, it has also been extended to services in almost all VAT operating countries. An outstanding feature of VAT is its focus on the real tax base, which is value addition by the payer. The conventional indirect taxes work on bases like entry, transaction, production and so on. They all converge on the value of goods and services that includes taxes paid on inputs and intermediates. By identifying the actual base of value addition, VAT ensures neutrality and efficiency. Instead of becoming a constraint to growth, it acts as a real facilitator by eliminating the cascading and other harmful effects of indirect taxation. VAT can generate adequate revenue from goods and services proportionate to the rate of consumption. Some essential exemptions for achieving equity goals can also operate within its ambit. Briefly stated, VAT is the most versatile tax capable of curing the congenital defects of commodity taxation.

VAT defined

VAT is the tax levied on the actual value added by a firm or individual on goods and services purchased from others. It is a tax on an economic activity rather than on the end products. In its comprehensive form, VAT is applicable to producers, wholesalers and retailers. For adapting to the statutory requirements, several countries have implemented variants of VAT. Some confined it solely to manufacturers but the more daring ones extended it to wholesalers and retailers. The distribution of the powers of taxation is the deciding factor in a federal set up for introducing a suitable form of VAT. The main interest is to reduce the cascading and other adverse effects of indirect taxation. It is the only remedy for removing the negative impact of multiple tax regimes.

An important feature of VAT is its flexibility to adapt to the

18

requirements of all socio-economic conditions, legal frameworks and the existing administrative institutions. While introducing any kind of VAT, modifications in the existing tax laws are necessary to give legal support for the smooth transition to the new system. In some countries, all products could not be brought under VAT at one stroke for ensuring equity. In some others, a differential rate structure had to be prescribed for protecting industries in sensitive sectors or for other considerations. Fortunately, VAT can adjust with all such requirements without endangering its basic features like transparency and input tax relief. The calculation of tax liability on a commodity or service is also easy and intelligible. There is no special expertise required for ascertaining the tax payable or for the refund of excess payment.

Variants of VAT

The three major varieties of VAT are, consumption VAT, income VAT and gross product VAT. All of them can be operated on either "origin" or "destination" principles. For computation of VAT, there are different routes such as subtraction, tax credit and addition. VAT can also accommodate multiple or single rate regime depending on the requirements of administration. Tax inclusive or exclusive value can be used for calculation and in the case of the latter; tax payable will be on the price without tax addition by applying the method of zero-rating. Certain sensitive sectors or commodities can be excluded from VAT for favorable tax treatment. The first step in adopting VAT is the selection of a suitable base that could achieve tax objectives in a harmonious manner. Among all the variants of VAT, the most favoured one all over the world is consumption VAT.

Consumption VAT

As the name signifies, it is applicable to value addition on goods and services·consumed. The value added by a firm to the goods and services purchased from others becomes the tax base. There may not be any direct value addition for services. For commodities, value addition may be on any inputs, intermediate goods or final goods. Consumption VAT can be extended to value addition at wholesale and retail points. Invariably, the final tax is collected at the retail point where the values added at all the previous stages of production and transactions converge. This variant of VAT allows deduction of tax on all purchases including capital assets. The tax covers the total private consumption in a country, which is the chosen target for an ideal indirect tax.

In a closed economy, which is a rarity in the modern world, the sum of the values added at various stages should equal to the aggregate of all retail sales. The stock of inventories and creation of capital goods remain constant in such static economies where the total value of sales to consumers at the retail stage would reflect all economic activities. But in developing economies characterized by accelerated growth in all sectors, economic activities are more dynamic and openness prevails in all spheres. An advantage of consumption VAT is that it does not interfere with investment decisions capital formation in any manner.

In open economies, consumption VAT may not give a correct picture of the total value addition in the economy, as goods produced in other countries can distort the tax incidence. An import duty at the point of entry or at the first wholesale stage immediately after importation becomes imperative to maintain parity. The use of imported goods may exaggerate the domestic value addition if it is not segregated from total sales at the retail stage. Similarly, export goods should not become a part of the value addition in the producing country. To keep a convenient balance, the normal practice is to impose a VAT on imports and exempt export from all kinds of taxation. If the value of exports equals the value of imports, the value added domestically can be inferred from the aggregate of domestic retail sales. Such equalized import-export trade regime is very rare in modern economies. But for such marginal distortions, we can safely assume that the base of consumption VAT is more or less equal to the estimates of national income. If foreign trade and capital goods are excluded from the ambit of taxation, consumption

VAT can catch the entire range of taxable economic activities at the retail sale stage.

Another advantage of consumption VAT is that it is total neutral to methods of production, capital and current expenditure, savings and consumption. This quality of VAT enhances economic efficiency, as it does not distort consumers' preference or producers' choice. Besides, the transparency in transactions makes it the easiest tax for the administration to enforce. The taxpayer knows exactly what burden he is bearing for the country. In comprehensive VAT, deduction of tax paid on all business inputs including capital goods is allowed. Normally, either no tax is levied on exports or they are zero rated while the full value of imports gets taxed at the point of entry. These attractive features have made VAT the most popular form of indirect tax in the world.

Income VAT

It is another variant of VAT, which collects tax on all sales but allows deduction only for the depreciation of capital goods. The value taxed roughly represents all economic activities of a country during the period of taxation. The tax base of income VAT is identical to that of comprehensive income tax that includes investments and gives deduction only for the depreciation of capital goods. Very few countries in the world operate income VAT. It is generally not favored for the practical difficulties in computing depreciation of capital goods. In an inflationary economy, the taxpayers may not be happy with the mandatory calculations that allow lower rates or deferred depreciation. More over, it does not give the industry any relief from the burden of cascading effect of multiple levies.

Gross Product VAT

In this variant of VAT, deduction is not allowed even for the replacement of capital goods. Relief is given only for purchases of current consumption goods. The value addition in the case of Gross Product VAT is much more than the aggregate of retail sales in a particular year. Presently, only two countries use modified versions of Gross Product VAT. The main drawback of Gross Product VAT is its discriminatory treatment to capital goods. It adversely affects investment and industrial growth. There is no relief from double taxation of capital goods. Consequently, the replacement of old and worn out plant and machinery is very slow, which leads to stagnation.

VAT Computation

Since VAT is a very versatile tax, it offers several methods to calculate the quantum of tax payable. The commonly used methods of calculation are addition, subtraction and tax credit. In addition method, all factor payments including profits are aggregated to arrive at the total value addition. The applicable rate is then applied on the tax base to calculate the tax liability. This type of computation is used mainly with income VAT. Addition method cannot easily accommodate exemptions of intermediate firms. It is also difficult to exempt exports and do correct valuation of imported goods. Another drawback is that it does not facilitate matching of invoices for detecting tax evasion.

Subtraction Method

This is the simplest method for computing tax liability. The value added by a firm is calculated by subtracting total purchases from sales. Tax is easily ascertained by applying the rate on the value addition. In the case of direct subtraction, tax is levied on the difference between the aggregates of tax exclusive sales and purchases. In an intermediate subtraction method, tax is levied on the difference between tax inclusive values of purchases and sales. Tax credit method is generally preferred to subtraction as it is easy to calculate tax liability and export refund entitlements.

Tax Credit or Invoice Method

VAT operating countries mostly employ the tax credit or invoice method for computing the actual tax payable. It is widely used in conjunction with comprehensive VAT. In this method, deduction of taxes paid on inputs is allowed from the taxes payable on sales on the basis of the aggregates of the taxes indicated on all invoices. The invoices received for the purchase of inputs and sale of value added commodities give correct indication of the actual tax liability. Even intermediate firms in the chain of transactions can be zero rated or exempted under this scheme. It also eliminates the distortion caused by a differential rate structure. Another advantage is that it can tax the full value of imported goods under the destination principle at the time of import or at any subsequent stage.

This method allows easy access to auditors for matching invoices electronically. With suitable software, tax evasion can be detected more quickly and efficiently by an error alert. Normally, there should be no temptation for misrepresenting VAT liability as the consumer ultimately bears the tax burden. Of course, deliberate tax evasion is possible if a nexus is established between the buyer and the seller for suppressing the real invoice value and sharing the unpaid tax. If the consumers do not insist upon a correct invoice or colludes with the retailer for under invoicing, evasion becomes intractable. In a large stream of economic activities variations in individual transactions cannot be detected by ordinary means. It is possible to discover willful manipulations only by comparing prices of similar commodities sold by other retailers. Deterrent penalties may also discourage tax evasion by delinquent firms. But taxpayers are normally not tempted to evade VAT if the rates are reasonable and very few products and sectors are exempted.

Origin Vs. Destination Principle

For implementing a suitable VAT, we can choose from two principles relating to trade. Under the "origin" principle, value added domestically on all goods, whether they are exported or internally consumed, is subjected to taxation. Consequently, tax cannot be levied on value added abroad. The tax is confined to goods originating in the country of consumption. In principle, exports are taxable under this scheme while imports are exempt. The origin principle is used normally in conjunction with income VAT and is unpopular for obvious reasons.

On the other hand, the destination principle allows computation of value addition irrespective of the origin. The principle is that all goods consumed in a country should pay the tax. In this regime, exports are exempt while imports are invariably taxed. It is normally used with consumption VAT and is preferred particularly in a federal form of government. Unlike the origin principle, it treats imported goods at par with domestic products. The origin principle gives, indirect protection and preference to the producers abroad. Once the goods are imported, subsequent domestic value additions are invariably taxed. Destination principle is generally chosen for retail sales tax levied by states or local bodies.

Exemptions under VAT

Taxation may be an unavoidable evil but exemptions are its loyal accomplices. In any country and in all tax situations, certain products, firms or sectors are to be excluded from the purview of taxation. General exemptions are given to essential goods consumed by low-income groups and also to export goods for achieving a beneficial foreign trade regime. Similarly, certain firms and sectors are excluded from the tax liability on account of low revenue potential compared to the cost of production or for any other compelling reason. In India, it is not economical to collect taxes from cottage and small industries in view of the large number of assesses and excessive cost of collection. It is difficult to compute value addition particularly in case of some services like banking and insurance. In developing countries, VAT is not advisable at the retail stage for want of suitable administrative machinery for collection. For giving exemption under VAT, either zero rating or direct exclusion can be applied.

Tax exemption is generally granted to firms falling below a specified turnover limit stipulated as the tax threshold. But all exemptions give rise to serious administrative problems and economic inefficiencies. It will be difficult to allow tax credit on inputs from the exempted sector. Consequently, tax-paying users avoid exempted materials, as they could distort calculations based on credits available on inputs. It actually produces the unintended adverse effect of losing the market share of small enterprises. Zero-rating adopts a different approach to exemption. It is, however, not favored in developing countries for reducing the claims for tax refunds. Normally under VAT, exports are zero rated to make them more competitive in international trade.

VAT Rates

Another advantage of VAT is that it can operate efficiently either with a single rate or with multiple rates. Zero rates can be used for exempting goods and low rates can give various kinds of tax concessions. Preferential treatment can be given to certain essential commodities, sensitive sectors and loss making firms by allowing tax refunds. In many instances, higher than normal rates are applied for curbing luxury or harmful consumptions. Such deterrent rates can also be used to divert factors of production from demerit goods like cigarettes and alcohol to other essential items.

The impact of multiple rates would be felt only at the retail level in tax credit method when the commodity or service is finally passed on to the consumer. With lower rates, the producer or wholesaler has to pay lesser tax on his value addition. The retailer gets a smaller tax credit against the standard rate, which is invariably higher. Penal rates for curbing consumption have substantial price impact and the margins are also much less for the dealers. In subtraction method, it is possible to apply different rates at each stage of transaction. The multiple rate structure gives a heavy burden to the retailer, as he has to keep a complete account of exempted goods, concession rated goods, standard rated goods, etc. It makes the cost of compliance much higher and some times leads to unintended evasion.

There is no uniform rate structure in VAT operating countries. Some prefer single rate despite its inherent inequity. One commonly witnessed phenomenon is the upward revision of rates after introduction of VAT with a low rate. More than 50 per cent of the VAT operating countries now use two to four rates. The highest rate is about 30 per cent and the lowest is one per cent. VAT rates are applied either on a tax base exclusive or inclusive of tax. In either case, the revenue would be the same but the rate should be kept lower in the tax inclusive form to offset the price effect on account of the presence of tax in the price. The public perception of the tax burden in such cases would be less, which makes it politically more acceptable. For the taxpayer, the tax inclusive price is easy for computation but for the consumer, tax exclusive invoice is more transparent as it is free from any hidden tax.

It is seen that all over the world the tax exclusive rates are now heavily favoured. Both types can make the tax liability transparent by indicating it clearly in the invoice. Generally, the consumers are not keen to get a break up of the tax paid at different stages of transaction, which ultimately get passed on to them. But the compliance patterns that exist at the time of introduction of VAT normally decide the kind of rates inclusive or tax exclusive rates.

Options for all Reasons

The best advantage of VAT is that it offers several options depending on the distribution of the powers of taxation and other constraints. In a federal democratic system, the powers of taxation are invariably distributed among different levels of government. From the practices prevailing in VAT operating countries, it is seen that the coverage of the base is clearly distributed across three distinct stages namely, manufacture, wholesale and retail transactions.

Manufacturers' VAT ends with the completion of the process of manufacture. It does not extend to other stages of transactions. This is the easiest form of VAT, which offers maximum administrative convenience. It has minimum contact points and the cost of compliance is also at the lowest. However, it is not generally preferred due to the extremely narrow base that gives limited potential for revenue buoyancy. It is prevalent in some South American and African countries.

In fact, manufacturers' VAT is the first step in the evolution of indirect taxation in a country. As the economy develops over time, the tax system becomes more competent to extend the base to other transaction points. In an industrialized economy having a well-defined network of transaction points, a comprehensive VAT is the ideal choice. But if unaccounted transactions are more at wholesale and retail stages and tax administration is unable to access a large variety of assesses, it is better to confine VAT to manufacturing stage. The cost of collection becomes too prohibitive if it has to reach several inter-firm sales and sales to related persons. In developing countries where under-valuation is pervasive, manufacturers' VAT is a preferable option for reducing evasion.

The second stage in the evolution of VAT is when it reaches the wholesale transactions. The value addition from the manufacture to the wholesale stage offers substantial revenue but it also entails a bigger tax base and more assesses and accounting practices and problems. In most of the countries where wholesale transactions are included, small wholesalers are kept outside the tax net for administrative convenience. A suitable tax threshold takes care of such exclusions.

The retail VAT is a fully evolved tax where the base is extended to all value additions until the last transaction point. It is a highly preferred form of taxation, which reduces distortions and simplifies the tax structure. The entire range of transactions becomes transparent to the consumer, tax administration and the taxpayer. Moreover, it minimises the incentive for tax evasion, as there is no advantage at any stage to avoid payment. The main drawback of the retail VAT is that it can be applied only in countries where the retail stage is easily approachable and all transactions are documented. The problem of compliance is acute in less monitorised economies. Such difficulties can be overcome by confining the VAT to the wholesale stage.

VAT on services

In many countries, VAT has already been extended to various services. The service sector in developed countries has assumed great significance in generating considerable national income. In fact, currently services constitute the second major economic activity in the world with immense value addition. The main consideration for exempting the service sector earlier was the inadequate documentation at the transaction stage. However, with the advent of electronic documentation, even the smallest service provider keeps sufficient data of services rendered and the consideration received.

In comprehensive VAT on services, the tax is levied on all kinds of services rendered for monetary consideration but the tax rate is invariably kept low for obtaining better compliance. In selective approach, only specified services are taxed and others are kept out of the scope of taxation. Some of the specified services which are favoured for VAT in developed countries are personal services like laundries, beauty parlours, entertainments, repair works, telecommunication and transportation. In the European Union, an integrated approach is prevalent in conjunction with the commodity VAT. Unlike commodity VAT, it is difficult to administer exemptions to any service on the basis of a turnover limit. The selective approach is preferred in many developing countries as it brings only firms or persons offering a specified service under the tax net. It is interesting to note that in the 2003-2004 budget, service tax has been made fully vatable with a massive increase in the tax rate.

The Ideal VAT

The wide variety of choices available under VAT sometimes confuses tax administration. The problem is that the administration has to identify the objectives of taxation and harmonize prevalent practices before choosing a compatible combination. A survey of the country specific VAT schemes show that the majority has chosen consumption type of VAT with destination principle, tax credit method and tax exclusive multiple rates. A large number of countries opted for tax relief method of outright exemption rather than zero rating. Origin principle cannot easily work with tax credit method or consumption VAT. In a federal system origin principle offers certain advantage for reducing border controls and valuation disputes.

Any variety of choice can always accommodate tax inclusive or tax exclusive rates; multiple rates or single rates are also compatible with all features of VAT. The advantage of consumption VAT is that it has all the important features of VAT except the origin principle and certain types of exemptions. Addition method is normally not favoured with consumption VAT. Income VAT does not work smoothly with destination principle, zero rating, exemption and multiple rates. The general aversion for origin principle is that it is incompatible with consumption VAT and many essential requirements for an equitable tax system.

The main consideration for a workable VAT in any country is to avoid incompatibility with the objectives of taxation. If savings and investments are to be encouraged, the best instrument will be consumption VAT with destination principle. For promoting exports, the destination principle is a better option than the origin. A comprehensive survey of various choices in VAT operating countries indicates that the most favoured combination is consumption VAT with destination principle and a single rate. The single rate gives maximum administrative convenience and economic efficiency but in some countries multiple rates are prevalent for reasons like equity. Political compulsions concede tax exemptions for preferential treatment to weaker sectors and sensitive products. Tax credit method has several advantages as it combines well with other features of VAT. The choice of VAT base will eventually depend on several factors such as administrative convenience, objectives of taxation, powers of taxation and the legal framework and institutions available during the transitional period. In the initial stages, the VAT adopting country should also be prepared for certain minor setbacks in revenue collection and compliance. But such apprehensions did not materialize in many countries probably with the sudden drop in tax evasion.

❑❑

CHAPTER IV

INDIAN TAX IMBROGLIO

Corruption is the most infallible symptom of constitutional liberty.

[Edward Gibbon]

Where are we?

The Indian tax system, particularly the indirect tax regime, has the rare distinction of being the most complex one in the world. To start with, it hardly leaves anything untaxed. The union, the state and the concurrent lists of the constitution of India covers the entire range of possibilities for levy of different types of direct and indirect taxes. The taxable events are also described in detail in the constitution. The fiscal needs of the Central and State Governments periodically evaluated a Finance Commission, which is a constitutional functionary. In Annexure I, the relevant provisions of the constitution that deal with taxation are enumerated for easy reference.

The constitutional provisions envisage a comprehensive tax system comprising of both direct and indirect taxes. They deal with income, wealth, production/manufacture of tradable commodities, services, national, inter-state and local entries and so on. It is in fact a continuation of the pre-independence entities. Many of the present statutes are actually modified versions of the original enactments of the British government. But the phenomenal expansion of the tax system has been an exclusive post-independence development. The intensive tax efforts in the first few decades after independence have improved the total tax to GDP ratio to reach the highest level of 15 per cent. Even when GDP growth was sluggish, tax revenue showed considerable buoyancy thanks to the rapid expansion of base and upward revision of rates.

The tax ratios (please see table I) reveal that compared to direct taxes, revenue from indirect taxes improved considerably

Table I : CENTRAL TAX–GDP RATIO

Year	Excise Revenue	Customs revenue	Direct taxes	Percentage of GDP
1974-75	4.82	1.99	2.37	9.18
1975-76	5.40	1.99	2.92	10.31
1976-77	5.52	2.03	2.85	10.40
1977-78	5.09	2.09	2.54	9.72
1978-79	5.69	2.61	2.59	10.89
1979-80	5.87	2.85	2.67	11.39
1980-81	5.31	2.78	2.30	10.39
1981-82	5.18	3.00	2.41	10.59
1982-83	5.06	3.21	2.36	10.63
1983-84	5.47	2.99	2.25	10.71
1984-85	5.35	3.38	2.15	10.88
1985-86	5.55	4.08	2.30	11.93
1986-87	5.59	4.43	2.33	12.35
1987-88	5.58	4.66	2.25	12.49
1988-89	5.36	4.49	2.47	12.32
1989-90	5.52	4.44	2.42	12.38
1990-91	5.15	4.34	2.27	11.76
1991-92	5.10	4.03	2.70	11.83
1992-93	4.40	3.40	2.60	10.40
1993-94	3.70	2.60	2.4	8.7
1994-95	3.70	2.65	2.7	9.05
1995-96	3.40	3.00	2.8	9.2
1996-97	3.30	3.10	2.85	9.25
1997-98	3.20	2.60	3.2	9
1998-99	3.10	2.30	2.7	8.1
1999-00	3.20	2.50	3	8.70
2000-01	3.30	2.30	3.2	8.8
2001-2002	3.19	1.80	3	7.99
2002-03(BE)	3.3	1.80	3.4	8.8
2003-04(Prov.)	3.3	1.80	3.8	9.2

Source: 1. National Accounts Statistics (New Series)
2. Budgets of Union & State Governments
3. Kelkar Committee report

since independence till 1992. On the other hand, direct taxes remained sluggish with hardly any expansion of base or levels of income. However, in recent times, direct tax revenue has started showing significant upward trend. But indirect taxes still continue to be the main source of revenue for the exchequer. Out of the total tax revenue of the central government in 2003-2004, Central Excise duties contributed 3.3 per cent while revenue from Customs duties was only 1.80. The total contribution of all direct taxes has improved to 3.25 per cent. Out of the three major indirect taxes in India, the foremost one is still central excise duties. It reached the peaks in 60's and 70's thanks to massive tax efforts to meet the fiscal demands of the five-year plans.

A scrutiny of the latest statistics of national tax revenue shows that the central excise is still ahead of all others. During the last five years, there has been a steady decline in the contribution of central excise revenue. In view of the massive reduction in Customs duty rates to comply with WTO requirements the share of import revenue has been on a steady declining trend. However, there is considerable improvement in the revenue from direct taxes particularly during the last five years. But what is really alarming is the steady fall of tax to GDP ratio. Such a miserable collapse could be avoided if tax reforms were implemented in time to remove inefficiencies. A brief review of the complexities and inefficiencies of the tax system will reveal how unscientific policies and practices affect the mobilization of revenue.

Structural Deficiencies

The constitution of India assigns the tax base of production/manufacture of commodities to central excise duties to be levied by the central government. Certain specific exclusions are also provided in the constitution. At the time of independence, only 14 commodities were dutiable. But the levy got extended to 137 commodities by 1985. Since 1986, excise tariff has been aligned with the harmonized system of classification of commodities, which brought all identifiable and marketable commodities under the tax net (please see annexure III for the chronological data of base expansion).

Presently, the excise base consists of about 1300 distinct commodities. Its phenomenal growth since independence does not show any systematic or selective expansion nor has it been consistent with the growth of domestic production/manufacture. The data of additional revenue mobilization indicates that almost 90 per cent of the growth since independence reflected only the intensive tax efforts. This situation has led to indiscriminate taxation on inputs, intermediates and even on capital goods. While the revenue showed some buoyancy the immediate outcome was the severe cascading effect and low responsiveness to GDP growth.

In addition to the steady expansion of tax base, tax rates have also been constantly hiked in the first four decades. Initially, specific rates dominated the tax structure as against rates based on the value of goods. But since 1994-95, there has been a deliberate switch over to value based rates to improve the elasticity of revenue. Although a large number of goods are excisable, more than 50 per cent of the revenue comes from just 15 commodities. The distribution of revenue in 2001-2002 shows that 62 per cent comes from 16 per cent rate of duty. Only 3.12 per cent of revenue is raised from 8 per cent rate of duty and only 7 per cent is collected from 32 per cent rate. Special rates of duty account for about 26 per cent of the revenue. The structural complexities of excise can be attributed to the indiscriminate expansion in the 70's and 80's. Since 1994-95, with the adoption of invoice based assessment and ad valorem rates, the tax system has been well-tuned for better performance in terms of revenue and compliance. Table III to VI presents the slow but steady transformation of the archaic excise system to a modern VAT during the last decade.

Low buoyancy and elasticity

There have been several studies to identify the factors responsible for the low responsiveness of central excise revenue.

It is well established that the elasticity co-efficient of central excise revenue has been less than unity since independence. But the buoyancy co-efficient showed some periodical upswings due to the rigorous tax efforts for additional revenue. One study revealed that less than 50 per cent of the total tax revenue is obtained from the automatic growth of the tax.

Another study indicated that excise revenue has not been responsive to rate variations although it showed some responsiveness to price variations. It is seen that ad valorem rates are more responsive than specific rates. In fact, the low responsiveness of excise revenue in the early days was mainly due to the predominance of specific rates. At one point of time, specific rates accounted for about 60per cent of the aggregate revenue. The strange fascination for specific rates was probably on account of the convenience for levy and collection. Ad valorem rates give rise to innumerable litigations related to the valuation of goods. The taxman never trusted the price declarations of the manufactures. The taxpayers always try to undervalue highly taxed goods for capturing market share and avoid payment liability.

But the incompetence of tax administration to face litigations cannot be a valid excuse for sacrificing the natural growth of revenue. With the introduction of invoice value and MRP based assessment, valuation disputes have now almost disappeared. The apprehensions of large-scale manipulation of invoices have also been belied. Further, with the acceptance of full-fledged VAT, the transactions are now extremely transparent, which reduces the scope for evasion. In some early studies, consumer durables showed less elasticity and buoyancy as compared to inputs. It clearly reflected the impact of the heavy cascading effect of the tax on inputs before the introduction of the modified form of VAT.

Price effect

I have examined the shifting pattern of tax burden of excise duties with reference to pre-tax and post-tax commodity prices.

The transmission of tax burden did not follow the possibilities envisaged in price theories and the patterns noticed in VAT operating countries. There has been almost uniform price shift across different types of commodities and market conditions. The demand elasticity was a major determinant in the shifting of the aggregate tax burden. The tax incidence and the availability of competing products also played an important role in deciding the quantum of tax burden being shifted to the consumers. After the imposition of tax, there was no time lag in shifting the burden to the consumer. The administration also collected taxes immediately after the levy was announce in the annual budget.

In many instances, commodity taxation in India resulted in extending consumer price much beyond the tax inclusive value of goods. The multiple rate structure on inputs, intermediates and finished goods snowballed into a much higher final price, which also included the interest on sales on credit basis. The hidden tax burden has always kept the final price misleading and the consumer could never get a complete breakup of the various elements of cost. The total transparency of the tax credit mechanism of VAT can remove such confusions and keep the consumer fully informed about the exact tax involved in the final price. After the adoption of VAT at state level, the transactions are likely to be much more transparent for all concerned. The certainty and transparency of tax structure will be an attractive incentive for investment, particularly of FDI. It can also reduce the high level of corruption in tax administration.

Production effect

The profitability of a firm and its choice of optimal production levels are always subject to the imposition of a fresh levy or change in the existing rates. Many changes are required in the output levels and the new consumer price after ascertaining the post-tax market demand, availability of substitutable and competing products, and so on. The producers find it difficult to decide the output levels as several factors influence the market. When the taxed products are particularly non-essential consumer items, realistic demand projections are difficult to obtain from a competitive market. Since the powers of taxation are vested in different agencies that frequently alter the rate and base for additional revenue, uncertainties of tax liability always affect the producer's choice. In a study of the tax effects on production it has been indicated that production levels invariably increased when a tax incentive in the form of reduction in rates was given to boost output.

When the higher production relief scheme was in operation in the 70's, it has been noticed that the output levels improved considerably for most of the commodities during the incentive period. But the upward trend was temporary as the initial spurt in production gradually declined for some commodities like iron and steel products. If the pre-tax production was sluggish or the capacity was under-utilized for one reason or other, the incentive scheme improved the output level. But such schemes unjustifiably discouraged efficient units, which had already reached the peak levels of production. The result was that inefficient and badly managed firms cornered unwarranted and perhaps undeserving tax benefits.

Several tax-induced distortions were created in the domestic industry in the first four decades of taxation. The rate structure complexities within the same industry prescribed for achieving multiple tax objectives affected the production pattern in many key sectors. Excise and sales tax exemptions were liberally given to provide relief to essential commodities, specified sectors, products and firms, ostensibly for maximizing equity or for administrative convenience. In the case of sales tax, tax holidays were given to attract industries to backward and undeveloped areas of a state. Deferred payment of sales tax is pervasive in many states even now to attract industries to migrate from the neighboring states. The state tax structure shows the ridiculous efforts made to develop trade and industry at any cost.

Agriculture Sector is one of the holy cows of the Indian tax system. It enjoys maximum relief from all kinds of taxation in addition to the open and hidden subsidies availed on the inputs.

37

The green revolution is attributed to the tax free era and the liberal support prices of agricultural products. Small and cottage sectors are the other holy cows that cannot be touched by the taxman. In the case of match industry, it is seen that differential rate structure has led to severe distortions in the production pattern. On account of the preferential tax treatment the organized industries were completely wiped out from the market and the small sector became the only player. However, the revenue from the match industry is still negligible and it should have been completely exempted from excise levy. But the small sector did not want total exemption that would have brought the organized industries back into reckoning.

Similar preferential treatment in sugar industry did not increase the market share of the small sector. It shows that the dispensation for matches did not hold good for sugar. In cigarette industry, it is seen that differential tax structure favoured the production of low taxed varieties, which are evidently more injurious to health. The higher incidence of duty for curbing consumption actually produced the opposite effect. It promoted cheaper brands that endanger consumers' health. The interest of revenue also suffered badly, as cheaper varieties fetched much less revenue than the high-priced ones. But the manufacturers were happy with the tax-induced brand promotion at the cost of revenue.

Tax effects seriously distorted the production pattern in the textile sector. The artificial classification of fabrics for tax purposes and differential rates for fine, super fine, medium and coarse varieties of cloth put the organized sector out of business. The heavy tax burden on super fine cloth curtailed its output while improving the production of medium and coarse varieties bearing lower tax rates. The differential tax burden and cascading effect of both central excise and sales tax induced migration of the factors of production to favored sectors. Preferential treatment to small and non-power operated firms definitely provided incentive to sustain and improve their production levels. However, if a cut-off limit was prescribed for exemption, the real growth of the favored sector got stunted.

The exempted sector always tried to remain within the turnover limit for enjoying continuous protection of preferential treatment.

It is not possible to point out all tax-induced distortions that affect production. But the clear conclusion that emerges from many studies is that the excessive burden of taxes levied by different authorities fall on the same base affecting the optimal production. The cumulative impact of various commodity taxes is further compounded by structural complexities of direct taxes. Only a tax system like VAT, which has an inbuilt device for automatic tax credit can relieve production from the unbearable tax burden. The producers should have the freedom to choose the output levels acceptable to the market on the basis of demand and supply factors rather than on tax induced distortions. The textile industry in India is a classic example of the growth according to tax pattern that ultimately had a negative impact on revenue. It really helped the unorganized sector to expand and take over the total market.

Tax Incidence

Equity considerations enshrined in the Constitution of India make it imperative that the tax burden should be progressive in relation to the taxable capacity of the population. The progressive or regressive nature of the tax is indicated by the quantum of tax burden in the consumption expenditure of different classes of the population. Several studies have been undertaken in the past to ascertain the per capita consumption of taxed goods. They used different dimensions such as rural/ urban, agriculture/non-agriculture, income and gender for estimating the incidence. The findings indicate that the rural/ agriculture sector is definitely under-taxed, which shows a satisfactory degree of progression. The Indirect Taxation Enquiry Committee, 1978, which conducted a comprehensive incidence study covering state, central and local taxes found that excise duties were more progressive than state taxes.

The variations in the incidence estimates in different studies reveal that they are at best rough approximations of the trend in the distribution of tax burden. The marginal progression seen in the urban sector is perhaps due to higher levels of consumption of heavily taxed commodities like cigarettes, and petroleum products. About 70 per cent of the tax incidence of rural sector and low-income groups was found to be on account of central excise duties. Essential consumer articles like textile, sugar, tea, kerosene and tobacco products are the main culprits for creating the regressive distribution. It is also seen that the tax burden on inputs and intermediates take a large share of the total incidence on consumer goods. The multitude of taxes falling on the same base irrespective of the taxes paid at earlier stages is yet another reason for the highly regressive nature of indirect taxes in India.

TAX EVASION

The structural complexities of taxation inevitably lead to conditions conducive to large-scale evasion. With the prohibitive tax rates, temptation to avoid payment becomes irresistible. Successful detection is very rare, but even after a case is made, the intricacies of the tax system renders prosecution and conviction of culprits a very protracted affair. The evader exploits the loopholes in the judicial system to avoid payment of duty, fine and penalty on one pretext or the other. There are also several subjective criteria for determining liability on the basis of end-use, source of production, nature of inputs and so on. These are areas where collusion between the taxpayer and the tax collector is pervasive. It is extremely difficult to unearth any evidence for establishing evasion if the taxman is involved in sharing the loot of the exchequer.

One of the common methods of evasion is suppression of actual production. In addition, under-valuation and misclassification of commodities are important means for avoiding payment of taxes. Suppression of production is mostly prevalent in the small sector enjoying tax concessions on the basis of a turnover criterion. When actual production is understated, borderline units easily escape tax liability. The evader not only avoids excise, but also other taxes like income tax and sales tax. In the organized sector, where a large number of persons and different

40

stages are involved in the production and sale of taxable goods, suppression is normally not possible. But even in the organized sector manufacturing products like cigarettes on which excessive rates are applicable, suppression of production is rampant to obtain huge monetary gains. Many unscrupulous taxmen are also involved in the massive evasion of excise duties on products like cigarettes and state taxes on alcoholic liquor.

Under-valuation is another attractive means of evasion when tax rates are based on the value of the goods rather than on specific characteristics like volume, number etc. In vertically integrated units, under valuation is more prevalent as documents can be manipulated conveniently through all stages of production and sale. In such cases, it is easy to share the unaccounted money generated with the collusion of officers. Under valuation cases are difficult to discover as the real value seldom gets reflected in any document. In fact, manufacturers of identical goods create cartels for declaring similar prices to avoid detection. Automobile sector allegedly indulges in such price equalization methods to maximize profits.

The acute problem of under valuation is the main cause for the prevalence of specific rates which are based on some physical criterion. However, this easy remedy for curbing under-valuation has resulted in considerable loss of revenue, as specific rates do not reflect the automatic growth of the tax base. With specific rates, suppression of production is the main source of evasion instead of under-valuation. Value Added Tax is an effective solution to combat the menace of under valuation by checking prices through invoice matching methods. It has been successfully tried in the Republic of Korea when VAT was introduced. India can take advantage of the audit pattern in VAT operating countries to control evasion and corruption.

With multiple tax rates, some adventurous evaders resort to incorrect classification of taxable products. It is particularly rampant in situations where differential tax structure gives preferential treatment to the same commodity based on some criteria like end-use, source of production etc. Some of the products prone to such modes of evasion are cotton, man made fabrics, yarn, soap and vegetable products. There is no reliable data for quantifying the extent of evasion of indirect taxation. Unlike VAT, central excise and sales tax data of clearances is not amenable to matching of invoices.

A very crude estimation of evasion is possible on the basis of number of offence cases booked by the administration. SRP Review Committee tried to quantify evasion on the basis of the data of the record of offences, loss of revenue and production. They also tried to cross check the data supplied to different tax authorities. The Committee concluded that evasion in respect of unmanufactured products like tobacco and coffee declined during the last 25 years, but during the same period, manufactured products became more prone to evasion. From the revenue involved in such cases and the number of prosecutions launched, it has been concluded that evasion has not declined in spite of the removal of most of the evasion prone products from the scope of taxation.

Another study conducted by the National Institute of Public Finance and Policy estimated evasion in respect of three select commodities namely, Copper, Plastics and Cotton Textile fabrics. They concluded that the probable amount of evasion was about 18 per cent of the revenue in the case of pipe and tubes of copper and 13 per cent for copper as a whole. The study suggested further rationalization of tariff structure for reducing the scope of evasion. They could not, however, estimate the extent of evasion in plastic industry, in view of the complexities of the tariff structure. Evasion through misclassification of textile fabrics was estimated to be about Rs.5 crores and loss of revenue from under valuation by the mill sector was placed around Rs.40 crores. It was estimated that evasion in textile fabrics was about 47 per cent and in the case of yarn, it was about 7 percent.

The conclusion that emerges from the various studies reveal high incidence of evasion in many sensitive commodities manufactured by widely dispersed sectors. They estimate evasion of about 10 to 20 per cent of the revenue collected. However, with the harmonization of the tariff and the reduction of rates, the scope for evasion has definitely narrowed. But successful prevention of evasion is possible only when we introduce self-checking systems like VAT with suitable software for auditing invoices. In Korea and Indonesia, substantial reduction in evasion was noticed after the introduction of VAT. It is true that the initial investment required for creating administrative infrastructure for introduction of VAT is substantial. However, the returns on investment are likely to be huge even if we accept evasion at the most modest level of 10 per cent of revenue. Moreover, VAT will create new patterns of tax compliance that can sustain high revenue yield. The latest data on tax evasion (please see table XVI) shows that the present practices are conducive to large scale avoidance of even moderate tax burden with liberal input tax relief.

In India the traders are up in arms against the adoption of VAT. There are no protests from the manufacturers and consumers. The state governments are also fully convinced about the positive impact of VAT on revenue. The traders are mostly worried about the possibility of exposure of fudged transactions and massive tax evasion. Since tax credit is available at every transaction stage, if the chain is broken, it is likely to be detected in audit. No wonder that the traders want continuation of the archaic system even at the cost of economic growth.

Customs duties

After central excise, customs is the major source of revenue for the Central Government. Since exports are exempt from all duties, customs revenue is derived mostly from imported goods. The main objective of import duty is to protect the indigenous industries against unfair foreign competition. While achieving this goal, massive resources are also mobilized for the exchequer. The customs levies also contribute to a favorable balance of trade position by restricting imports.

Before independence, Customs duties contributed the major

share of revenue. Since the import duty rates were substantially higher in the 50s and 60s, customs revenue maintained a high growth profile despite the fall in the volume of imports. Since the rates were mostly ad valorem, revenue responded adequately to the changes in the base. Customs revenue accrued mainly from raw materials and intermediates rather than from final products. Final products and baggage items contributed only about 10 per cent of the total revenue. It is seen that import duties achieved the main tax objective of protecting the indigenous industry by restricting successfully the import of many finished products.

The various tariff and non-tariff barriers that existed before the liberalization of the economy in 1991 have definitely boosted the indigenous production of import substitution products. A study of the import duty incidence on major commodity groups prior to 1991 indicated that tax burden on imports had been at a very high level. The maximum rates of import duties on baggage items and consumer goods were in the range of 150 per cent to 300 per cent.

Although they have been reduced to 85 per cent in the 1993-94 budget and further to 65 per cent in the 1994-95 budget and to about 35 per cent in the last budget, the rates are still substantially higher than those prevailing in other Asian countries. With the progressive reduction of tax rates, the domestic industries are loosing the hard cover of protection. They are made to compete with the products of foreign manufacturers both in quality as well as cost. But domestic industries have been demanding a level play field with considerable reduction in excise and sales tax and better infrastructure facilities for gaining a competitive edge.

Import duties are imposed mainly under two categories. The basic Customs duty is the major tax component in the duty structure. On an average the revenue raised under this head is about 50per cent of the total revenue. Additional duty of customs which is popularly known as countervailing duty (CVD) is imposed to provide protection to domestic industries.

The CVD rates are equivalent to the Central Excise duty on similar products when manufactured indigenously. The tax base for CVD is the total value of imports including the basic customs duty. Customs duties have contributed immensely to the cascading effect of the tax, as majority of the imports are inputs and intermediates. When MODVAT scheme was introduced, tax relief for only CVD was allowed. It was intended to boost the production of inputs by the domestic sector. But such pious expectations did not materialize due to unfair pricing and acute competition by importers.

Import duties have preferential and standard rates for accommodating bilateral and multi lateral trade agreements. There are several liberal exemptions for inputs and final products imported for humanitarian purposes. In the past, the rate structure was kept at fairly high levels even for capital goods and essential inputs. Consequently, it affected modernization of industries and export promotion. While the manufacturing sector suffered from the high incidence of import duties on raw material, capital goods and intermediates, agricultural and mining sectors enjoyed many tax concessions.

The liberalization of the economy since 1991-92 provided some relief to the manufacturing sector and removed many anomalies that affected competitiveness. The opening up of the economy also created a sustainable export trend in recent times. The reduction of peak rates from 150 per cent to 35 per cent and further concessions for capital goods and essential inputs boosted the growth of indigenous industries. But the cumulative burden of import duties is still considerable as the existing mechanism does not ensure full tax relief at every stage of transaction. Several developing countries have given complete or partial tax relief of customs duties paid on inputs and intermediates in their VAT system. While implementing full fledged VAT, a suitable procedure will have to be evolved for providing adequate tax relief of all import duties. At the same time care should be taken to protect the interests of indigenous industries manufacturing substitutable goods

SALES TAX

In India, sales tax is the major source of revenue for the States. It covers all inter state and intrastate sales of goods. Article 246 of the Constitution of India empowers the states to make tax laws for items enumerated in the State List. The State List authorizes levy of duties of excise or CVD on alcoholic liquors made for human consumption, Indian hemp and other narcotic drugs. The states can also levy tax on the entry of goods into the local area, taxes on consumption and sale of electricity and taxes on the sale or purchase of goods other than newspapers. Advertisements other than newspaper advertisements, taxes on passengers carried by road or inland waterways, motor vehicle taxes, tolls, taxes on animals and boats, entertainment tax, betting and gambling taxes etc., are some other avenues for their revenue.

The two major components of sales tax are the Central Sales tax and State Sales Tax. The Central Sales tax which is known as CST is origin-based and it is applicable to inter state transactions. It is collected by the State Governments at 4 per cent from registered dealers. The main drawback of CST is that the industrially advanced states producing taxable goods collect bulk of the revenue leaving the consuming states with little income. The consignment tax system created additional problems for the industrially backward states as they got much lesser share of the CST. All states and Union Territories levy the state sales tax known as General Sales Tax (GST). It also includes purchase taxes on sugarcane and so on. The states collect sales tax from importers, manufacturers, whole-sellers and retailers. In some states, sales tax is a single point levy, but some others maintain a multi point system for certain commodities. By April 2003, all states were expected to adopt a variant of VAT.

In 1950-51, revenue from the GST was a meager amount of Rs.58 crores. It reached about 18,000 crores by 1990-91. The growth rate of GST revenue was not as impressive as that of central excise revenue. The tax base of GST was also not responsive to automatic growth. The growth reflected only the

46

massive tax efforts during the developmental period. It is not easy to isolate the impact of sales tax in view of the presence of several other taxes and deferment of tax incidence in many states. The single point tax normally ranges from 5 per cent to 15 per cent and the multi point tax lies between 7 per cent and 9 per cent. Differential rates are commonly applied on the basis of criteria like essentiality, preferential sectors etc.

CST has been considered a clear aberration as the tax collection was based on origin principle. It was introduced for ensuring uniformity of tax rate all over the country. But over a period of time the states found it difficult to accept the CST procedure and rates. In the VAT regime CST will have to be phased out and the centre has already reduced it to 2 per cent in 2003-2004 fiscal. An assurance has been given that it will be phased out in three years and that the states will be fully compensated for the revenue loss. It means that the centre has to pay up the loss of revenue to the states. But the states are still unwilling to abolish all other levies and accept the VAT rates suggested by the centre.

VAT Misunderstood

There are some serious misconceptions about the impact of VAT on state revenues. Many states have introduced entry taxes like octroi on select commodities as a compensatory measure. They consider it legitimate to have entry tax even under the VAT regime. The underlying assumption is that a fully 'vatable' entry tax levied at a rate equal to the VAT rate on sales will not have any cascading effect. But the idea is an outdated perception as any entry tax or toll involves avoidable detention of cargo and prepayment of sales tax at the state rate even before the transaction is concluded. It is an aberration that should be avoided like plague.

Such a scheme will block the capital until the tax credit is available on sale. Some of the states allow tax free entry for goods meant for re-export or goods passing through the state. They also apprehend that inter-state branch transfers and imports being tax free would result in serious erosion of revenue. Practically every state wants to convert itself into a sovereign nation by imposing entry restrictions of the kind that existed in the middle ages. The states of Karnataka, Rajasthan, Madhya Pradesh and Tamil Nadu have already imposed compensatory entry taxes to offset the VAT losses. In West Bengal, a surcharge on the existing sales tax has already been enforced. Many states want to continue entry taxes and all other state levies even after introduction of VAT for protecting revenue.

If we accept the real spirit of VAT, all other taxes should be abolished. Entry tax is not a tax on value addition and it has no place in the VAT scheme. The concept of border check is applicable only for importation of goods into a sovereign country. It is inconceivable that border checking could be done during the movement of goods within a country. In fact, countries in the European Union have removed all border checking mechanisms when they accepted the VAT regime. If the goods are moving on consignment basis, payment of duty can be insisted upon at the first value addition stage and tax credit can be given for subsequent wholesale or retail sale. If the manufacturer pays the sales tax the wholesaler is entitled for the tax credit. Abolition of entry taxes do not lead to tax evasion. Some of the states are levying it under the mistaken notion that they are sovereign countries allowing importation of goods from other states. The only entry tax leviable in India should be the customs duties and all other levies on entry, into states should be discontinued.

Sales tax is not confined to final goods. It is applicable to all raw materials and, intermediate goods whether they are indigenously manufactured or imported. The state tariff is much more complex than central excise due to the multitude of exemption schemes. The State Governments have to accommodate a wide variety of local interests seeking exemptions and concessions. They include incentive schemes for backward areas and concessional rates or deferment for attracting new industries. Such state specific exemptions and

48

concessions should be standardized for effective implementation of VAT. If every state is free to follow its own preferences in rates and exemptions, VAT is not likely to give any benefit to the trade and industry.

The cascading effect of taxation is very high with multipoint taxes as it compounds the tax effect of central excise and import duties on inputs, intermediates and final products. With the imminent switch over to VAT, the domestic manufacturing sector is expected to get substantial relief from the convergence of taxes and rates. It would have been better if the model legislation suggested by the central government were accepted by all states. Presently, 10 per cent VAT rate has been suggested for states in the Northern India and 12.5 per cent for the South. These are supposed to be revenue neutral rates and in addition four more rates are suggested for VAT. Defense and strategic goods are allowed nil rates and one per cent is prescribed for precious metals. Demerit goods will attract 20 per cent and agricultural products will be taxed at 4 per cent. The states will also be empowered to levy VAT on sugar, textiles and tobacco, which are now subject to additional excise duties in lieu of sales tax. The revenue neutral rate of 12.5 per cent has already been reduced to 4 per cent in the case of drugs and medicines. Another concession given to the traders was an option for paying a composite tax of one per cent of the turnover in lieu of VAT. However, it will be available only to traders with an annual turnover of Rs. 25 lakhs.

Retail Sales

Retail transactions are not a fully exploited tax base for want of administrative capabilities for obtaining compliance. This sector is inaccessible to administration as documented transactions are simply not available. The cost of maintaining a huge collection machinery to reach the retail level is not commensurate with the revenue potential. Mostly, the states get out of the problems of taxing this sector by exempting outlets on a turnover basis. They try to maximize revenue by taxing imported and indigenous goods heavily at the first point of sale.

The state taxes are now actually a duplication of excise and customs levies with a different nomenclature. The tremendous scope for taxation on value addition at the wholesale and retail stages is forgone in view of the practical problems of reaching large number of assesses. The fiscal arrangement envisaged under the Constitution is to assign taxes accruing from value addition till the manufacturing stage and imports to the Central Government. Value additions at the wholesale and retail stages are meant for the State exchequer. But the practical problems of administration compel the States to go for backward integration that invariably overlap with the tax base of the Central Government. Only a full fledged VAT, can bring the wholesale and retail outlets under the tax system. It will ensure revenue from the automatic growth of the economy. For this purpose, the tax system and collection procedures should conform to VAT requirements. Tax credit will have to be liberally given for all payments made at the previous stages. If VAT is not implemented in the real spirit, it is not likely to improve the revenue or GDP growth.

SERVICE TAX

In the recent past the pattern of GDP growth has given rise to serious apprehensions. The industrial growth rate declined to about 4 per cent and agriculture was growing more clumsily at less than 2 per cent. But service sector has grown at a higher level of about 8 per cent during the same period. Some people consider it as an unhealthy trend that reflects mainly the wage increase in the government sector. The slow down in the industrial growth is particularly noticeable in the last decade. It is whether service sector growth without matching industrial growth in rate is sustainable in the long run.

The expansion of IT sector may be one welcome sign but we cannot simple survive on sporadic growth surges in service sector. Service sector in India is another area that has not been sufficiently explored for raising revenue. However, the considerable growth of services during the last two decades has now focused attention of the Central Government on this new tax base. Some identified services have been brought under the indirect tax regime in the 1994-95 budget. Selective extension of Service tax has been attempted later. Presently, we have 61 services under the tax net and the revenue estimate for 2002-03 was Rs.5000 crores. The Service tax can save the commodity tax base from the excessive tax burden. The growth of services taxes from 1994 is presented in Annexure IX.

The centre has now agreed to amend the constitution by inserting a new article 268A to enable the states to collect service taxes. It will have two lists of items on which the centre and states can levy service tax. A negative list of services will indicate the government and social services that fall outside the scope of tax. To ensure uniformity, the center will be empowered to prescribe the rates of service tax. The states could collect the tax as certain services to compensate the revenue loss on account of the introduction of VAT. In the 2003-2004 budget the service tax rate has been enhanced from 5 per cent to 8 per cent. Service tax has also been imposed on ten new services. In 2002-2003, service tax has been made 'vatable' for the same category of input and out services. In 2003-2004, the centre has announced tax credit of all service inputs. It is a great improvement that reduces the cascading effect of service tax.

The new Finance Minister, while presenting the 2004-05 budget, reiterated the need for implementing VAT, which according to him, is a modern and efficient trade tax that incorporates the best international practices. He welcomed the decision of the Empowered Committee to introduce VAT in all states from 1st April 2005. The states were urged to pass the relevant VAT legislation and sufficient compensation was promised for any consequential loss of revenue. An Expert Committee has also been proposed to assist the states to move towards the stage of implementation.

WAY OUT OF THE MUDDLE

The brief overview of our major indirect taxes reveals several structural deficiencies and tax-induced distortions. The cumulative impact of all the wrong policies and practices has finally pulled down the industrial growth rate. The high fiscal deficit, lack of reforms relating to labour, power and infrastructure are some relevant factors that keep the growth rate sluggish. The way out of the muddle has to be a comprehensive growth plan. Another glaring anomaly is the inability of taxes to achieve multitude of objectives for ensuring equity and protection. Not only that, they also fail to meet the challenges posed by the rapid growth of the developing countries in Asia and Latin America. For realising the tremendous revenue potential from enhanced economic activities particularly in E-commerce, we have to convert taxes to a flexible and dynamic system.

In the budget 2004-05, a major step was taken to integrate the tax on goods and services by extending credit of service tax and excise duty across goods and services. The rate of service tax was also raised from 8% to 10%, ostensibly to keep the impact of the integration revenue neutral. In addition to the hike in the rates, some new services were also included in the tax net. Some existing taxable services were redefined to include all service providers in that category within the tax·base. The administration has been made more customer friendly by removing mandatory verification of self assessment and the mandatory penalty for non-registration.

The experience of VAT in many countries clearly establishes the fact that it is the only tax that can give India an adequate tax to GDP ratio. The salient features of VAT, which can easily bring about the much-needed reforms in the tax structure, will be discussed later. Before that, we will briefly see the suggestions made by KTF that looked into the deficiencies in the prevailing central indirect taxes. It is the last in a chain of expert groups and committees that examined the deficiencies of the tax system to suggest changes for raising the revenue and competency of administration. We will also see how the proposals for major tax reforms were implemented in the 2003-2004 budget.

❑❑

CHAPTER V

KELKAR'S QUANTUM JUMP
AND QUIET FALL

Mr. Speaker, Please sympathize with me. I endeavour to make easy that which Einstein found so difficult.

[Jaswant Singh presenting Budget 2003-2004]

The Last Doctor

True to the axiom that bureaucracy revels in committee culture, we have the report of yet another Task Force (KTF) on the state of the tax system. The mandate for KTF on Direct and Indirect Taxes was to take advantage of the advancement of information technology to bring the tax systems at par with the best international practices. As I mentioned earlier, it is the latest in a series of committees and groups that have been looking into the complexities of our tax system. In the annexures I am presenting some relevant extracts of their recommendations to remove the inefficiencies of the tax system. Here, I do not propose to examine the suggestions on direct tax reforms, which are mostly for marginal changes in the rates and administration.

The macro perspective of KTF was conditioned by the concerns of deteriorating fiscal deficit and the weak performance of exports and FDI. KTF was deeply worried about the declining tax to GDP ratios of all central taxes and state taxes. In actual terms, there has also been a perceptible fall in India's share of exports in world trade from 2per cent prior to independence to the current level of 0.6per cent. Our FDI flow is currently at a dismal level of about $ 2 billion as compared to China's $ 46 billion. In the introduction, I presented a brief glimpse of the deplorable levels of our economic activities as compared to the recent outstanding performance of China.

With the ever increasing total fiscal deficit estimated over 10 per cent of GDP and keeping in view the declining tax credit ratio, KTF made several sweeping recommendations. The objective was obviously to create a user friendly and transparent tax administration that could raise the tax ratio to reasonable levels. The most important suggestion was the immediate removal of the plethora of exemptions granted on import and excise duties for a variety of reasons. Expansion of the service tax base and improving tax compliance were the other major recommendations for improving revenue. The export incentives also came under close scrutiny and it was agreed that input tax relief should be given for all export production.

They wanted to reduce the transaction cost involved in trade and business activities in India. To achieve this objective, they suggested modernization and automation of procedures comparable to international standards. Specific mention was made about the removal of the impediments that prevent smooth inflow of FDI. They referred to an EXIM bank study that placed the transaction cost of Indian exports of textile and garments, and pharmaceuticals at 10 per cent and 8 per cent respectively. By introducing automated systems and procedures, the estimate is that a 50 per cent reduction in transaction costs can be achieved. The Task Force did not favour the direct tax exemptions, which are obviously intended to improve savings and investment.

The methodology

KTF held extensive dialogues with the trade, industry and the bureaucracy concerned with tax administration. They also examined the best international practices in critical areas of administration. The reports of other expert committees and groups that studied the functioning of the indirect tax system in the past were also referred to for guidance. While admitting that the government has recently initiated a wide variety of steps to improve the tax administration, they felt that nevertheless the general perception of the trade and industry was that much more reforms were needed at this critical juncture. They did appreciate the introduction of transaction value for excise duty assessment, MRP based levy on certain consumer goods, simplification of procedures like dispensation of pre-clearance requirements, fortnightly payment of duty, discontinuation of statutory reports, and so on. On the Customs, the switch over to EDI based assessment for clearance of import and export cargo was appreciated.

After reviewing the structural complexities and examining informed opinion and reports of other committees and groups, KTF concluded that there was perceptible lack of public confidence in tax administration. It was attributed to too much of discretionary powers, absence of accountability and a clear pro-revenue bias in all administrative decisions particularly in quasi-judicial orders. Taxpayers are alienated from the administration due to complex procedures that led to low level of compliance. As regards tax policy, it was observed that uncertainty about tax liability and the absence of time bound decisions affected the business prospects in the economy. They found that complex laws and procedures created an environment of distrust and corruption. Conditional exemption notifications made compliance difficult and caused serious delays in conducting transactions. Another observation was that unscrupulous taxpayers and dishonest administration exploited the absence of transparency for evading taxes.

The Quantum Jump

In spite of the complexities and problems, they were confident about introducing a modern, transparent and efficient tax system even in the short term. It was admitted that mere tinkering with the existing laws and procedures could not create such a desirable system. A macro-jump was urgently needed to remove all hurdles at one stroke and achieve fundamental changes in tax rates and administration. The strategy was to transcend to a trust based administration by allowing all clearances of goods on self-certification or appraisal. The checks and controls to be exercised on clearances should be made only on the basis of intelligence or post-facto audit in a specified time frame. To reduce the transaction cost, they wanted to do away with all securities and create mandatory systems for time bound resolution of disputes. They suggested completion of the automation of procedures yet to be digitized for increasing the transparency, accountability and efficiency of administration.

It was suggested that online acceptance and assessment of documents should be introduced to reduce the number of public contact points. Lastly, it was recommended that the tax administrators should be given intensive training to restore confidence and to create a new mindset required for modernization. All discretionary powers should be taken away from the departmental officers for reducing the scope of subjectivity and corruption. They relied on the principles of simplicity, transparency and stability for the formulation of the recovery package. Apart from these conventional economic principles, they also incorporated the principles of trust, best international practices and service to make comprehensive recommendations. They expected that the recommendations would change the face of India's tax administration. It was also estimated that drastic changes in administration and reduction of structural complexities would also improve the tax to GDP ratio.

Customs Scenario

As regards Customs, KTF noticed that there had been a steady decline in revenue during the last decade and the tax to GDP ratio has fallen from 3.6 to 2.3. During the same period the central excise ratio also fell from 4.3 to 3.3. It was easy to account for the loss of excise revenue, as the share of the manufacturing sector in the GDP has been perceptibly shrinking for some time. On the Customs side, although the duty rates had been reduced considerably, a plethora of exemptions particularly export promotion schemes were found to be eroding the revenue base. To arrest the deteriorating revenue collections, they targeted on the immediate withdrawal of all unnecessary

56

exemptions. They also wanted to reduce the number of rates and types of taxes to make administration less complex and improve compliance. Another important step mooted to augment revenue was to expand the coverage of service tax comprehensively and introduce VAT for removing the cascading effect of indirect taxes.

They observed that the Customs tariff consisted of a bewildering array of levies and multiplicity of rates and recommended that only three types of duties should remain in the tariff namely, basic customs duty, additional duty of customs (CVD) and Anti-dumping/safeguard duties. As regards rates, the government already laid out the policy objective that by 2004-2005, there would be only two rates of 10 per cent and 20 per cent for Customs. The lower rate would be applicable to raw materials, inputs and intermediate goods and the higher one would be for final goods. Certain demerit goods like cigarettes and alcohol would attract a much higher rate than the standard rates and agricultural products might fall in a special category outside the scope of the standard rates. It was suggested to adopt (i) 0 per cent for life saving drugs, sovereign imports (security related goods, etc.) and Reserve Bank imports (ii) 10 percent for raw materials, inputs and intermediate goods (iii) 20 per cent for final goods. A higher rate of up to 150 per cent was suggested for specified agricultural products and demerit goods. To safeguard the interest of domestic industry, a staggered move towards lower rates had been recommended.

It was not found possible to estimate the effect of different kinds of tax exemptions or to quantify the revenue involved. Certain exemptions require certification, verification, etc. which result in delays and higher administration cost. There are also several undesirable side effects of exemptions, which cause loss of transparency and give opportunities for widespread corruption. For the end-use based exemptions, there are several certifying authorities. In addition to certification, there are also post import verifications for releasing the bonds or bank guarantees. While recognizing the need for continuing certain essential exemptions, KTF recommended that there should be only four categories of exemption applicable to: (i) life saving goods (ii) security related goods (iii) goods meant for relief and charitable purposes, and (iv) for discharging international obligations and contracts. If an exemption was justified under one of the chosen categories, it should not be conditional or end use based. For protecting the domestic manufacturers, it was suggested that countervailing duty (CVD) should not be subject to any exemption. They did not favour the continuation of specific rates of duty currently applicable to a few items. Specific rates are not acceptable in a modern tax system that follows well-documented value based transactions for collection of revenue.

Same Medicine for Excise

The prescriptions for customs were repeated in the case of excise duty exemptions with certain modifications. While appreciating the declining trend of exemptions during the last five years, it was observed that the number of notifications might not be the correct pointer to the revenue forgone in various tax concessions. They noted the absence of a mechanism for periodical and comprehensive reviews to justify exemptions. It was recommended that exemptions should not be given to any luxury goods even if they were manufactured in the small sector. Another criterion for granting exemptions would be the cost of compliance and collection. Since demerit goods are taxed at high rates all over the world, it was also suggested for the Indian system. A justifiable kind of exemption was for products requiring use in environmental protection. As in the case of Customs, instead of exemptions, they recommended a budgetary mechanism for giving tax rebate.

No Sops for SSI

SSI sector came up for a close review in view of the liberal tax exemptions given to them on equity consideration. There are about 40 lakhs units in SSI sector that represent 95 per cent of all industries in the country. The value addition from this SSI sector comes to about 40 per cent of the total value addition by the manufacturing sector. In exports, its share is about 34 per cent and the contribution to GDP is about 7per cent. But it was noted that the excise revenue from SSI is only 3.5 per cent. At present, units having clearances up to Rs.1 crore in a financial year are exempt from duty. More than 90 per cent of the SSI units are now enjoying duty free status that adversely affects the revenue. In addition, they also get out of the reach of income tax, sales tax, etc., as the production and sale are not documented. Another difficulty in administering the exemption is the misuse of Cenvat credit by duty paying sector using exempted inputs from SSI. Exemptions giving massive benefits to inputs and intermediates also affect the functioning of a full fledged VAT as they break the credit chain in many places. As they try to remain perpetually under the cut-off limit, it has a decelerating effect on GDP growth. It is the major cause of the stagnant growth rate.

In many countries, the threshold of exemption is generally Rs.30 to 40 lakhs. Since the SSI sector pays other taxes like income tax, it was recommended that they should also pay excise duty if the turn over exceeded Rs.50 lakhs. The exemption limit could be lowered from the current level of Rs.one crore gradually for giving them time to adjust with the new tax liability. They also wanted to modify the eligibility to exemption by calculating the total turnover of all goods manufactured in a unit excluding export production. A negative list was proposed to deny exemption to certain white goods and a declaration to the department was also recommended when the value of clearances reached the threshold of Rs.50 lakhs.

Considering the complexities of assessment and collection of duty on matches, they recommended that the present practice of using excise stamp for paying duty should be discontinued. They found that there was widespread corruption and inefficiency in the operation of the excise stamp system and the extension of small sector exemption to matches would take care of the majority of manufacturers. Since only large units would be in the dutiable sector, an ad valorem levy could be imposed with Cenvat credit. It was also recommended to discontinue exemptions based on geographical locations. Such schemes should be replaced by a budget subsidy or other non-tariff supports.

Multiple Duties and Rates

There are different kind of duties like special duty of excise, additional duties of excise (textile and textile articles act, 1978), additional duty on motor spirit and high-speed diesel and cess. They distort the tax structure and create uncertainties leading to innumerable litigations. Continuation of AED (Additional Excise Duty) in lieu of sales tax has also been adversely affecting the possibility of the introduction of a national VAT. KTF was of the view that Cenvat should be the only duty in the tariff. Alternatively, if a product attracted multiple levies, it was suggested that the total tax leviable should be indicated against a particular item. The task of breaking up the total tax into individual heads should be done by the department and not by the taxpayer. The Cenvat credit rules should also be simplified to accommodate multiple levies, but preference should be given to abolish as many levies as possible and if practicable, just keep only the Cenvat.

Ideal Rate

KTF analyzed the proportion of revenue accruing from different rates and found that 62 per cent of the total revenue came from 16 per cent rate and 8 per cent rate yielded only 3.2 per cent of the revenue. Revenue from the higher rate of 32 per cent was only 7 per cent and 26.7 per cent of revenue came from special rates. They recommended four rates starting with 0 for life saving drugs, security related items and 8 for food items and 16 for all other items excluding agricultural products and tobacco and tobacco related products. Transitional arrangement of staggered rates was suggested as a buffer and 4 per cent without Cenvat was indicated as a starter. Duty rate of 32 per cent should be reduced to 16 in a sliding scale of 4 points per year. Separate rate structure was proposed for petroleum products and textiles.

As regards textile sector, the recommendation was to remove the exemptions that distorted the production pattern. It was proposed to put all unprocessed woven/knitted fabrics as well as yarns under the general SSI exemption. Handlooms and handloom fabrics should also be given the same benefit. Duty should be levied on all other processed fabrics whether using power or not. The excuse for not entering this sector being the cost of compliance, they suggested suitable simplifications of procedures. It was not found necessary to give any special rates to the textile sector and the abolition of deemed credit facility was also recommended to keep parity with other commodities.

Trust is Best

Several basic reforms have been suggested for simplifying tax collection procedures and reducing functional deficiencies. As compared to clearance practices prevailing internationally, the Indian system depends on excessive documentation. There is also inadequate automation and application of information technology. In place of the transaction based documentation, they suggested a Trust Based System (TBS) that would give universal green channel to all imports. To facilitate automation, the EDI network should be expanded to all ports/airports by 1st January 2004. Routine examination of goods should be done away with and if any examination was found necessary, it should be on the basis of risk profiling and risk assessment techniques. Department should maintain detailed profiles of all importers and exporters. Risk profiling could be done using parameters like high import duty, imports from countries other than the country of manufacture, and related party transactions. The declarations made prior to clearance should be verified only after clearance, unless some risk factor was apprehended.

Multidisciplinary audit was recommended on post clearance basis at the importers' premises. A revolutionary recommendation was for self-assessment of bill of entry by the importer followed by the computer system giving clearance after payment of duty. It was suggested that instead of transaction based bills of entry, the importer should be allowed to file a period bill of entry to reduce the cost of individual assessments. In the case of established importers having good track record of compliance, goods should be cleared on the basis of minimum specified information with or without examination and after payment of duty. Regular assessments could be done subsequently after all requisite documents are received within a specified period of time. The process of automated verification of import declarations should rely solely on system software to avoid human intervention.

They also suggested many minor procedural modifications for improving the tax administration. They include, interalia, changes in Custom House Agents Licensing Regulations and empowerment for enforcing IPR and formulation of export valuation rules. The introduction of full -fledged VAT was strongly recommended with suitable modifications in the definition of manufacture. It was suggested that guidelines on determination of cost of production should be issued at the earliest and MRP based valuation must be extended to other commodities. A permanent committee on MRP abatements was suggested to fix the extent of abatement for the items brought under MRP.

All Credits Together

An important recommendation was to abolish the distinction between capital goods and inputs and allow credit on all inputs brought into the factory. Cenvat credit should be denied only for items such as office furniture, motor spirit, high speed diesel, etc. that could constitute a very small negative list. Capital goods should be given full credit of the duty paid as in the case of other inputs. Cenvat credit should not be denied on technical or procedural violations and provisions should be made to delegate authority for condoning lapses. The Task Force strongly recommended against Cenvat credit being allowed on deemed credit basis. The credit should be allowed even if the goods were stored outside the factory in an identified place. As regards sealing of export consignments, it was suggested that the practice of container sealing by the officer should be replaced by self-sealing by the exporter.

Another recommendation was to replace the fortnightly payment of duty with monthly payment. In case of defaults, there should be automatic charge of interest and penalty. Removal of Budget day restrictions and several other procedural simplifications were suggested to simplify tax administration. An institutional setup for the guidance of small manufacturers was envisaged to improve customer relations.

Bogus Exports

Export promotion schemes were taken for a microscopic scrutiny and it was found that precious revenue had been lost in the misutilization of incentive schemes. Actual physical exports were not found commensurate with the duty foregone. In 2001-2002, all schemes for export promotion cumulatively cost the exchequer about Rs.21,799 crores. Total neutralization of the tax element in export production is internationally accepted, but multiplicity of export promotion schemes and the loopholes in the law created scope for bogus claims for export benefits. It was recommended to replace multiple export promotion schemes involving tax relief with a new one having only two channels for incentives.

The first channel would be for special export zones and EOUs and the second one for duty free clearances of capital goods and raw materials with refund of duties paid through drawback. All notifications pertaining to EOU/EPZ schemes should be consolidated into one and domestic market sales by EOU/EPZ units should be progressively reduced. Since large numbers of bills of entry are involved in export outstanding statement, it was suggested that there should be electronic exchange of information between the RBI and the customs. They should also accept bank certificates as proof of realisation.

In the case of drawback, several procedural simplifications had been suggested for the schedule and declarations. The recommendations also envisaged creation of an import and export co-ordination committee to examine and resolve all issues and to cut out the delays. Both the customs and directorate

63

general of foreign trade had been asked to make use of EDI technology to create the database for an effective interface with exporters.

All customs and central excise commissionerates had been asked to complete automation immediately for online processing of returns and applications, risk analysis, profiling and management, message exchange with related agencies, etc. Not only the field formations, but CBEC and its directorates should also be automated and facility for video conferencing between the CBEC (central board of excise and customs) and the Chief Commissioner could be created for the smooth flow of information. The commissionerates should offer their customers online facilities for filing of documents and returns. The taxpayers could file the data through a web based application from their own premises or from a service centre instead of the department entering the data. The systems directorate should be revamped to lay down the road map for automation and for procuring the necessary resources. The automated processes should identify the share of individual heads in the total duty paid.

Tax Ombudsman

An indirect tax ombudsman was suggested for resolving tax-related grievances of the public. Another independent body was envisaged for carrying out investigations relating to safeguard duties and anti-dumping. They sought replacement of adjudication of offence cases by a single officer by a bench consisting of two officers of the same level. The Tribunal was asked to finalize cases in a time bound manner and any stay given should stand automatically vacated if it was not finalized within six months. The Chief Commissioner should be authorized to appoint counsels beyond the monetary limits prescribed for commissioners. As regards revenue targets, the recommendation was to fix them realistically by including drawback disbursed and refunds sanctioned. The central excise revenue should take into account duty paid both in PLA and Cenvat credit in addition to the refunds paid. All customs formations were asked to obtain ISO certification by 1st January 2005. The Task Force also made some other important recommendations relating to administration, human resources development and training.

In respect of value added tax and service tax, it was recommended that the state governments should be told to announce a time bound action plan for implementation of VAT by 1st April, 2003. The multiple tax regimes of the state governments should be converged into a single VAT on goods and services. In the case of service tax, the scheme of tax credit should be extended to include all services. Presently, it is allowed only if the input and output services are in the same category. Ultimately the service tax credit should be amalgamated into the Cenvat scheme for a total integration of all tax credits available to a taxpayer.

I mentioned the highlights of the recommendations of KTF mainly for focusing attention on the inadequacies of the current indirect tax system in India. The desperate hurry indicates that the patient is really sinking and the life supporting systems may not hold on for long. True that such critical situations cannot be tackled with conventional palliatives and pious hopes of changing the mindset of the tax collectors. Marginal changes of this kind have already been suggested and implemented in the last three decades. In fact, I am presenting in the annexures a brief overview of the tremendous efforts to make structural and functional changes in the administration of indirect tax. (Please see annexure IV to VII). Evidently, recommendations of KTF reveal where we reached with all the marginal reforms adopted on expert advice. I am presenting the relevant extracts of the budget speech (2003-2004) that deal with the recommendations of KTF. It confirms that our marginal approach to reforms is an incurable affliction.

Direct Taxes

In respect of direct taxes, the main recommendation of the Kelkar Committee was to exempt taxpayers with income below

Rs.one lakh on equity consideration. Some marginal reductions were given, but most of the existing exemptions were not favoured. It was conceded that the consumption tax burden borne by such taxpayers would be adequate contribution to the public cause. What they probably forgot is the fact that Rs.one lakh exemption does not give sufficient subsistence income to the taxpayer. It seems that equity was the main consideration for recommending the elimination of exemptions particularly those related to savings. I do not know whether KTF considered the fact that our domestic savings is at the miserable 24 per cent level as compared to the saving rate of 42 per cent of China.

Another lopsided argument was that since the corporate profits would bear the full burden of corporate tax, the effective burden of individual shareholders could be substantially higher in spite of the elimination of tax on dividend and long-term capital gains. KTF's obsession with progressivity and revenue neutrality probably conflicted with the objectives of economic growth and improving tax to GDP ratio. Like the tax collectors, KTF also approached the basic issues of reforms with revenue blinkers. No wonder the next committee will also find the tax system as ailing as before.

KTF accepted that under the existing law the maximum marginal rate of personal income tax was leviable at a low income level i.e. Rs.1,50,000/-. The recommendation to levy the highest rate of 30 per cent only on incomes above Rs. 4 lakhs was to benefit the young generation of taxpayers. While reeling out the huge tax-cuts accruing to senior citizens, salaried and non-salaried taxpayers in each income group, the committee forgot the fact that they were also supposed to pay the indirect taxes. The package of recommendations relating to corporate tax is actually revenue positive. It does not make much sense to give a marginal reduction from 36.75 per cent to 30 per cent for domestic companies and to 35 per cent for foreign companies. The only substantive recommendation is regarding exemption of dividend from taxation in the hands of the shareholders and exemption on long-term capital gains on listed equity. The proposal to eliminate minimum alternate tax under Section 115

JB is an already accepted position. Although the expectation is that the recommendations are revenue neutral, the committee hopes to generate buoyancy by widening the personal and corporate income tax bases. The justification for abolishing tax incentives for investment and savings is based on the view that such incentives are inefficient. Another strange conclusion is that elimination of such exemptions will improve economic efficiency by reducing the interest rates. When saving rate is stagnating at the 24 per cent level, the proposal to abolish tax incentives would mean removal of the life supporting systems. True, the patient will not require further medication.

The recommendations of the Task Force do not reflect an open-minded approach to the complexities of direct tax system. First they did not adopt an appropriate conceptual framework to correlate the incidence of direct and indirect taxes. They did not converge the tax burden on a typical individual or family paying direct taxes as well as consumption taxes like excise and sales tax. It seems that the committee was more concerned with transparency in tax administration than on the impact of the recommendation on savings and incentives required for economic growth.

They were also more obsessed with the revenue neutral nature of tax reforms and reduction of transaction costs. As in the case of indirect taxes, the recommendations were mostly based on individual perceptions rather than on empirical studies of the probable impact of the tax rates on economic growth. Removal of exemption Raj was the most important concern of the committee than the introduction of basic reforms for improving productivity and value addition. One interesting feature of the quantum jump was that it was made within the confines of the conventional ambit of committee reforms. They did not find it expedient to recommend any revolutionary departure to achieve accelerated growth.

All that we find from such periodical reviews is that systemic reforms are now unavoidable. The tax regime may be a small issue, but it is a crucial one to start the basic changes in the economy. A holistic approach with lot of trust on the taxpayer is undoubtedly the need of the time. I will give an outline of an ideal recovery package in the conclusions along with my views on some of the recommendations of the Task Force. But before that, let us delve deeper into VAT and see whether it can really show the way out of our tax muddle. In Annexure X the relevant extracts of the budget speech (2003-2004) are presented to indicate the acceptance of some of the recommendations of KTF. It is evident that even the KTF package, which did not incorporate many of the pressing needs of the economy also met with the usual bureaucratic burial.

❏❏

CHAPTER VI

WHY THE WORLD IS ON A VAT MODE?

For deriving all from nothing there suffices a single principle.

[Lebniz]

We are now at the threshold of the promised wonderland of VAT. The thrice postponed deadline for a national switchover to VAT at the state level was definitely an ambitious one. If it materialized, we would have joined a band of about 120 VAT operating countries in the world. Not only that, the VAT regime would have integrated our tax system with the tax payment patterns of more than 70 per cent of the world population. In India, it is all the more important that VAT should immediately replace the regressive and unfriendly taxes like entry tax, luxury tax, turnover tax, single point or multi point sales tax and so on.

Many states have already enacted laws for introducing VAT at the rates suggested by the empowered committee. For classification of goods, the states are presently not following the harmonized system prevalent in central excise and customs. They have been demanding immediate compensation for the probable loss of revenue. Some of them are keen to get compensation rather than the economic benefits of VAT. In the guise of revenue protection, some states have re-introduced entry taxes and turnover taxes. It is definitely a confusing scenario for the hapless public. Whatever reforms are suggested, the taxman will not forgo his revenue obsession! And the traders do not want the transparency of VAT to expose their murky deals.

The fact that VAT has been accepted in most of the countries in the world shows that it has many attractive features which are not found in other tax systems. In the 70's and 80's there has been large-scale tax reforms all over the world for accelerating GDP growth rates. Massive tax efforts in the developing countries distorted the tax system, which tried to mop up maximum revenue from a narrow base. Following the American initiative, developing countries attempted broadening of the direct tax base and reducing the rates in anticipation of higher revenue collection. But having realised the limited impact of direct taxes for raising adequate resources, tax reforms began to focus on the evolution of a comprehensive and non-cascading indirect tax like VAT. The progressive and non-intrusive features of VAT are so attractive that even some of the developed countries are contemplating the replacement of direct taxes with a simpler model of broad based VAT.

No Debt Traps

In recent times public finance reforms have become the main concern of governments all over the world. President Reagan introduced certain unprecedented fiscal reforms in the 80's. They were followed by many changes in the monetary policies to reduce fiscal deficit. But developing countries instead of reforming tax system, took the easy route of market borrowing from external and internal sources. The result was uncontroll-able inflation and all pervasive poverty. Serious law and order problems ensued with violent protests against governments' policies for inflation.

Many countries in Africa and Latin America are still in deep debt traps for want of suitable mechanism to reduce fiscal deficits. Taxpayers in developing countries invariably resent imposition of personal income taxes. They try to avoid payment at any cost and only salaried employees get caught in the tax net. Most of the countries in the world have now switched over to VAT for collecting taxes unobtrusively through an elastic and transparent system. VAT has been universally acclaimed as the panacea for correcting the fiscal imbalances as it works well within all political and legal constraints.

One important lesson from the tax reform experiences of developing countries is that for a successful outcome in terms of revenue and other objectives it should apply to the entire economy. A partial replacement of a few components of federal taxes with modern VAT may not achieve the objectives of tax reform. From the experiences of VAT operating countries, it is seen that the revenue and the tax ratio to GDP increased considerably after switch over from conventional taxes. In the preceding chapters, we have seen the deficiencies of the Indian indirect tax system and Dr Kelkar's bitter pills for a quick cure. They show the urgent need for comprehensive reforms to avert the impending collapse of the economy in about ten years' time. We cannot attribute the low GDP growth rate entirely to the defective tax system but a thorough overhaul of the fiscal policies would definitely go a long way in rejuvenating investment and growth. In this chapter, we take a brief look at the attractive features of VAT that can correct the economic inefficiencies created by the archaic taxes.

Goodbye to Tax on Tax

VAT is the only tax that offers positive alternatives to the negative impact of indirect taxation. It is an accepted fact that commodity taxes create severe cascading effect as the taxes levied at earlier stages of production and distribution get taxed again and again at subsequent points. Consequently, instead of paying taxes on the value addition by a manufacturer, wholesaler or retailer, tax is paid on an inflated value, which includes taxes already paid at earlier stages. Such anomalies escalate prices and encourage vertical integration, where the manufacturer himself tries to wholesale and retail the goods. Vertical integration has been responsible for recession and unemployment particularly in developing countries. VAT has an inbuilt device for reducing the cascading effect by restricting the levy to actual value addition. It encourages growth by confining tax burden to the net economic contribution of the taxpayer. Moreover, since the capital investment also gets tax relief, VAT can accelerate economic growth by encouraging modernization and replacement.

71

Simple and Transparent

There is no other tax that can be as transparent and simple like VAT. At every stage of transaction, VAT indicates the quantum of tax payable after adjusting tax credits. The taxpayer, the ultimate consumer and the administration are all fully aware of all the details of tax payment. In the conventional system, only the taxpayer and administration know the tax liability. If there is a nexus between the department and the payer, it is possible to distort the element of tax without the knowledge of the ultimate consumer. The transparency improves compliance as it becomes difficult to evade taxes successfully at every transaction stage. Cross-checking of tax credit taken earlier can make it difficult to avoid payment. After deducting the tax credit, the tax payable is a small amount at any point of time. In conventional taxes, there is ample scope for evasion as the documentary requirements are not as elaborate and inter-related as in VAT. In figure III, a typical VAT audit system is presented for illustration.

More Revenue

The immediate objective of VAT in developing countries is to improve the tax to GDP ratio. It is adopted when conventional taxes fail to provide elastic revenue for meeting the increasing demands of public expenditure. In all VAT operating countries, it has earned the reputation of being a dependable revenue raising instrument. VAT can easily access the incremental income generated by the expanding economic activities without altering the rates or base in every budget. When VAT was introduced, it yielded more revenue than the initial estimates in countries like New Zealand, Portugal, Korea and Indonesia. The average revenue contribution of VAT ranges from 5 to 10per cent of GNP depending on the rates and requirements. That should allay the apprehensions of the Indian states that they are about to lose considerable revenue.

Several studies conducted in European countries indicate that revenue from VAT increased steadily since its inception. In developing countries like Korea, Indonesia and Chile, the first three years after its inception showed substantial increase in the tax ratio. The substantial rise of revenue in these countries has been attributed to better tax compliance and reduced scope for evasion. The revenue is also closely related to the cost of collection and compliance. In the initial stages, VAT is definitely more costly to administer than other conventional taxes for its requirements of infrastructure and detailed documentation. The administration also has to invest heavily on automation to deal with the scrutiny of returns and matching of invoices. But once the infrastructure is provided, the cost of collection and compliance gradually declines.

The very low cost of collection of conventional taxes only reflect the inability of the administration to tap the vast potential for revenue. The British experience shows that operating cost of VAT came down from 2 per cent to 1per cent in less than 10 years time. If the VAT rates were low, it would not be economical to incur the cost of maintaining a huge establishment for revenue collection and tax payment. It has been estimated that any rate below 7 per cent would not be worthwhile for developing countries contemplating the adoption of VAT. A basic rate of 10 per cent is the minimum that is required for implementing a manufacturers' VAT of the type that was adopted in Indonesia and Columbia.

More important than the cost of collection is the compliance cost of the taxpayer. For compliance at the retail level, details of daily transactions in exempted goods, taxable goods, and tax credits on purchases are to be maintained even by very small establishments. Every sale will involve the issue of a proper invoice indicating the tax in the price. If the literacy rate is low, such requirements lead to serious problems of documentation. Many retailers and wholesalers may have to hire help for maintaining accounts, which increases the overheads. Since the margins available for retail and wholesale transactions are not much, the burden of VAT may become unbearable for small enterprises. But the alternative is to continue overtaxing a narrow base repeatedly by different agencies. It is difficult to

73

raise revenue properly unless taxpayers make some sacrifices in the initial stages.

Price Neutral

There have been serious apprehensions about the inflationary impact of VAT. Prospective VAT users went on postponing implementation for fear of serious political fallout particularly during the transitional period. However, the initial inflationary impact of VAT was found only in very few instances. If it were introduced to replace an existing commodity tax, the price rise would be hardly noticeable. The tax relief from the abolished tax could offset the price impact. Inflationary pressures are expected in VAT regime as it allows exemption to very few products, firms and sectors. But we should not forget the fact that it also brings in more revenue for supporting the welfare programmes of the government.

The price effect of VAT depends mainly on the elasticity of demand and supply of the taxable products and the conditions in the factor markets. If traders pass on the entire tax, the consumer price index would rise exactly to the extent of the tax levied. In fact, in the Indian context, introduction of a comprehensive VAT to replace the existing indirect taxes both at the state and central level, should in every likelihood, reduce the consumer price. The study conducted in 35 VAT operating countries showed that its introduction had very little effect on consumer prices. If VAT substituted an existing tax with no additional revenue objective in the short run, it would not have any inflationary impact. On the other hand, a reverse effect could be felt due to the input tax relief, which was not available earlier.

Equity Ensured

Policy makers are a worried lot when it comes to the distributional impact of tax burden. Incidence studies try to estimate the distribution of tax burden across various income groups for indicating whether the tax is collected according to the capacity of the payer. To reduce the regressive impact of commodity taxes, VAT rate has to be less than that of the substituted taxes like central excise or sales tax. Some empirical conclusions on the distribution of VAT burden indicate that its overall impact is marginally progressive. Vat has been found progressive in the UK in view of zero rating of essential consumption articles. However, it had a regressive effect in France due to higher incidence on consumption.

In Korea also the lowest income groups had to bear a heavier tax burden than the high-income groups. The progressive effect of VAT is visible only in countries that totally exempt essential consumer articles like food and medicine. But the comfortable fact is that its incidence is generally less regressive than that of other commodity taxes. In comparison to conventional indirect taxes, VAT can be more equitable by exempting articles of essential consumption. The tax policies will have to be adjusted to the requirements of the country having regard to the existing patterns of distribution of income in the population.

Neutrality and economic efficiency

The most important feature of VAT is its neutrality, which is the benchmark of an efficient tax system. With uniform rates, VAT is neutral to producers' preferences and consumers' choice. It treats all inputs uniformly to avoid any tax-induced distortion. There is also no interference that influences the choice between present and future consumption. On the other hand, taxes on income encourage present consumption and consequently savings get affected. VAT does not influence consumers' preferences for commodities, whether they are taxed or untaxed or even when they are taxed at different rates. It also keeps total neutrality between capital and labour. If the exemptions are kept at the minimum level, the impact of neutrality will become more visible. But even if a few products are left untaxed, it does not alter the overall efficiency of the tax system.

The optimal tax theory seeks to tax different commodities at the most appropriate rates based on price elasticity. The assumption is that a differential approach would improve economic efficiency. If the elasticity of a commodity is low, higher rates are prescribed and nominal rates suffice for goods having high elasticity. Conceptually, VAT is not compatible with differential rate structure based on optimal tax theory. The emphasis of VAT is more on reducing the cascading effect and improving neutrality rather than prescribing differential rates for improving economic efficiency. Moreover, economic efficiency cannot be measured only in terms of tax revenue.

In a democratic set up, the tax system has to serve many objectives other than revenue. It is not practicable to have a large variety of rates based on certain assumptions of elasticity of demand. The cost of collection will become prohibitive if too many rates are prescribed particularly in countries where evasion is rampant. With multiple rates, matching of invoices will be a more time-consuming and costly affair. The positive features of VAT can be improved if the rate structure encourages smooth and effective administration and better compliance. At the present level of understanding of tax effects, neutral taxes like VAT are definitely preferable to the conventional taxes that may offer a differential structure based on price elasticity.

Tax evasion

It is well-known that conventional commodity taxes are highly prone to evasion. If luxury consumption is heavily penalized with deterrent rates, evasion and corruption become uncontrollable. The cascading effect of conventional commodity taxes and the delays involved in detection and litigation makes it easy and profitable to get away with tax-related crimes. Even law-abiding citizens and firms are tempted to try their luck in making a fast buck through evasion. Successful events of tax evasion attract many followers who attempt to replicate them with more ingenious methods. They call evasion euphemistically as "legal avoidance". The evaders not only escape payment of commodity taxes with impunity, but avoid all kinds of taxes related to the chosen base. The honest taxpayers who bear a heavy burden ultimately perish in competition with the powerful

·evaders. With the adoption of VAT, the evasion scenario undergoes a drastic transformation.

Consumption type of VAT with tax credit method of collection does not give much scope for evasion. Evader cannot escape detection with the thorough auditing of invoices unless all transactions uniformly reflect lower value addition. The clear possibility of discovery at one stage or other is a deterrent for habitual offenders who may find it difficult to pay heavy fines and penalties. The evaders are not likely to be benefited individually, as large amount of tax does not get collected at any stage of transaction. With rigorous auditing of documents, chances of detection can be further increased. In conventional taxes, audit is confined to manual data checking, but VAT uses the speedy electronic medium for matching of invoices. VAT operating countries have lower non-matching ratio of sales invoices than that of purchase invoices. This indicates the trend to fully utilize tax credit on purchases. In many countries, errors and non-matching ratios have considerably fallen after the introduction of VAT.

One major worry on the evasion front is that computerized checks cannot easily capture cases of fictitious tax credit using forged invoices. Even the most ingenious tax administration will have to learn how to cope with problems of forgery particularly when the trust imposed on the taxpayer is abused. They have to be fully alert to such new methods of evasion. Unscrupulous elements in trade and industry are always on the look out for fresh pastures to make more black money at any risk. To deal with them, VAT will have to be equipped with more stringent deterrents like black listing and deregistration.

Economic growth

As indicated elsewhere, in the first two decades of the post war period, policy makers all over the world resorted to massive rate changes and base expansion for resource mobilization. Tax incentives were lavishly given ostensibly for promoting savings and investment. But after an initial spurt in economic activities,

77

the growth became stagnant due to inefficiencies arising from wrong policies and practices. It was realised later that the cause of economic growth can be served better if the tax system was left undisturbed to pursue its primary objective of revenue. A heavy tax burden restricts growth while lower taxes not only promote savings but also ensure better revenue and improved compliance. In fact, indirect taxes do not have any direct bearing on the incremental saving ratio like the taxes on income.

The increasing mobility of capital and the emerging E-commerce necessitate lowering of rates of income and corporate taxes. Tax reforms for achieving higher growth rates will have to aim at improving the domestic after-tax rate of return to capital as compared to that of neighboring countries. Tax rates will have to be attractive and its administration should be transparent enough to prevent migration of capital and improve FDI. Luxury consumption is always taxed at high rates in many developing countries on the assumption that saving ratios can be improved. But a heavy tax burden imposed on luxury articles generally leads to distortions in the choice of the producers and consumers. It also provides an incentive for evasion. A uniform VAT is preferable to differential rates as it allows uninterrupted flow of economic activities. In fact, VAT can definitely achieve faster economic growth unlike other indirect taxes.

We have seen some of the positive features of VAT that made it an acceptable alternative even to the ubiquitous income tax. Now let us proceed to the actual Indian experience of a watered down version of VAT. MODVAT was introduced in 1986 and it evolved into a full fledged CENVAT in 2000. The transition from a crude form of VAT to a highly evolved tax instrument is an interesting episode in our economic growth. It can guide the states in their choice of a suitable VAT variant. The model of Cenvat and its institutions are worthy of emulation by the states to avoid possible pit falls in the implementation of VAT in 2003.

❏❏

CHAPTER VII

THE INDIAN FORERUNNERS

Public money is like holy water; everyone helps himself.

[An Italian Proverb]

Modified value added tax, popularly known as 'MODVAT' was introduced in India in 1986 as the forerunner of a full fledged VAT. In fact, it had only consolidated various input relief schemes like proforma credit, set off, and Chapter X procedure etc., which were available in the excise system. In 1986, as suggested by a technical study team, a new set of rules was framed to simplify and bring together the various input exemptions in a legal framework of VAT. It was issued as Rule 57A of the Central Excise Rules.

Initially, Modvat applied only to commodities covered by 37 chapters of the Central Excise Tariff. In 1987, it was extended to all commodities except tobacco, textile products, petroleum products, matches and cinematography films. In the 1991-92 Budget the scheme was extended to manmade fibers, filament yarns, and aerated waters. The coverage was further extended to capital goods and some specified petroleum products in 1994-95. The various modifications and extensions effected from time to time are indicated in detail in table VI.

As mentioned earlier, since independence, excise duties were extended indiscriminately even to raw materials and intermediates for mobilizing additional resources. In certain cases, input taxation was administratively more convenient than taxing final products manufactured in widely dispersed sectors. However, the administration was very well aware that levies on inputs and intermediates create cascading effect in the final stage of transaction. Several input relief schemes were devised to give set off of taxes already paid. They were presumably meant to mitigate the hardships of taxpayers of final products.

The practice followed prior to 1962 was to issue individual exemption notifications to reduce the duty liability on the final product to the extent of duty paid on components or raw materials used in its manufacture. The procedure was found cumbersome as an advance notice was required to be given to the excise officer about the arrival of duty paid inputs in the factory and a complete account had to be kept about the use of such materials. There was another scheme for in-bond movement of inputs without payment of duty at the initial stage. However, the processes involved for availing any kind of concession entailed laborious documentation and frequent interaction with the administration for inspection and other purposes. The public called the system of rigorous controls the "Inspector Raj" to indicate the stranglehold of the administration on production and clearance.

The actual precursor of Modvat was a scheme for input relief introduced in 1962. It was known as proforma credit applicable to certain notified commodities. The manufacturers were permitted under the scheme to obtain duty paid materials as inputs or intermediates. Similar to tax credits in VAT, proforma credit also could be utilized by the manufacturer for the payment of duty on the final product. Credit was allowed on the entire amount of duty paid on the inputs without the requirement of a one to one correlation between the input and the final product. Under another scheme known as the Chapter X procedure, a manufacturer could receive goods without payment of duty for special industrial purposes. The manufacturer of inputs could send his goods under Chapter X procedure without paying the duty or passing it on as a proforma credit. But all these input relief schemes operated with lot of interference by the administration to check the correctness of the claims.

In 1977, the indirect taxation enquiry committee specifically examined the question of adopting value added tax to replace the Central Excise duties. The committee however, found it premature to introduce a comprehensive VAT in India. They suggested a model of VAT at the manufacturing level to eliminate the cascading effect of Central Excise duties on inputs and intermediates. Tax credit method was recommended for input relief but they did not favour credit for import duties.

In 1985, a technical study group looked into the question of cascading effect of Excise duties. They suggested the introduction of a broader variant of proforma credit scheme to all excisable goods including packing materials and consumer durables. Petroleum products, cigarettes, matches, etc. were kept outside the ambit of tax credit. The net revenue effect of the extension of proforma credit was estimated to be about Rs.6000 crores. The long term fiscal policies announced by the government in 1985 also considered various aspects of input tax relief and declared that effective measures would be taken to reduce the cascading effect of excise duties.

The Modvat scheme introduced in 1986 was applicable to goods falling under 37 chapters of the Central Excise Tariff. The tax credit obtained for the payments already made on inputs and intermediates could be utilized for payment of duty on the final product. Later, Modvat was extended to packing materials and some consumables. A further extension of Modvat was made in 1987 but no input relief was given to capital goods. Certain procedural modifications were also made in 1987, which allowed refund of import duty in cash for exports and credit for the stock of inputs, etc. In 1995, the government admitted that the coverage of Modvat was incomplete as it excluded petroleum products, textiles, matches, tobacco products and capital goods. There had been persistent demand from the industry to make the scheme more comprehensive and consequently it was extended to certain capital goods and petroleum products in the 1994-95 Budget. Capital goods duty relief was one major step taken to adopt the consumption kind of VAT.

Total switch over from Modvat to a full fledged VAT was

suggested by an expert committee headed by Dr. Raja Chellaiah. They recommended a time frame of three to four years for extension of excise to all manufactured goods and also to some services like advertising, stock broking, insurance, etc. The Modvat scheme was recommended for all inputs and end products. Extension of Modvat was also suggested for wholesale dealers having a turnover of Rs.50 lakhs. A special feature of the Modvat scheme was that it did not cover all high revenue yielding commodities. A "deemed credit" facility was made available under Modvat, which is normally not given under the regular VAT.

An important feature of the Modvat scheme was its simplified compliance requirements for availing input tax relief. No prior permission was required from the administration for taking Modvat credit other than a simple declaration. Under the proforma credit scheme there was a stipulation of filing D3 intimation for the receipt of duty paid goods in the factory. Other procedural irritants like separate storage of inputs and visits for verification by the administration have also been discontinued under the Modvat. The credit was not only available for the basic excise duties but also for special excise duties and countervailing duties paid earlier. Modvat credit could also be availed on documents other than gate passes.

The concept of "deemed credit" was an innovation of the Indian tax system. The manufacturers of final products have to buy many duty paid inputs from the open market without sufficient documentary proof of initial payments. It was felt necessary to assume that inputs and intermediates procured from the open market would have discharged duty liability at the appropriate rate and stages. In the matter of documentation also, Modvat simplified the procedural requirements. Only two registers were required, one for showing the details of inputs received and another for the credit availed by the manufacturer. When Modvat was introduced, the estimated revenue loss on account of tax credit was about Rs.6000 crores. But the actual revenue forgone in the first few years of Modvat was much less than the initial estimates. This can make the states feel much comfortable that their apprehension of loss of revenue is not likely to materialize.

With the steady extension of Modvat, revenue forgone reached about 20 per cent of the gross excise revenue by 1990-91. It is now almost 40 per cent of the total revenue, which indicates the very high cascading effect of indirect taxation. The same kind of estimates can be applied to sales tax revenue, which also contain 30 to 40 per cent input taxes. The conclusion is inevitable that almost 60 per cent of the entire national tax revenue is derived from the cascading effect and not from the value addition which is the real target base for taxation. Only a comprehensive VAT can mobilize more revenue for the central and state Governments by exclusively taxing the real base of value addition. That will allow the economy to grow without sacrificing scarce resources to the revenue-starved exchequer.

Ever since its inception, the Modvat scheme has been extended steadily to goods initially kept outside its purview. By April 2000, Modvat has already reached almost all taxable goods. In April, 2000, it was rechristened as "Cenvat" which is an acronym for Central Value Added Tax. A new series of simplified rules, which are more liberal, and user friendly have also been introduced. The "Cenvat" is applicable to all inputs other than HSD and Motor Spirit. It is also available for all final products except matches. Even tobacco products including cigarettes are eligible for "Cenvat" credit. Most of the capital goods were also covered under the new scheme.

The scheme applies even to indirect inputs like paints, packing material, fuel, lubricating oil, grease, cutting oil, etc. The availment of credit is automatic on receipt of goods on a proper invoice. The assessee is required to keep only very simple accounts of receipt, disposal, consumption and inventory of the duty paid goods and to give a monthly return to the department. All types of duties such as BED, SED, AED and CVD could be taken credit of and utilized for payment of the duty on final products, capital goods cleared as such, or even on inputs. Under the Cenvat scheme, there is a provision for sending duty paid goods for job work. The only condition is that they should be received within 180 days. Otherwise, proportionate credit has to be reversed, and it can be restored again after the physical receipt of goods.

On export goods, the credit taken for inputs can be utilized for payment of duty on other final products sold domestically. If an exporter does not have any domestic sales the input credit could be claimed as a cash refund. If common inputs are used for dutiable and exempted final products, the assessees are required to maintain separate books of accounts for receipt, utilization and inventory. If a factory changes ownership on account of sale, merger, amalgamation, etc. and the stock of inputs are also transferred, the credit is allowed to the new owner. Cenvat scheme for capital goods is much more simplified than MODVAT.

On capital goods 50 per cent of the credit can be taken on receipt and the remaining 50 per cent on any subsequent financial year. The only condition is that the capital goods should be in the possession and use in the subsequent years in which the remaining 50 per cent credit is taken. In case depreciation under Income Tax Act is claimed on the credit portion, the credit is disallowed. When capital goods are sent for job work or repairs, the credit is allowed on the condition that they should be returned within 180 days like in the case of inputs. If they are exclusively used for manufacture of exempted goods, credit of duty paid is not available under Cenvat. Unlike in the MODVAT, the Cenvat scheme does not require installation of capital goods for taking credit. There is also no requirement of filing declarations under Cenvat. The limitation of 6 months for input invoices has also been discontinued. In fact, Cenvat introduced several procedural modifications and simplifications probably learnt in from the experience of the performance of its forerunners. On the whole, it is an ideal system that has been functioning efficiently in the Indian context. The states can emulate the Cenvat provisions for introducing their variant of VAT. It is a well tested and trusted tax welcomed by all concerned.

TABLE II : SHARE OF MODVAT CREDIT IN GROSS EXCISE REVENUE

(Rs. in Crore)

S.No.	Year	Net Revenue	Modvat	Gross Revenue	% of Modvat to Gross Revenue
1	1986-87	14470.00	1913.59	16383.59	11.68
2	1987-88	16462.00	2819.91	19245.91	14.65
3	1988-89	18841.00	3809.01	22650.01	16.82
4	1989-90	22406.00	5278.93	27684.93	19.07
5	1990-91	24514.00	6495.56	31009.56	20.95
6	1991-92	28110.00	7965.35	36075.35	22.08
7	1992-93	30651.22	10840.23	41491.45	26.13
8	1993-94	31711.14	11896.40	43607.54	27.28
9	1994-95	37415.95	21686.74	59102.69	36.69
10	1995-96	41658.77	29951.20	71607.97	41.83
11	1996-97	46916.04	34221.88	81137.92	42.18
12	1997-98	48137.19	35164.52	83301.71	42.21
13	1998-99	52723.65	35489.39	88213.04	40.23
14	1999-2000	61981.26	43643.88	105625.14	41.32
15	2000-2001	68917.60	44986.37	113903.97	39.49
16	2001-2002	72383.99	47509.40	119893.39	39.63
17.	2002-2003	82253.06	53039.12	135292.18	39.20

Source: Budgets of the Central Government

From table II, it is evident that the share of tax credit has been steadily increasing in the gross revenue from central excise duties. The initial hesitation of the government to implement a full fledged VAT prevented the units from availing the entitled tax credit. In fact, in the first few years only less than 20 per cent of the tax credit was allowed. Subsequently, with further liberalization, we find that about 40 per cent of the tax

Figure I : MODVAT CREDIT UTILIZED AS % OF GROSS REVENUE (PLA+MODVAT)

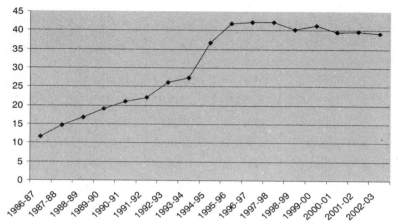

Source: Union Budgets

collection is now accounted by tax credit. Applying the same data base to sales tax, we can surmise that with the introduction of VAT at state level about 40 per cent tax credit will be available to the taxpayers. It will give a tremendous boost to our economic activities, which are currently saddled with the heavy cascading burden of sales tax.

❑❑

CHAPTER VIII

IN THE WONDERLAND OF VAT

No one would have remembered the Good Samaritan if he had only Good intentions. He had money as well.

[Margaret Thatcher]

In a preceding Chapter, we have seen several admirable features of VAT and its Indian variant at the central level. The most appealing aspect is its adorable flexibility to adjust with the widely varying political, legal and economic requirements of an adapting country. Some of the country specific modifications might have marginally compromised on its qualities likes efficiency and neutrality. But its overall positive impact in the developing and developed countries all over the world encourages non-VAT countries to accept a suitable variant. Some of the specific experiences of the adapting countries are mentioned here to give an insight into the prospects and problems of the introduction of state level VAT in India.

BRAZIL

Before the introduction of VAT, the Brazilian tax system consisted mainly of a personal income tax levied and collected by the federal government. The states were authorized to collect a sales tax on turnover basis. The federal government also collected revenue from imports and excise duties on liquor and tobacco.

In 1966, Brazilian tax was divided into four categories, namely (i) tax on external trade (ii) tax on income and wealth (iii) tax on production and, (iv) special taxes. Each category was assigned to a specific authority of government. The turnover tax levied by the states was replaced by a state VAT. A federal VAT was introduced in place of the federal wholesale tax. The local bodies like municipalities were assigned a service tax on business and trade. Fuel, electricity, exports, imports and minerals constituted the tax base of the federal government. As a part of the reforms, the states were deprived of their powers for imposing new taxes. In India it is seen that the states are clamoring for compensation even before the introduction of VAT.

Brazil introduced a comprehensive VAT having several unique features. Brazilian experience is comparable to the conditions obtaining in India like the federal structure and distribution of taxation powers. The federal VAT in Brazil, which is comparable to the Indian Cenvat, is a selective tax on certain manufactured products like cigarettes, beverages, automobiles, etc.

In Brazil, exports are totally exempted and VAT is collected using the tax credit method. Imports are also 'Vatable'. At the time of introduction of VAT, tax revenue accounted for about 50 per cent of the federal tax revenue. But other new taxes like taxes on gross revenue and wage contributions reduced the revenue share of VAT to about 20 per cent. Another important development was the upward trend in revenue from income taxes from 21.85 per cent of the federal tax revenue in 1968 to more than 59 per cent in the 90's. The state VAT extends from production to distribution including the retail level. The capital equipments are generally exempt from VAT and cash rebate is allowed for exports. The service sector is excluded from the state VAT but only very few exemptions are allowed, which are mainly for agricultural produce.

The rate of state VAT in Brazil was about 17 per cent in the beginning and on inter-state sales, tax rate was 10 per cent. The tax paid to the state of origin was given a set off against the tax payable in the state of destination. The importing state gets the difference between the internal and inter-state rate. The VAT base of the states excludes fuel, sale of energy and minerals, transportation and communication and other activities tax at the federal level. Agricultural inputs like fertilizers and seeds were exempt and most of the revenue was derived from industry and trade. The services, which were exclusively taxed by municipalities, were outside the purview of the state VAT. There were many grey areas that created conflicting cross-country exemptions and exclusions. Since many authorities were empowered to levy tax on the same base, disputes are prevalent in the Brazilian tax system. But in course of time many of the anomalies were removed and the VAT became an efficient means for revenue collection.

Problems of federalism

In the Brazilian VAT, the states were initially kept on a tight leash with a narrow base and no powers to alter the rate or give exemptions. Consequently, they did not have the fiscal autonomy of the types enjoyed by Indian states. Since the taxes were destination based, it avoided problems of valuation in inter-state transactions. The more industrialized states in the south got better revenue from the VAT. There had been persistent demand from the state for more fiscal autonomy by restricting the federal VAT on items like cigarettes, beverages and automobiles.

Brazilian VAT is a relevant experience as its 1965 conditions are now perceptible in the Indian tax scenario. At the state level, India has multi-point GST and CST for inter-state and intrastate sales. The central excise duties in India are identical to the Brazilian consumption tax. It is true that the introduction of VAT has not solved many problems of the Brazilian tax system because of the spate of disputes between the centre and states. Since the state had no authority to change the rates and base, some of them suffered serious setbacks in the developmental efforts. Later on, a consensus has been reached for giving more freedom to the state governments to legislate on VAT rates and extend the tax coverage. Such complex situations would not come up in India as the powers of taxation are more specific in giving the states lot more freedom and fiscal autonomy.

ARGENTINA

Argentina replaced its sales tax in 1974 with an income type of VAT having destination principle. The repealed sales tax had multiple rates for a wide variety of commodities. Sales tax was collected at the manufacturing stage and deduction was given for the input excluding capital goods. The VAT rate in 1974 was 16 per cent which was raised to 20 per cent in 1980. Before the introduction of VAT sales tax revenue was 1.6 per cent of GDP and the total tax revenue was 9.7 per cent. Since the VAT rate was lower than the sales tax rate, a sharp fall in revenue was apprehended in the transitional stage. But VAT revenue steadily increased and reached 4.8 per cent of GDP by 1981. There has also been a steady upward trend in the number of tax payers. It indicates better compliance and a steady decline in tax evasion.

Argentinean VAT was fashioned after the models of Denmark, France, Germany and Netherlands. Instead of implementing consumption VAT Argentina went for income VAT, to make it probably less regressive. The agricultural sector was exempted till 1983 and initially many sensitive commodities were also excluded from VAT. Most of the initial exemptions were withdrawn later. Exporters were entitled for a refund of the VAT on inputs. Even in the beginning, the exemptions involved only 2 per cent of the VAT revenue. But the figures are probably misleading, as the firms not paying any tax normally do not submit VAT statements.

The Argentinean experience of VAT has not been as impressive as that of many other VAT operating countries. The revenue has not shown much improvement although there has been a steady growth in the number of taxpayers. Tax evasion and corruption became rampant in view of the large variety of exemptions. The choice of income type of VAT and frequent changes in the base and rates could have been responsible for the low elasticity of VAT revenue. But several improvements have been introduced later including a switch over to consumption VAT and removal of exemptions based on regional considerations.

REPUBLIC OF KOREA

Republic of Korea is the leading Asian country that introduced VAT as early as in 1976. Prior to introduction of VAT, Korea had 11 indirect taxes out of which VAT substituted eight. The major tax replacements were on commodities, textiles products, petroleum products and business taxes. Taxes on liquor, telephone and stamp duty continued as separate entities. Before introduction of VAT Korea conducted a feasibility study in 1972 by comparing the experiences of other countries. In 1975, a report prepared by Allen Tait suggested the taxes that should be replaced by VAT and the rate structure and exemptions required for a smooth switch over.

Prior to the actual implementation, dry runs were taken for filing tax returns. More than 99 per cent of the potential taxpayers filed dummy returns in three trial runs. In view of the elaborate preparations, the problems that normally arise at the transitional stage were settled much before the introduction. The national tax administration was also reorganized to take care of the huge infrastructure. To minimize any adverse impact on the prices, the government enacted a price stability law, which controlled the prices of 41 items and gave price guidelines to more than 851 items.

Tax Rates

When VAT was introduced in Korea, the rate was kept at 10 per cent, which was lower than the legally leviable rate. The rate was chosen after careful research to identify the most acceptable rate for the industry and trade. Small business firms whose annual gross sales did not exceed a prescribed ceiling was given a lower rate. The regressive nature of the single rate was compensated by special excises on 33 groups of items. Some of the interesting items being taxed with special excise rates are admission to race course, sauna baths, golf courses, casinos, night clubs, etc. In place of about 50 tax rates that prevailed before the introduction of VAT, only one general rate and two special rates were allowed. The special excise had ten rates with the maximum at 100 per cent and the minimum at 5 per cent.

Tax Base

Korean VAT covered both goods and services. The definition of goods included even intangible objects having some taxable value. The service sector was taxed comprehensively. The tax base more than trebled within a span of five years while the GNP growth for the corresponding period was only 24 per cent. The number of taxpayers also increased by 25 per cent during the same period. It shows that trade and industry readily accepted VAT as its positive features were more favourable to higher value addition.

Many categories of goods and services are exempt under the Korean VAT. They include items like unprocessed food stuff, agricultural and marine products, piped water, coal, passenger services, etc. Some cultural and sports related activities are also outside the purview of VAT. Non-resident foreign corporations that provide international transportation by ship or aircraft get the benefit of zero rating if the foreign country has reciprocal arrangements. The small sector is excluded from the rigorous documentary requirements if they pay a low rate of two per cent on the turn over.

Revenue and Incidence

When VAT was introduced, it contributed 20.5 per cent of the total Korean tax revenue. The special taxes introduced along with VAT did not yield much revenue. The retail sector in Korea did not respond favorably and contributed only ten per cent of the VAT revenue. VAT was introduced at a time when Korea was undergoing severe inflation of about 15 per cent. After the introduction of VAT, the price index showed a decline mainly because of the controls effected during the transitional period. The government published the recommended prices of certain essential consumer items much before the introduction of VAT. The change in the tax system did not impose any dispropor-tionate burden on the taxpayers. VAT was more regressive than the conventional indirect taxes but the special excise that fell exclusively on the high-income groups improved its equitable impact.

VAT Administration

The quality of Korean tax administration has considerably improved after the introduction of VAT. The total number of invoices issued showed a steady upward trend and the number of re-assessments of tax difference was greatly reduced after the implementation of VAT only 13 percent of the tax returns were corrected by the government whereas it was 51 per cent earlier. Very stiff penalties were awarded for non-registration, non-issue of invoice, late submission of returns, matching errors in the invoice, etc. The clear possibility of easy detection and the rigorous penalties that followed detection virtually removed all incentives for tax evasion.

The small sector had great temptation to continue in the lower category in spite of their increasing turnover. The service sector also tried to confine to the lower limits by filing false returns or by refusing to issue or accept invoices. India has to learn lot of lessons from the Korean model of VAT particularly about the adoption of a practical system for matching of invoices through computers. Manual auditing and preventive operations can only increase the cost of compliance and administration without improving the revenue. The successful application of special rates on small and medium firms in Korea deserves emulation. A very sensitive and evasion prone small sector in India contributes more than 50 per cent of value addition in the economy but refuses to pay proportionate revenue.

INDONESIA

In 1983, Indonesia replaced an outdated turnover tax with a variant of VAT. It was initially confined to manufacturing sector, imports, construction and mining. The rate structure was also rationalized and tax exemptions and holidays were removed. With the adoption of VAT, the income tax has also been simplified with low rates and a broad base. After the introduction of VAT, the revenue increased from 5.4 per cent of GDP to about 19 per cent. The improvement in revenue was mainly due to better compliance, as tax evasion was brought down considerably with the uniform rate. Import of capital goods and raw material was given tax relief at the time of introduction. The Indonesian VAT used destination principle and tax credit method. However, there had been lot of objections, as VAT was considered more regressive than the repealed sales tax. But a separate luxury tax on a number of consumer durables inspite of the uniform VAT rate improved the progressivity of the tax system.

Administration

Indonesia introduced an integrated taxpayer identification system for facilitating submission of returns, checking and cross verification of invoices. The returns were audited on the basis of an objective selection criterion. Small firms were also exempted on the basis of annual sales turnover and capital investment. Introduction of VAT was a huge success mainly because of large scale computerization following the model of the Republic of Korea. The competence and continuity of tax administration while implementing major tax policy changes was another important factor that contributed to the success of tax reforms. The economic policies of the country remained almost unchanged for almost two decades and tax reforms were only meant for simplification of tax structure and better compliance. The introduction of VAT did not cause any inflation as apprehended by many detractors. Revenue showed more responsiveness to changes in national income than the conventional tax revenue.

CHILE

In 1973, the Chilean economy was in total shambles with inflation reaching about 400 per cent. There was a sharp fall in industrial production and balance of payments situation also became precarious because of trade restrictions and declining exports. In 1974, the tax system was simplified with introduction of VAT and integration of personal income tax with corporate tax. In 1975 VAT replaced all indirect taxes, Agriculture was initially excluded from VAT along with some

94

sensitive products like chemicals, petroleum, electricity, water and gas. The indexation system allowed readjustments of income tax brackets on the basis of a price index and the same scheme was applicable for deciding the VAT liability. Small firms got preferential tax treatment only at the final consumption stage. The transition from the outdated indirect taxes to VAT has been smooth and eventless due to the simplification of tax returns and extensive training to administrators and taxpayers.

COLUMBIA

Following the 1974 tax reforms recommended by the Musgrave Commission, many elements of VAT were introduced in Columbia. The reforms covered the national sales tax and taxes on services like insurance, international travel, photographic development, photo copying and communications. Initially, no tax credit was allowed for capital goods. A differential rate schedule was used for making the tax system more progressive. Essential consumer items were taxed at the low rate of 6 per cent while luxuries attracted 35 per cent. Selected agricultural machinery and most of the food items were outside the scope of VAT.

In 1983, Columbian VAT was extended to retail sector through a simplified procedure. The new system was designed to reduce the cost of compliance and facilitate administration. More services like computing, rentals, hotels and maintenance was also brought under VAT. A major drawback of the Columbian VAT was the non-deductibility of tax paid on capital goods. The extension of VAT to retail stage did not improve the revenue to the expected level. Small firms did not accept new simplified scheme and they preferred to remain below the specified turnover limit. In spite of the turnover getting adjusted to the level of inflation on an annual basis, most of the firms resorted to understatement of sales to stay out of the tax net. Fragmentation of small units is another common practice followed in Columbia to avoid tax liability.

EUROPEAN UNION

VAT has been accepted very early in the EEC for replacing the sales tax levied by member states. It was intended to ensure unfettered movement of goods and services among the members. Import duties were abolished in the EEC in 1968. Harmonized VAT rates were accepted by the members after the October, 1992 meeting of the Finance and Economic ministers of the EEC. The agreement was to implement a 15 per cent floor rate in all member states, one or two reduced rates were also permitted for special category of goods and services. A small select list of products was agreed upon for reduced rates. They included food, water and drugs. There has also been an agreement on the minimum duty of excise on alcohol, tobacco, heating oil, etc. The only country that had a rate lower than the floor rate was Germany. Transitional arrangements were allowed to continue on destination principle until 1997.

Border tax adjustments

The main problem of VAT in the European Union was the differential treatment for foreign and domestic goods. Since border controls were not in conformity with the spirit of the common market, the initial trend was in favour of adopting origin principle but in view of the serious problems in the implementation of origin principle the destination principle was accepted for inter-state tax adjustments. Some states in India have already imposed entry taxes to offset the probable revenue loss from VAT. They should learn from the experience of European Union to evolve the document-based control for appropriating tax revenue.

The destination principle allows the consuming country to retain the VAT revenue. VAT is collected through records and returns. The acquisition tax is the VAT liability or receipt of goods from another member state. The term `import' was confined to goods coming from non-member countries. Similarly the term `export' also meant dispatching goods from EC member state to a non-EEC country. Exports attracted zero rating and within the

member states the movement of goods were called 'dispatch'
VAT can cater very well to the requirements of independent and
sovereign nations who are members of the European Union. If
the will is there, we can also establish a harmonious tax system
at the central and state level by following the EU model.

❑❑

CHAPTER IX

IDEAL VAT FOR INDIA

The King shall bestow on farmers only such favours and remissions which will enrich the exchequer and not endanger the treasury reserves.

[The Arthashastra]

We have seen that the worldwide adoption of VAT has proved beyond doubt that it is the best candidate for becoming a global tax. The European Union has established that a uniform VAT in contiguous countries can prevent migration of factors of production and encourage all round investment and growth. It has also been proved that development in information technology makes it feasible to extend the VAT even across continents. A comprehensive VAT based on destination principle can be made functional on a global basis with the producing and consuming countries arriving at bilateral or multilateral agreements to share the tax proceeds.

Global identification of tax payers and the location of sources of production and consumption and share of the tax proceeds can be worked out on a mutually acceptable tax treaty. The European Union has abolished border taxes and operates VAT without any major hitch. An intra-EU clearance system allocates the tax revenue to member countries and a single legislation has introduced a simplified procedure. The entire European community has become one market that gives immense freedom and mobility for goods, services, persons and capital to create value addition without hassles.

If the European Union, which comprises of several sovereign nations could transcend all ethnic, linguistic and economic barriers and establish a harmonized tax system, there is no reason for the Indian states to persist with outdated taxes. At the central level, a full fledged VAT has been established with the introduction of Cenvat in 2000. The forerunners of Cenvat imposed several restrictions on tax credit. It took about four years for the central government to create a full fledged central VAT with almost complete tax credit on capital goods, packing materials and consumables. Since the states have undertaken to introduce VAT in place of sales tax, they should not consider it necessary to continue with entry taxes and surcharges. Such aberrations can reduce the positive impact of VAT, which is being ushered in to stimulate growth.

We can emulate the experiences of Brazil and Korea to control evasion. Brazil has faced several administrative problems in adopting a federal VAT along with a state VAT. Korea has also successfully implemented VAT by controlling prices and reducing the scope for evasion. These practical lessons are more relevant than the theoretical speculations on the probable impact of VAT on federal relations or fiscal autonomy of the states. The extracts of the recommendations of various committees that examined the issue of input tax relief (please see the annexures) present a comprehensive perspective of the problems existed and the solutions suggested even before the introduction of Modvat.

Many Models

One solution suggested by the Tax Reforms Committee was to introduce uniform VAT at the central level for all goods and services with certain specified exemptions. The VAT should reach up to the retail stage replacing most of the indirect taxes except some protective duties and deterrent taxes. The taxes to be replaced should include central excise, sales tax, octroi, goods and passengers tax and duty on electricity. It was suggested that the tax proceeds should be shared among the different levels of government according to an agreed formula. The initiative for adopting VAT can be taken by the Finance Commission or the National Development Council.

Such a model would lead to two major taxes, namely, the income tax and VAT, both administered by the central government. It would also ensure uniformity of rates, collection procedures and compliance requirements. The cost of compliance be much less and evasion would be easily discovered. It is an ideal model, which should have been implemented immediately after independence. Presently, the constitutional constraints do not allow a national tax system as state taxes are fully established collecting massive revenue through an administrative setup having several decades of experience. The various taxes at different levels have created powerful lobbies of political, economic and bureaucratic interests. The immense economic benefits that accrue from the continuation of the status quo make any substitution proposal impossible to implement. Despite the forecast of dire consequences in the economy, there is no likelihood of the state governments agreeing for a national VAT which is the real solution suggested by several expert committees and eminent scholars. I have presented a workable model of National VAT in my book published in 1994.

Another model suggested by the Tax Reforms Committee was a mixture of VAT at the central level with a rationalized sales tax at the state level. In this scenario, the Modvat was recommended for extension up to the wholesale level and tax credit on the sales tax collected at the raw material stage should be given as part of the tax payable at different stages. This suggestion was vague and impractical, as it has not given any clear indication as to how the central VAT can be extended to the wholesale stage. Sales tax is already established and the intrusion of central VAT would create overlapping jurisdiction with no relief from the cascading effect.

The model of VAT, which is now being implemented, consists of separate central VAT and state VATs to substitute union excise duties and sales tax. The central VAT has already begun functioning since 1986 and in 2000 it became a full fledged VAT. The transition to VAT in the states would be hopefully completed by April, 2003. The states may have differential rate structure while the central VAT will have minimum rates applicable to all commodities. But it is the only practical solution within the existing constitutional framework. Separate VAT regimes may not give us a simplified tax structure with adequate revenue and compliance. Since each state will have its own rate structure the competitive advantages of the consuming states and the originating states may not equalize. The states will continue with all sorts of schemes for attracting entrepreneurs by giving liberal tax exemptions and other benefits. But it is a welcome change from the chaotic sales tax system with its GST, CST and Turnover taxes.

A variant of this model is also being mooted for service taxes. An agreement has already been reached for amending the constitution to give away some more powers of taxation to the states. Consequently, the states will be empowered to collect tax on certain specified services. A further variation of this scheme can be suggested for central excise duties. The central government may continue to collect VAT at the manufacturing stage and share the revenue proceeds with the concerned state governments in accordance with the recommendations of the Finance Commission. The tax collected at the manufacturing stage may be allowed as credit at subsequent stages. The inter-state transactions can still be operated on the destination principle.

Best Model

Alternatively, the central government can give up the powers of taxation even at the manufacturing stage except on a few specified articles that yield substantial revenue to meet its resource requirements. Presently more than 60 per cent of the revenue is raised from about 15 commodities. Since 40 percent of the excise revenue is being distributed to the state governments, the central government can retain the powers of taxation for 15 commodities and pass on the rest to the state governments. There will be no revenue loss and the states can implement a regular full fledged VAT beginning with the manufacturing stage and ending at the retail stage.

The obvious merit of this proposal is that the existing

distribution of powers of taxation between the centre and states need not tampered with. Instead, it involves the surrendering of some central revenue to the states, which would be roughly equal to what they are already getting from the shareable taxes. The states, particularly the industrialized ones, are likely to agree with such a proposal. However, the drawback of this model is that it will not bring about the degree of uniformity in tax system that would be desirable for economic development. Some states are likely to get a competitive edge over others because of the existing uneven pattern of industrial growth. The reverse effect of such a situation was seen in the Brazilian model that gave rise to several disputes and litigations between the states and federal government.

The ideal variant that retains all positive features and advantages is a comprehensive national VAT. It can substitute all indirect taxes on goods and services like central excise duties, sales taxes, taxes on goods and passengers, tolls and entry taxes, and so on. The main problem is that the present distribution of the powers of taxation and the fiscal policies of the central and state governments cannot accommodate a national VAT. Such a system can make use of the administrative expertise and institutions functioning at different levels. The tax can be a single non-overlapping VAT at uniform rate on all goods and services throughout the country except for a few commodities on which penal rates are necessary for discouraging consumption. It is possible to distribute the revenue collected from the uniform rate and sumptuary levies to all claimants.

The constraints of the federal system will not allow the tax administration to be kept under the direct control of either the centre or the states. It is preferable to entrust the national tax administration to a statutory and autonomous body like the Reserve Bank of India. The tax administration should be on par with a corporate entity to maximize efficiency and avoid delays and corruption. Any system of government control can render only substandard service, which is detrimental to public interest in the long run. A neutral body answerable only to the legislature can impart the much-needed objectivity to tax administration and keep the rates and base free from political interference. The existing administrative setup can be merged to create a national VAT administration that can adopt the features of the Korean system.

The most difficult challenge of a unified VAT is to allay the apprehensions of state governments about the loss of financial freedom and political leverage. Presently, more than 50 per cent of the resources of the state government are raised from sales tax and about 40 per cent of the central government's revenue comes from central excise duties. Out of the total tax revenue of the country, the state governments' share is only 34 per cent. It is difficult to convince the states about the economic benefits of a centralized tax system if they are not given a higher share of revenue. In this connection, the Tax Reform Committee, 1992 suggested that the trade and industry should exert pressure on the state governments for an immediate change in the sales tax system. It will be difficult to change the status quo that has many beneficiaries feasting on the spoils of an anachronistic tax system.

Ideal Base

The tax base of any country is the income generated by the economic activities. Value addition on factors of production is the basic economic activity that traditionally creates income and wealth. The direct taxes take away a part of the individual and corporate income arising out of such activities. The indirect taxes levied on consumption reach the value addition through the back door. In fact both direct and indirect taxes reach the same base through different routes. While the former hits you on the face, the latter sneaks in through the back yard to steal your purchasing power.

Presently, both central excise and sales tax indirectly share the same base of value addition. Most of the revenue is collected at the manufacturing stage. It is done to collect more revenue and avoid chances of evasion at later transaction stages. Value addition on certain demerit goods like cigarettes, tobacco products, and alcohol deserve penal levies to discourage consumption. All over the world, such goods attract high rates of duty while commodities of common consumption are taxed at low rates on equity consideration.

The ideal coverage of VAT is up to the retail stage where maximum value addition is available for taxation. But even for retail transactions, a suitable tax threshold is necessary to keep the small retailers out of the tax net. Similarly, small scale industries and exports will have to be taken out of the purview of VAT on economic considerations. Services like electricity, transportation, entertainment and hospitality are already subject to various taxes at the state level. They can be integrated into a comprehensive service tax along with other services. The service tax can be given input tax relief under the VAT scheme. In addition to services, an item of special importance is alcohol which is now exclusively within the domain of the state. There are elaborate arrangements in all states to control its production, distribution and sale. There is no need to change the system of controls that are required for a volatile product like alcohol. It is an effective way of discouraging demerit consumption.

Ideal Rate

If a single rate of duty is acceptable for VAT, it could be 15 per cent. This issue was specifically examined by the recently by KTF. They found that the maximum revenue is derived from 16 per cent rate and special rates. If special rates are applicable only for demerit goods and agricultural products, the remaining single rate for maximum revenue mobilization should be 16 per cent. Since the rate of 16 per cent is not amenable for easy calculation and in view of the abolition of other lower rates, it would be preferable to fix the single rate at 15 per cent.

If more than one rate is required for a uniform VAT, a lower rate of 5 per cent can be adopted for articles of mass consumption and sensitive goods that require concessional treatment. Most of the inputs and intermediates can be given the lower rate that will give incentive for the production of final products. For goods, which are injurious to health and social welfare like cigarettes and liquor, maximum rates of 35 per cent to 150 per cent can be applied. But higher rates induce evasion through illegal manufacture or suppression of production. Prohibition of alcohol consumption is a classic example of the misguided initiative for controlling individual preferences and choice. It would immediately give rise to a new industry for illicit production and clandestine sale of alcohol. In the case of cigarettes, heavy tax rates promoted large scale evasion despite the strict physical control on its production and clearance.

The VAT rates in various developing countries does not indicate acceptance of any ideal rate. But the outstanding fact is that most of them fall below 20 per cent. Only in a few cases 25 and 30 per cent exist with lower rates for essential goods. The developing countries have the rates ranging from 5 to 20 per cent. Some developed countries go far beyond 20 per cent for financing heavy social security commitments.

As far as the services are concerned, applying VAT rate will not be advisable in the initial stages. The limited access of the administration to the widely dispersed service sector is a major constraint in extending service tax to all services. Moreover, services are also a part of the value addition in the economy and a tax on any value addition at one stage should not exceed 10 per cent. Most of the states now charge more than 10 per cent on the services specifically allotted to tnem. In the interest of equity and for curbing conspicuous consumption it is advisable to have separate rates for each service rather than a uniform rate for all. But the rate structure should begin at the lowest level of 5 per cent for most of the services and it may be levied at the rate of 10 per cent for certain services catering to luxury consumption. If a uniform rate is preferred, 10 per cent would be appropriate for mobilizing revenue commensurate with the cost of compliance and administration.

Minimum Exemptions

A major hurdle in the introduction of VAT in the states is the problem of collecting taxes from sensitive sectors and products. The small scale sector is already exempt from central excise duty on the basis of a turnover criterion despite the fact that it contributes to more than 50 per cent of the value added in the manufacturing sector. Similar exemptions are also available for sales tax on various considerations ranging from the size of the firm to locational disadvantages, sensitivity of the product, etc. It is necessary to harmonize the exemption schemes of the central and state governments and set a uniform criterion for tax exemption. A uniform approach can be evolved for exemption not only for small-scale units but also for sensitive products. One common case is for the total tax exemption on all export production.

In addition to the total exemption for exports, for small scale units, a turnover criterion will have to be fixed keeping in mind the rate of inflation and other relevant factors. The experiences of developing countries indicate that there can be no universal criterion for exempting small units. An element of arbitrary estimation is involved in granting exemption on the basis of turnover. It is difficult to verify the declarations of gross sales or turnover of a unit which may not be maintaining documentary proof of sales and purchases. A practical solution is to follow a simplified version of the regular VAT that was tried in Chile for small enterprises.

Follow the Leader

At the central level, the introduction of Cenvat 2000 has already heralded the completion of the transition from Modvat to a full fledged VAT. Cenvat is a kind of comprehensive VAT being applied at the manufacturing stage. Cenvat rules are more simplified than the Modvat rules and tax credit is now available on all inputs except some fuels. All finished goods including matches are now eligible for Cenvat. Even tobacco products including cigarettes get tax relief and the scope of capital goods for availing tax credit has also been clarified. The credit is now available on duties like BED, SED, AED and CVD. Credit earned can be utilized for payment of duty on final products, inputs, and capital goods cleared as such from the factory of receipt. The raw materials on which credit has been taken can be sent for job work to other factories. In the case of capital goods, there is a scheme of staggering of credit utilization to two instances. The only exception is that credit is not allowed if the capital goods are exclusively for the manufacture of exempted goods.

By accepting the basic features of the full fledged central VAT now under operation, the states can implement a similar system with no adverse impact on revenue. Since VAT will be replacing sales tax at the wholesale or retail stage, the tax payers are already used to the more rigorous kind of compliance that can be simplified for VAT requirements. If the compliance required is more or less compatible to the one in existence, VAT will be welcomed by all tax payers.

Transitional Problems

In the federal system in India it is difficult to introduce any variant of VAT acceptable to the governments and the trade and public. The VAT rates proposed show about 40 items attracting zero per cent and one per cent for four items, 4 per cent for 41 items, 8 per cent for 50 items and 12 per cent for 37 items. A higher percentage of 20 per cent is reserved for motor spirit including ATF, liquor, narcotics, molasses and rectified spirits. There is also no unanimity regarding a revenue neutral rate as many of the states are presently levying higher sales tax. The claim for compensation for the states is reasonable if they accept 10 to 12 per cent tax rates.

Some states like Maharashtra, Tamilnadu, Gujarat and Haryana are likely to suffer huge revenue loss with the abolition of CST. Since destination principle will be accepted for state VAT, the consuming states are likely to end up in heavy losses after adjusting the tax credit to the exporting state. It will be difficult to settle the disparities unless the pattern of industrialization becomes more or less uniform across the country. The states are unwilling to give up other taxes such as entry tax, luxury tax, etc. even though in principle they agree for a multi point VAT system with destination principle. Although a time bound reduction of CST has been agreed upon, it will take some time before the transitional problems can be sorted out.

The central government has suggested a model value added sales tax bill to facilitate state legislation. However, many states have not followed the model for defining and harmonizing tax heads. It has been pointed out that even the definition of the charging section is different in different states. Consequently a dealer in one state may not become a dealer in another state. Such anomalies are probably of transitional nature that will be sorted out in course of time.

The VAT adopting state has to be extremely vigilant about its impact on prices during the initial stages. Prices may tend to rise if VAT rates are higher than the rates of the replaced taxes. In countries like Argentina, Korea and Mexico, prices were kept under control even by using statutory intervention. The state governments may keep such provisions handy if VAT introduction creates any unjustifiable price rise. Care should be taken to ensure that the price rise is not disproportionate to the input tax relief, which makes the total tax incidence much lighter.

The states had ample time to create legal framework required for implementing VAT. They could have prepared VAT return forms and developed a system of taxpayer identification. Moreover, the administration could train the staff to cross check the invoices using the electronic medium. The assessees can also be given proper training for entering the data at the VAT website. The advantages of VAT could be highlighted through the media to increase public awareness of its positive impact on the economy. But they lost precious time for preparation.

Some Essential Steps

The first step in the implementation of VAT is the creation of a system for taxpayer identification. If a unified system is developed for all taxes, it will facilitate the cross checking of returns, invoices and tax credit. National taxpayers ID can consolidate all registrations done at divisional or state level and convert them into a permanent code like the PAN number. The main problem in creating an ID system is to persuade all the potential taxpayers to register with the authority. In some countries, keeping the exempted sector out side the scheme reduces the workload. In India, it is advisable to identify even the exempted sector. A 13-digit registration system can bring in all the potential taxpayers in a national identification system.

Less Records

The conventional indirect taxes like central excise and sales tax demand elaborate documentation by the assesses. The statutory requirements have been recently relaxed for central excise duties, but state taxes insist on several documentary evidences of transactions from the payers. They include evidence of the receipt of inputs, daily production, sales, stock transfer, internal consumption and so on.

In VAT regime, such details of transactions are not necessary for compliance. VAT requires only the invoices of all transactions and production data for audit. Tax is paid on the basis of invoice value, which is normally not under stated. Of course, there is a possibility of collusion between buyers and sellers in a chain of transactions but such possibilities are much less under VAT. The Korean experience has clearly established considerable reduction in evasion. In Cenvat 2000, invoices are accepted as the basis for collection of revenue. The same Patten can be used for the state VAT.

But the main problem at the retail stage and with the small firms is the fear of getting out of exemption if real turnover is disclosed. In Latin American countries, consumers are encouraged to insist on invoices from retailers. A resent survey reveals that many buyers use invoice as a bargaining tool for getting a lower price from the retailers. If the buyers are tempted with a much lower price with out invoice, they do not normally insist on it. Some malpractices of this kind can be detected by comparing invoices of similar goods and duty payments at different stages. But the best solution is to keep small firms out of VAT on the basis of the turnover threshold. Actually, non-issue of invoice is not meant for tax evasion but for continuing the benefit of registering lower turnover.

Returns

There is no uniform practice for filing returns in VAT operating countries. In Argentina, taxes are paid on monthly basis and returns are filed annually. But in several other countries, monthly payment and returns are insisted on for immediate collection of revenue. KTF suggested the replacement of fortnightly payment of excise duties with a monthly payment system. It has been accepted in the 2003-2004 budget. In some of the states, sales tax returns are not required on monthly basis.

In the past, central excise duties were payable at the time of clearance of goods. It was a major irritant for the assessees as they had to pay the tax before recovering the sale proceeds. Small firms having meager working capital found it extremely difficult to pay the duty at the time of clearance. In a full fledged VAT, monthly payment system is advisable instead of paying duty with every dispatch. It will reduce the interest burden of taxpayers and release resources for more value addition. Whatever system is adopted, it should be followed uniformly all over the country for the convenience of trade and industry.

More Teeth With IT

An important requirement for the successful implementation of VAT is efficient and expeditious processing of information. For this purpose, an advanced computer system using the latest

110

Figure 2 : AN IDEAL MODEL OF INDIRECT TAX SYSTEM

Custom Tax Base   **C Excise & Sales Tax**

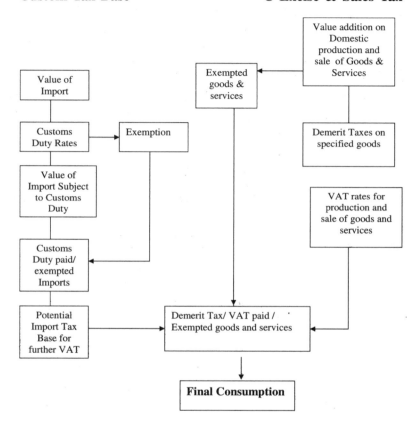

available software is absolutely essential. Manual system cannot process voluminous information with the accuracy and speed of the computer. In developed countries, dedicated systems and exclusive software are used for tax assessment. But in developing countries, computer applications are limited to certain areas. In Korea and Indonesia, extensive automation was completed before the introduction of VAT. VAT returns were processed using electronic facilities. But the most important achievement was the cross checking of invoices to pick up suspect cases of evasion. Special auditing feature of the software enabled the administration to focus on suspect firms rather than wasting the expertise on routine kind of investigations. But total tracking and crosschecking was not initially attempted for want of complete automation.

Among the industrialized nations, the European union uses very sophisticated technology. The returns are processed and correlated using the data emerging from the registered dealers in all member countries. In Canada, a detailed auditing system is used for matching the returns with other documents to ascertain accuracy of declarations. The French applies several parameters to select units that require special attention and scrutiny. In India, certain areas of indirect taxes are now fully automated. A national center is required for processing returns at the central and state level. Online facilities will have to be offered to the trade and industry before attempting a complete switch over to VAT.

VAT Audit

The underlying assumption while introducing VAT is that the efficiency of processing of the returns would enhance revenue and compliance. The self-checking mechanism reduces the scope for evasion and improves the revenue. But it has been found that the evaders have resorted to innovative methods like bogus invoicing, suppressing of turnover and faking of refund claims. New auditing methods are required to detect such advanced modes of evasion and to short-list habitual offenders.

It is true that under VAT the auditing system is more accurate and reliable. But only in some counties all returns and firms are audited comprehensively. The resource constraints do not permit cross-checking of all invoices and transactions. Some countries concentrate on sensitive commodities and sectors to avoid unnecessary wastage. Only selected units are audited thoroughly by scrutinizing the stock, private documents, correspondence and competitors' price. Income tax returns are also verified to

Figure 3 : A VAT AUDIT MODEL

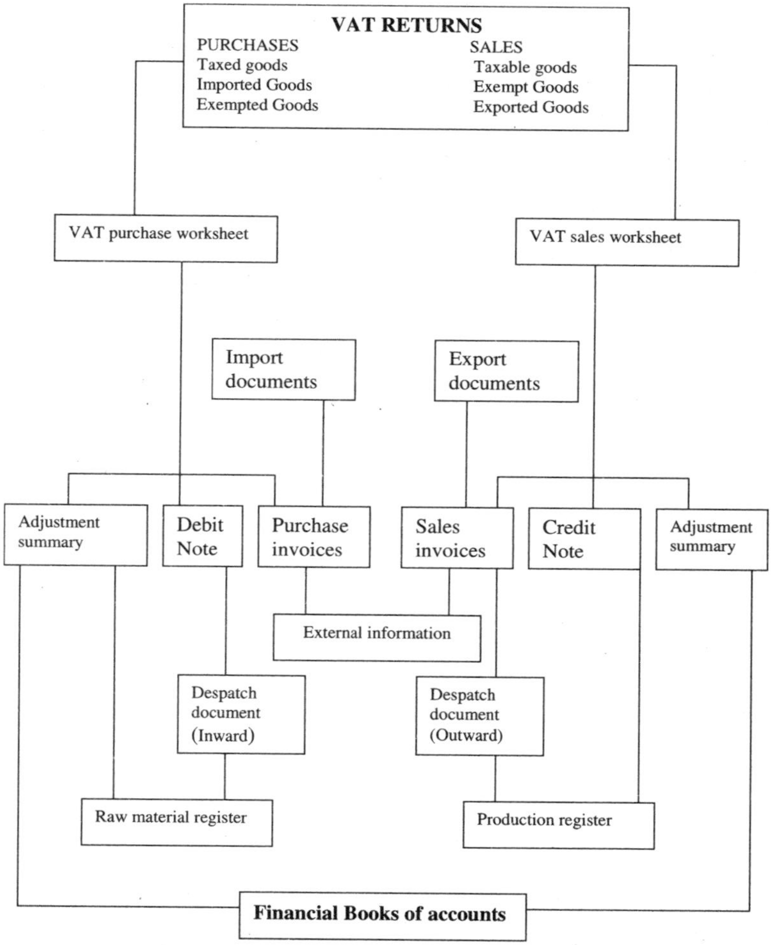

Adopted from IMF

ascertain whether they reflected undisclosed income accrued through evasion.

In India, tax returns are audited mainly by the collecting agency. An independent authority working under the Comptroller and Auditor General of India also audits them. But over a period of time, audit tend to become a routine check of returns and registers. They do not yield any significant results other than pointing out some arithmetical inaccuracies or deficiencies in documentation. Under the VAT scheme, audit has to be more sensitive to the possibilities of manipulation. It has to use the database of the system to unearth suspect firms and sales. Since audit is done on post clearance basis, regular processing wings should be separate from the audit. The concept of third party audit by the Comptroller and Auditor General of India will become redundant when automated system for audit is installed. The recommendation of KTF to abolish AG's audit is a sensible step towards reducing duplication of work. Frequent visits of audit parties belonging to different agencies for scrutinizing the same document over and over again is a major irritant to taxpayers. It can be dispensed with if electronic database is used by all agencies for any kind of enquiry. A typical audit model is presented here to indicate the broad outline of VAT audit.

Refunds

In VAT regime, refunds are normally given only when goods are exported or when the credit exceeds certain specified limits. Some countries allow credit to be carried forward with indexation for inflation. In conventional system, refund claims are manually processed which involve delays and corruption. The administration invariably tries to disallow payments on one pretext or other. They also ask for the proof of passing on the benefit of refund to consumers. This kind of impediments, which may be ethically justified but economically untenable, may not arise if cash refunds are replaced by credit allowed for duty payments. The administration need not bother to ascertain the actual beneficiary of refund since credit cannot be encashed. In consumption VAT, refunds some times arise as purchase of capital goods. The amount available as refund can be staggered by a depreciation formula for purchase of capital equipments. The usual practice in VAT operating countries is to refund the VAT collected from exporters, but there is also an alarming increase in the number of fraudulent claims. Instances of bogus exports claims and forgery of shipping documents have been detected in India even under the VAT regime. The tendency for evasion might continue unabated unless stiff penalties are imposed on habitual offenders.

Evasion

VAT reposes full trust on the firms and dealers to report the value addition correctly. Any attempt to defraud revenue is a serious breach of trust and offenders deserve exemplary punishment. It should act as a real deterrent to prospective lawbreakers. However, currently most developing countries do not impose stiff penalties on tax offenders. In some countries evaders get imprisoned, but generally, a light fine is the only punishment for tax offence. Temporary stoppage of production or suspension of sale is also resorted to as a punitive measure.

In India, tax offences involve protracted litigation. The fear of punishment is lost if it comes after long delay. Special courts will have to be setup to deal with tax offences in a time bound manner instead of leaving them to the general legal system. Evaders will have to be punished with imprisonment and heavy fines that should give a warning to all taxpayers. Otherwise, the sincere effort to modernize the tax system will end up in creating more lucrative avenues for evasion for the hardened criminals.

April came, and then June

The million-dollar question till April was whether all the states would adopt VAT by the deadline or not. All states except Haryana missed the target and only 7 out of 23 states have sent their legislation for Presidential assent. The thrice-postponed shift to VAT will get yet another deadline as the taxpayers are not ready in many states. Will the Centre coerce the delinquent states to fall in line? The scene is chaotic out there but let us hope that before the end of 2003, the sky will clear up and VAT will prevail. Taxpayers could have pressurized the states to accept VAT immediately to avoid flight of economic activities to more tax friendly lands. Unfortunately, traders have unleashed an unreasonable national agitation against VAT. In fact, it is the first time anywhere in the world that the taxpayers' protest against modernization. It reveals that transparency is not always welcome as it could expose rampant evasion and collusion.

❏❏

CONCLUSIONS

The core need in the country is of releasing national creativity.

[Jaswant Singh]

In the preceding chapters, we have seen the attractive features of VAT and the prospects and problems of adopting them to replace sales taxes. We also examined the structural and functional deficiencies of the existing tax systems at the central and state level. The experience of the implementation of a central VAT was seen in the transition of MODVAT to CENVAT 2000. The KTF that has recently scrutinized the inadequacies of the direct and indirect taxes and has given some path breaking suggestions for a thorough overhaul of tax administration. They want to transform the Indian system into a world class one to achieve accelerated economic growth. By revamping the administration, tax to GDP ratio is also expected to reach the level of developed countries. I have presented the extracts of the Budget Speeches in annexure X that clearly indicates the inability of the government to go for big bang reforms. I think we missed a rare opportunity to revamp the economy. We could have achieved miracles in this year if only some bold initiative was taken to bell the cat.

What kind of an ideal tax system could have achieved the twin objectives? I do not think that another dose of marginal reforms can give us better growth and revenue. That is what exactly KTF suggested and the government accepted. The same line of approach has been tried earlier with little success. We can slightly lower the tax rates; reduce their number, and give them new names. We can also give complete input tax relief through the VAT mechanism and exempt export and small enterprises. We can put the entire responsibility for the clearance of cargo on the importer or manufacturer, and ask the administration to focus on post audit and selective examination. But the basic question is can we achieve the objectives of more growth and revenue through such simplistic means?

The fiscal deficit is not the real villain. Even at the present high level, it is still within manageable limits. The foreign exchange reserves are comfortable to afford a big push for pumping more purchasing power into the economy. A timely incentive would have created more income and employment. It would have doubled the growth rate and mobilized about 15 per cent of GDP as tax revenue. I think the good doctor was taken for a smooth ride. With the blinkers of revenue neutral reforms, Kelkar saw the same gigantic complexities that bewildered his predecessors in the committee room. He was told the same old story of fiscal deficits that prevents all fundamental reforms. They allowed him to cut some taxes here and there by a few points when matching revenue gain was sighted elsewhere. He succumbed to the same temptation to prescribe drastic changes in tax administration like taking away all discretionary powers, ending inspector raj, exemption era and so on.

But the glaring fact is that he missed the basic cause of the malady. It could not be sighted in a maze of mind-boggling facts and figures. Eminent economists like Swaminathan S. Anklesharia Iyer and T.K. Arun pointed out that the government requires a holistic view on the fundamental issue of value addition in the context of taxation. Our stunted growth is not exclusively attributable to the inefficiency of administration. The major culprit is the inadequate appreciation of the fact that taxation should not take away more than a small proportion of the total value addition in the economy. It is evident that the after tax income of any entity in our country is currently too meager to inspire saving and investment. What is the reward left for the hard work of value addition after the babus appropriate almost the entire income?

Let us see the results of the lavish expenditure using the taxpayers' hard earned income from value addition and uncontrolled market borrowing. For those who care to look, it is a grim scenario out there. We have $71 billion in foreign exchange reserves, which is as good as that of Singapore and Hong Kong. We have food grains overflowing in godowns and a fairly stable democratic system in charge of governance. In spite of all these positive features, more than thousand people in the north recently died in a cold wave. Many farmers commit suicide all over the country to get out of the debt traps. Starvation deaths do not make news any more. How do we reconcile the dollar prosperity with abject poverty, unemployment and starvation deaths? Can we simply say that because of fiscal deficits, poverty alleviation programme cannot be supported any more? It is easy to state the facts but no solutions will emerge unless we are prepared for some basic reforms in our perception. The ideological solutions of the left are now no more relevant. The unholy thrust for globalization without a sound domestic economy has been equally suicidal. So what is the way out of the muddle?

I am sure that with some marginal reforms in tax rates or administration, we cannot get at the targeted growth even in the very distant future. We need more fundamental change of the mindset to stimulate growth with a new tax system capable of accepting the genuine demands of the economy. For that purpose, we have to go to the origin of the problem that retards the efforts for expanding economic activities. It is undoubtedly the productive activities that create employment, income and wealth. They add value to men and materials and create goods and services that should be consumed in a competitive market. What we really forget is that all our taxes whether direct or indirect converge on the same base of value addition. It is the base that creates salaries, wages and profits. In actual terms, we get the purchasing power only from some kind or other of value addition. Taxes on income, manufacture and sales tap the same source again and again for more revenue. The results are disastrous when many hands try to empty the kitty without improving the inflow of income generating activities.

A realistic approach to taxation does not mean pampering the rich. The flow chart of value addition reveals how the governments at the central and state level and even local

119

authorities reach the same base for revenue. The income generated by value addition is directly taxed through income tax and corporate taxes. Indirect taxes like excise duties and sales tax reach the same stream at the point of manufacture and transactions. Even entry taxes and professional taxes levied by local authorities touch the same base of value addition. Unless income is generated by more value addition in the economy, the source for the taxman to demand his share will definitely decline. That is why in many sensible Asian countries like Singapore, Hong Kong, Indonesia and Taiwan, the direct tax rates are kept at the lowest level (see table XV). I am presenting the tax slab applicable to the upper middle class in India and elsewhere. The main contributors to value addition in the Indian economy suffer more tax burden than similarly placed persons in the neighborhood. No more explanation is necessary for the stunted growth.

I request the policy makers to ponder about the maximum tax burden the economy can presumably bear after allowing the person or firms to survive and grow with comfortable margins of profit? Direct taxes on income collect on an average 30 per cent and corporate tax takes away another 35 per cent. The central excise and other taxes put together corner about 30 percent. It means that what is left out after all kinds of taxation is just 30 per cent of the value addition. They may say that there is a tax threshold to give us some basic income for survival.. But they conveniently conceal the fact that even the purchasing power of that negligible amount is further reduced when you buy highly taxed consumption articles. The taxman manages to cut your income in one way or other with unacceptable justifications. Such a huge tax burden does not leave much incentive to enhance value-adding activities. Nor does it give any room for improving the output levels. The real motivation for value addition is seldom altruistic. You cannot ask people to work for feeding some privileged persons with more perks. Taxes are essential but overtaxing will undoubtedly kill the goose. Simply stated, our problems begin from the excessive greed of the taxman.

The most important step in tax reforms is to estimate the optimal tax burden that would not decelerate economic activities. Assuming that the maximum tax element in value addition can be about 40 per cent, the tax system has to make all claimants to share it without exceeding the ceiling. Taxes on income and consumption will have to compromise for smaller pieces of the cake until the cake grows to a much bigger size. Let us first give an opportunity for the system to generate real incentives for enhancing economic activities.

First we will see the share of direct taxes. Before taxing individual income, we have to exclude from the base the minimum expenditure required for essential subsistence. Assuming that the average family size in India is 4 members, the subsistence expenditure is about Rs.12000 per month. The tax threshold should be given at the income exceeding Rs.2 lakhs. We should not forget the fact that consumption taxes erode income even below the taxable level. Beyond the threshold, the income can be taxed at the rate of 15 per cent up to Rs.10 lakhs. If there are equity compulsions, the rate can be raised to 20 per cent after Rs.10 lakhs. The maximum rate of 20 per cent will be conductive to accelerated economic growth as it gives enough incentive for higher output. Since the low income brackets do not contribute much revenue these rates and threshold are evidently revenue neutral.

The next question is about the ideal rate for corporate taxes. Corporate value addition is disbursed in the form of wages dividends and profits that are again subject to taxation. The income generated through various kinds of value additions cannot escape the consumption tax net. Assuming that on an average 15 per cent is directly taxed and 15 per cent is taxed indirectly, corporate taxes should not exceed 10 per cent. Lesser corporate tax boost economic activities by generating more disposable income for investment. The outer limit for income ad corporate tax should not be more that 20 and 10 per cent respectively. Some incentives can also be designed to encourage savings particularly by low income groups.

Now let us proceed to the ideal indirect tax rates that can accelerate economic growth. After appropriating minimum 20 per cent of value addition through income taxes, what is left for indirect taxation is about 20 per cent out of the total taxable limit of 40 per cent. The ideal rate of excise duties and sales tax for normal tradable goods should not exceed 20 per cent. For protection of domestic industries and revenue, the rates of import duties could be 10 per cent and 20 per cent. The higher rate should be applicable to all final goods other than alcohol, cigarettes and some agricultural products that deserve protection of a higher order. Only basic customs duty and countervailing duty, which is equivalent to the applicable excise duties, should continue in the customs tariff. The countervailing duty should be available as tax credit, if imported goods undergo any further value addition. Basic customs duty should continue as a protective cover for encouraging indigenous value addition.

The rates of excise duties should also be confined to the taxable limit on value addition. Two basic rates of 5 per cent and 15 percent can take care of the tax on inputs, intermediates and final goods. Like customs, separate higher rates can be levied on demerit goods and agricultural products can be taxed at lower levels for protection. The maximum value addition that can be tapped by sales tax and other taxes is about 10 per cent. We should not forget here that all taxes reduce the purchasing power of the taxpayer and too much of it is not good for encouraging further value addition. The disposable income beyond the tax threshold cannot be taxed entirely by the state. It is meant for saving and investment and not for lavish public expenditure. The basic reform for growth is to change the attitude of the taxman. He cannot, in any direct or indirect disguise, take away more than 40 per cent of the total value addition. How he shares it with others in the family is not the taxpayers' concern. The government simply cannot afford to appropriate all fruits of the labor of its population.

After presenting the model rate structure for the direct and indirect taxes in India, I would like to suggest some functional simplifications that can facilitate economic activities. Here, I am in full agreement with the liberalization thrust in the recommendations of KTF. In fact, I would like to go a step further to suggest more drastic changes on the basis of compliance and tax potential. It can be applied straight away to import and excise duties using the criteria of revenue and compliance. The idea is to introduce a two tier system of tax administration. But the 2003-2004 budget has only accepted some procedural reforms suggested by KTF. The basic structural changes were ignored to safeguard the precious revenue. And we still hope for tax to GDP ratio to reach higher levels! Our neighbours' tax rates are owner's pride.

For commodities yielding sizable revenue of say more than 500 crores, we can adopt a highly simplified procedure for assessment. Care has to be taken to ensure that such commodities are not manufactured in sensitive and dispersed sectors. They should not be attracting high rates reserved for demerit consumption. The simplified administration should allow online registration, posting of monthly production on the administration web site, and annual auditing on a selective basis. The administration can do regular auditing of clearances online to find if there are any deficiencies in tax payment. There should be no visit to the factory except for a comprehensive annual auditing if a firm is selected on the basis of the audit parameters No control of any kind should be allowed to create hurdles for value addition.

The simplified administration can also apply for imports. From table IX and XI, it can be seen that about 27 commodities yield more than 70 per cent of revenue. Established importers of such major commodities can be allowed to clear the goods without customs examination and on the basis of a declaration and payment of duty. For finalizing assessments on an annual basis, the administration can audit all documents to tally the receipt of imported good and consumption. Online auditing can be done to find out whether the declarations and duty payments are correctly made. The advantage of the system is that the goods are delivered at the factory on importation without undergoing any customs or port detention. It will ensure significant FDI and facilitate more value addition using imported or indigenous materials.

The benefit of such simplified administration for customs and excise can also be extended to state taxes. Initially, it could be done selectively and having regard to certain well defined benchmarks. The normal process should be a slightly modified version of the simplified system. The only difference should be to increase the periodicity of audit or compulsory examination in the case of very suspect firms and sectors. With the introduction of VAT and software for cross checking of all purchase and sales invoices, the simplified administration is not likely to give scope for large-scale evasion. I would like to present here a flow chart of the ideal tax regime that could achieve the twin objectives of growth and revenue.

You may ask at this point a very pertinent question. Can such basic reforms in rates and practices actually yield higher growth and revenue? Will they reduce fiscal deficits and usher in an era of double-digit growth? I can assure here that basic reforms of this kind can definitely stimulate growth if accompanied by some other bold measures. We need some revolutionary changes in our antiquated labour laws, exit policy, policies on infrastructure like power and monetary policies. We should also reduce market borrowing and strictly enforce fiscal discipline both at the central and the state level. The governments should assume the role of a watchdog and ensure that the institutions and individuals do not loot the public funds. Swift and exemplary punishments alone can exorcise the ghost of corruption from administration.

That brings us closer to the issue of corruption. The rating given by Transparency International shows that in a group of 96 countries we are placed at 71. We keep company with countries like Tanzania, Zimbabwe, Ivory Coast and Honduras. It is a very depressing perception that discourages FDI and even incentive for domestic value addition. The public cannot afford lavish kickbacks without losing heavily on the thin margin of profits. China has set a good example by strictly punishing the

Figure 4 : MODEL TAX STRUCTURE FOR INDIA

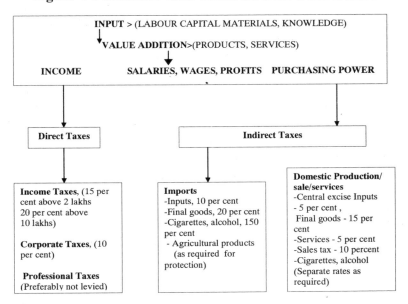

corrupt officials. But our courts take unduly long time to decide even cases of clear embezzlement and corruption. We have to do something urgently to change the rules and regulations that require constant interaction with government. Automation can do wonders. But ensure that it is used for public facilitation and not for babus to play games. Let us out source a new online system of tax administration and expenditure monitoring. There is more scope for corruption in expenditure than revenue. Expenditure reforms will involve more fundamental changes in the system of governance.

We are 127th in the human development index of the UN. It confirms that we will go on wallowing in poverty, corruption and backwardness unless we decide to make a clean break with the past. The way out of the quagmire is not only the adoption of VAT and other administrative reforms but also our willingness to leave something for those who add value to the economy. China achieved the double-digit growth rate with lot of fiscal discipline and transparent transactions. It has 42 per cent domestic saving rate whereas we have not even reached the half way mark. Do we need any more reasons for fundamental reforms in economic policies and practices? The figures stare at us day and night. They silently implore us to implement revolutionary reforms. For the sake of the poor and needy, let us try to move forward with some determination. We cannot simply wish away poverty without creating more income and employment. Empty slogans and meaningless demonstrations against globalization can only capture momentary attention of the news hungry media. To feed the hungry millions, we need some basic changes in policies and practices that can activate more value addition.

And those who add value to the economy would also like to have a better quality of life. We cannot afford to ignore them any more. Our neighbors pamper them and reap rich rewards. We should not envy their entrepreneurship. Let us emulate their farsighted statesmanship.

❑❑

THE CONSTITUTION OF INDIA

ARTICLES RELEVANT TO TAXATION

Subject matter of laws made by Parliament and by the Legislatures of States

Art.246 Not withstanding anything in Clauses (1) (2) and (3) Parliament has exclusive power to make laws with respect to any of the matters enumerated in List I in The Seventh Schedule (in this Constitution referred to as the "Union List").

(2) Notwithstanding anything in Clause Parliament, and subject to Clause (1) the Legislature of any State also, have power to make laws with respect to any of the matters enumerated in List III in the Seventh Schedule (in this Constitution referred to as the "Con-Current List").

(3) Subject to Clauses (1) and (2) the Legislature of any State *** has exclusive power to make laws for such State or any part thereof with respect to any of the matters enumerated in List II in the Seventh Schedule (in this Constitution referred to as the "State List").

(3) Parliament has power to make laws with respect to any matter for any part of the territory of India not

included (in a State) notwithstanding that such matter is a matter enumerated in the State List.

Duties levied by the Union but collected and appropriated by the State

Art.268 Such stamp duties and such duties of (1) excise on medicinal and toilet preparations as are mentioned in the Union List shall be levied by the Government of India shall be collected.

(a) in the case where such duties are leviable within any (Union Territory), by the Government of India, and;

(b) in other cases, by the States within which such duties are respectively leviable.

(2) The proceeds in any financial year of any such duty leviable within any State shall not form part of the Consolidated Fund of India, but shall be assigned to that State.

Taxes levied and collected by the Union but assigned to the States

Art.269 The following duties and taxes shall be (1) levied and collected by the Government of India but shall be assigned to the States in the manner provided in Clause (2) namely:-

(a) duties in respect of succession to property other than agricultural land;

(b) estate duty in respect of property other than agricultural land;

(c) terminal taxes on goods or

128

passengers carried by railway, sea or air;

(d) taxes on railways fares and freights;

(e) taxes other than stamp duties on transactions in stock-exchanges and futures markets;

(f) taxes on the sale or purchase of newspapers and on advertisements published therein;

(g) taxes on the sale or purchase of goods other than newspapers, where such sale or purchase takes place in the course of interstate trade or commerce.

(2) The net proceeds in any financial year of any such duty or tax, except in so far as those proceeds represent proceeds attributable to (Union territories), shall not form part of Consolidated Fund of India but shall be assigned to the States within which that duty or tax is leviable in that year, and shall be distributed among those States in accordance with such principles of distribution as may be formulated by Parliament by law.

(3) Parliament may by law formulate principles of determining when a sale or purchase of goods takes place in the course of inter-state trade or commerce.

Art.270 Taxes on income other than agricultural income shall be levied and collected by the Government of India and distributed between the Union and the states in the manner provided in the Clause (2)

(2) Such percentage, as may be prescribed the net proceeds in any financial year of any such tax, except in so far as those proceeds represent proceeds attributable to (Union territories) or to taxes payable in respect of Union emoluments, shall not form the consolidated Fund of India, but shall be assigned to the States within which that tax is leviable in that year, and such a manner and from such time as may prescribed

(3) For the purposes of Clause (2) in financial year such percentage as may be prescribed of so much of the net proceeds of taxes payable in respect of Union emoluments shall be deemed to represent proceeds attributable to (Union Territories).

(4) In this article-

(a) "taxes on income" does not include a corporation tax;

"prescribed" means – (i) until a Finance Commission has been constituted, prescribed by the President by order, and (ii) after a Finance Commission has been constituted, prescribed by the

President by order, and;

(c) "Union emoluments" includes all emolument and pensions payable out of the Consolidated Fund of India in respect of which income-tax is chargeable.

Charge on main duties or taxes for purposes of the Union

Art.271 Notwithstanding anything in Articles 269 and 270, Parliament may at any time increase any of the duties or taxes referred to in those articles by a surcharge for purposes of the Union and the whole proceeds of such surcharge shall form part of the Consolidated Fund of India.

Taxes which are levied and collected by the Union and may be distributed between the Union and the States

Art.272 Union duties of excise other than such duties of excise on medicinal and toilet preparations as are mentioned in the Union List shall be levied and collected by the Government of India, but if Parliament by law so provides, they shall be paid out of the Consolidated Fund of India to the States to which the law imposing the duty extends sums equivalent to the whole or any part of the net proceeds of that duty, and those sums shall be distributed among those States in accordance with such principles of distribution as may be formulated by such law.

Taxes on professions Trades, callings and employments

Art.276 Notwithstanding anything in Article (1) 246, no law of the Legislature of a State relating to taxes for the benefit of the State or of a municipality, district board, local board, or other local authority therein in respect of professions, trades, callings or employments shall be invalid on the ground that it relates to a tax on income.

(2) The total amount payable in respect of any one person to 73 the State or to any one municipality, district board, local board or local authority in the State by way of taxes on professions, trades, callings and employments shall not exceed two hundred and fifty rupees per annum:

Provided that if the financial year immediately preceding the commencement of this Constitution there was in force in the case of any State or any such municipality, board or authority a tax on professions, or the maximum rate, of which exceeded two hundred and fifty rupees per annum such tax may continue to be levied until provision to the contrary is made by Parliament may be made either generally or in relation to any specified States, municipalities, board or authorities.

(3) The power of the Legislature of State to make laws as aforesaid with respect to taxes on professions, trades, callings and employments shall not be construed as limiting in any way the power of Parliament to make laws with respect to taxes on income accruing from or arising out of professions, trades, callings and employments.

❑❑

ANNEXURE II

INDIRECT TAXES LEVIABLE BY CENTRAL GOVERNMENT AND STATE GOVERNMENTS AS PER SEVENTH SCHEDULE OF THE CONSTITUTION OF INDIA

1. UNION LIST

83. Duties of customs including export duties.

84. Duties of excise on tobacco and other goods manufactured or produced in India except:

    (a) Alcoholic liquors for human consumption

    (b) Opium, Indian hemp and other narcotic drugs and narcotics but including medicinal and toilet preparations containing alcohol or any substance included in sub-paragraph (b) of this entry.

89. Terminal taxes on goods or passengers, carried by railway, sea or air; taxes on railway fares and freights.

90. Taxes other than stamp duties on transactions in stock exchanges and future markets.

91. Rates on stamp duty in respect of bill or exchange, cheques, promissory notes, bills of lading, letters of credit, policies of insurance, transfer of shares, debentures, proxies and receipts.

92. Taxes on the sale or purchase of newspapers and on advertisements published therein.

92A. Taxes on the sale or purchase of goods other than newspapers; where such sale or purchase takes place in the course of inter-state trade or commerce.

97. Any other matter not enumerated in List II or List III including any tax not mentioned in either of those Lists.

2. STATE LIST

51. duties of excise on the following goods manufactured or produced in the State and countervailing duties at the same or lower rates on similar goods manufactured or produced elsewhere in India:

    (a) alcoholic liquors for human consumption

    (b) opium, Indian hemp and other narcotic drugs and narcotics; but not including medicinal and toilet preparations containing alcohol or any substance included in sub-paragraph (b) of this entry.

52. Taxes on the entry of goods into a local area for consumption use or sale therein.

53. Taxes on the consumption or sale of electricity.

54. [Taxes on the sale or purchase of goods other than newspapers, subject to the provisions of entry 92A of List 1].

55. Taxes on advertisements other than advertisements published in the newspapers.

56. Taxes on goods and passengers carried by road or on inland waterways.

57. Taxes on vehicles, whether mechanically propelled or not, 73 suitable for use on roads, including tramcars subject to the provisions of entry 35 of List III.

58. Taxes on animals and beasts.

59. Tolls.

62. Taxes on luxuries, including taxes on entertainments, amusements, betting and gambling.

63. Rates of stamp duty in respect of documents other than those specified in the provision of List I above with regard to rates of stamp duty.

3. CONCURRENT LIST

Item No.

44. Stamp duties other than duties or fees collected by means of judicial stamps but not including rates of stamp duty.

❑❑

ANNEXURE III

EXPANSION OF EXCISE TAX BASE

A CHRONOLOGICAL PRESENTATION

Year	Number of Excisable Commodities	Description of Commodities
1870	1	Salt
1917	2	Motor Spirit
1922	3	Kerosene
1930	4	Silver (17.3.1930)
1931	5	Power Alcohol (Added to "Motor Spirit")
1934-35	8	Matches, Mechanical Lighters (revised as 'Lighters N.E.S.' w.e.f.28-2-1982), Steel Ingots, Sugar other than Palmyra and Khandsari Sugar.
1941-42	9	Tyres
1943-44	11	Tobacco (Unmanufactured), (Cigars and Cheroots), Vegetable Products.
1944-45	14	Coffee, Tea, Betelnuts
1948-49	13	Cigarettes (Added to 'Tobacco' item)

Year	Number of Excisable Commodities	Description of Commodities
1949-50	14	Cotton Fabrics
1954-55	18	Machine-made Biris, Rayon or 'Artificial Silk' Fabrics, Cement, Soap (Power-operated), Footwear (Machine-made Biris added to 'Tobacco').
1955-56	24	Woolen Fabrics, Sewing Machines, Electric Fans, Electric Lighting Bulbs and Fluorescent Lighting Tubes, Electric Batteries, Paper, Pigments, Colours, Paints, Enamels, Varnishes, Blacks and Cellulose Lacquers and Cotton.
1956-57	30	Soap (Non-power-operated), vegetable non-essential oils, Refined Diesel and Vaporising Oil, (Diesel Oil not otherwise Specified, Furnace Oil, Rayon and Synthetic Fibres and Yarn Motor Cars.
1959-60	31	Asphalt and Bitumen
1960-61	39	Staple Fibre Fabrics, Component parts of Footwear, Motor Vehicles (including Chassis), Silk Fabrics, Parts of Cycles (other than Motor Cycles), Internal Combustion Engines, Electric Motors, Cinematographic Films Exposed, Aluminium, Tinplate, Pig Iron.

137

Year	Number of Excisable Commodities	Description of Commodities
1961-62 ("Diesel Oil not otherwise specified" and "Furnace Oil were given independent serial Plastics nos. in place of Fuel Oils" with effect from 1-10-60 under the Central Excises (Conversion into Metric Units) Act, 1960.	55	Soda Ash, Caustic Soda, Glycerine, Dyes derived from Coal Tar and Coal Tar derivatives, Patent or Proprietary Medicines, Cosmetics and Toilet preparations, (all sorts), Cellophane, Cotton Twist Yarn, "Industrial and Thread (all sorts), Woollen Yarn, Glass and Glassware, China and Porcelainware (all sorts), Copper and Copper Alloys, Zinc, Airconditioning machinery (all sorts) Refrigerators and parts thereof, Wireless Receiving Sets (all sorts).
1962-63 Two separate items i.e., Refrigerators and Air-Conditioning Appliances and Machinery and their parts were amalgamated into one as a new item entitled Refrigerating and Aircon-	65	All products derived from/of Crude Petroleumc or Shale, not otherwise specified (including refinery gases, lubricating oils and greases, wax and coke), Nitric, Hydrochloric and Sulphuric Acids, Gases, Rubber products, Plywood (changed to 'Wood and articles of wood w.e.f. 28-2-1982), Jute manufactured product, electric wires and cables, and Gramophones and Gramophone Records (w.e.f. 24-4-1962)

Asphalt and Bitumen definition altered So as to cover tar distilled |

Year	Number of Excisable Commodities	Description of Commodities
ditioning Appliances and Machinery, allSorts, and parts thereof w.e.f,, 24-4-1962 under Finance (No.2) Act, 1962.		from coal. 'COAL TAR DYES': Definition reworded to cover all synthetic organic dyes.
1963-64	65	No new excise was levied; in addition to changes in rates of a new items, selective surcharges were levied on several articles with a view to raise revenue exclusively for the Centre, which has to carry the burden of Defence.
1964-65	66	Sodium Silicate Duties were completely removed on number of items i.e., gramophone records, all glass other than carbon dioxide used for manufacture of aerated waters, low voltage electric motors and all acids other than sulphuric acid. Excise Duty was also withdrawn on soap manufactured without the aid of power)
1965-66	67	Lead unwrought (w.e.f 20-8-1965)
1966-67	69	Synthetic Organic products (known as Optical Bleaching Agents), Organic Surface Active Agents.

Year	Number of Excisable Commodities	Description of Commodities
1967-68	69	Rubber piping, tubing and belting were included for the first time as sub-items to item No. 16-A in the Central Excise Tariff.
1968-69	75	Confectionery and Chocolates, Artificial Leather Cloth, Embroidery, Sets, Steel Furniture and Crown Corks.
1969-70	80	Prepared or preserved Foods, Fertilizers, Domestic Electrical Appliances, Power Driven Pumps, Pilferproof Caps, and Wool Tops. Embroidery item deleted)
1970-71	91	Food products, Aerated Waters, Glucose, Dextrose and preparations thereof, Chemicals (namely, Calcium Carbide, Bleaching Powder, Sodium Hydrosulphite, Bicarbonate of Soda, Bichromates of Potassium or Sodium, Hydrogen Peroxide, Potassium Permanganate), Synthetic Rubber, Office Machines, Safety Razor Blades of Stainless steel, metal containers, Metal containers n.e.s Slotted Angles or channels of steel. Safes made of base metals, sparkling plugs omitted vide Finance (No.2) Bill, 1971.
1971-72	116	Maida, Blended or compounded lubricating oils and greases, calcined petroleum coke, Linoleum, Ready

Year	Number of Excisable Commodities	Description of Commodities
		made Garments, Typewriter Ribbons, Mosaic Tiles, Motor Vehicle Parts and Accessories, Fork-Lift Trucks and Platform Trucks, Cinematographic Projectors and parts thereof, Photographic cameras ('photographic apparatus and goods' changed through Finance Bill 1974', Roller bearings, welding electrodes, coated abrasives and grinding wheels, Bolts and Nuts and Screws Zip or Slide Fasteners and parts thereof, Pressure cookers, Vacuum Flasks, Playing Cards, Camphor, Menthol, Electric Insulating Tapes, Adhesive Tapes, all sorts n.e.s., Newspapers and Periodicals.
1972-73	120	Silk Yarn, Jute Twist Thread and Ropes, Yarn all sorts n.e.s., Textile Fabrics n.e.s. Tool Tips, Wire Ropes, Carbon Black, Rubber processing Chemicals
1-4-1973	123	('Newspapers' - Item deleted)
1-3-1974	128	Toothpaste, Electrical Stampings and Lamination Tape Recorders, specified Cutting Tools, Permanent Magnets
1-3-1975	130	Graphite Electrodes and Anodes, and all other goods, n.e.s.

141

Year	Number of Excisable Commodities	Description of Commodities
16-3-1976	132	Starch, Computers, Mineral Fibres and Yarn (Item No.45 - Safety Razor Blades of Stainless Steel omitted)
18-6-1976	136	(a) (i) Polishes; (ii) Flax yarn; (iii) Stereo systems; (iv) Watches; (v) Weighting Machines; (vi) Electric Lighting, Fittings.
		(b) (i) Slotted Angles and Channels (ii) Electric Insulation Tapes omitted
		(c) "Rayon and Synthetic Fibres and yarn, Yarn all sorts n.e.s., Rayon or Artificial Silk Fabrics and specified cutting Tools" replaced by "Man-made fibres and yarn, non-Cellulosic spun yarn, Man-made Fabrics, and Tools" respectively.
1-3-1978	138	Coal and Electricity
1-3-1979	140	Carpets, Locks, toothbrushes and Hookah tobacco added, but 'Cycle parts' deleted
10-5-1979	138	'Locks' and 'toothbrushes' deleted from Tariff on 10-5-1979
19-6-1980	139	Molasses
1-3-1981	140	Polyster Films (taken out from Tariff Item No. 15A w.e.f. 1-3-1981 and again merged with T.I.No.15A w.e.f. 28-2-1982)

Year	Number of Excisable Commodities	Description of Commodities
28-2-1982	141	(a) (1) Petroleum gases (2) Television image and sound recorders (3) Television Cameras (including Video Cameras) (4) Electronic Machines for games of skill or chance (5) Articles of all kinds used for sound or sound and image recording
		(b) (1) Calcined petroleum coke (2) Coal and merged with T.I.No.10
		(c) (1) Cellophane (2) Polyster Films omitted and merged with T.I.No. 15-A
1-8-1983	138	(i) Iron in any crude form T.I.No.25, (ii) Steel ingots T.I.No.26 (iii) Iron or Steel products T.I.No.26AA and (iv) Tinplates and tinned sheets have been merged to form new T.I. No. 25-Iron and Steel and products. Thereof, as consequence of a Notification issued in pursuance of provisions made in the Finance Bill, 1982 on 28-2-1983 and subsequently in the Finance Act, 1983.
11-5-1984 (date of enactment of Finance Bill, 1984 presented to Parliament)	133	The following commodities omitted from the Central Excise Tariff: (1) Maida (2) Blended or compounded lubricating on 29-2-1984) oils and greases

143

Year	Number of Excisable Commodities	Description of Commodities
		(3) Ready-to-wear Apparel (4) Mosaic tiles and
17-3-1985	137	(1) Pan Masala (2) Organic Chemicals (2) Marble (4) Travel Goods
28-2-1986		New Central Excise Tariff introduced. This is based on harmonized system of classification adopted for the Customs Tariff. All items are now listed in 91 Chapters (Chapters 2 to 96, with some Chapters being absent, as, like live animals, they are not pertinent for excise purposes of the Central Excise Tariff Act, 1986 (5 of 1986) which Replaces the 1st Schedule to the Central Excises and Salt Act, 1944.

❑❑

ANNEXURE IV

EXTRACTS FROM THE RECOMMENDATIONS OF TAX REFORMS COMMITTEE, 1992.

THE CASE FOR VAT

4.2. We have gained the impression that, in general officers of the Excise Department have not been properly informed about the rationale and justification for introducing a non-cascading and non-distorting type of indirect tax. It is now agreed among fiscal experts all over the world that any extended system of indirect taxation, that is, a tax that applies to all or most commodities, will have to be in the form of either a retail sales tax that does not interfere with the processes of production, does not affect costs and has the further advantage of capturing the entire value added. However, a retail sales tax (that is a tax that applies only to sales to non-producers) is found to be difficult to administer and may not be feasible for other reasons as well. The rational alternative is a VAT.

4.3. IT may be true to say that, administratively, it is east to tax just the inputs and leave out the final products. However, the criterion of administrative convenience will have to be balanced against the other more important criteria such as a desirable pattern of incidence, minimization of costs and of unintended interference with the choices of procedures. Besides, it is not possible to classify commodities into inputs and final products because that distinction depends also on the nature of use. A commodity purchased by a producer for use in manufacturing becomes an input, but the same commodity if purchased by a consumer becomes an output. As we show below, an extended system of excise or sales levied on a gross value basis, that is, one without the grant of credit for taxes paid on inputs, is undesirable from several points of view. If a VAT is to be avoided, then, as in the United States of America, excises must be confined to a few non-essential consumer goods such as tobacco, alcohol, motor cars and others. This is possible only of a major part of the tax revenue could be raised through direct taxes. Since that is not possible in India in the near future and since sales tax is leviable by the State Governments, the Government of India has no alternative but to resort to an extended form of excise taxation.

4.4.   An extended excise tax system of the cascading type, that is, one whose base at every stage includes the taxes paid at the earlier stages (gross value), can be shown to lead to four major types of undesirable consequences. First, such a system of taxation leads to an uncontrolled pattern of incidence on final products. With widespread taxation of both inputs and final products, it would not be possible to control the effective incidence of tax on different products and hence on different groups of consumers. The total effective incidence of any given final product at the end of the chain of production would be almost fortuitous and largely unknown to policy-makers. It is only after a great deal of research that one could get an idea of the pattern of incidence on consumers in different income or expenditure groups as at a given moment. But that pattern would keep changing with the changes in techniques of production, relative prices, etc. Nominal rates of taxes fixed for final products would give a misleading picture of incidence because the total effective incidence on different products could be vastly different. It is also to be noted that a heavy tax on an input for which no relief is given at alter stages generally tends to be regressive. It places a greater burden proportionate to price on the varieties of products consumed by the poor than on those consumed by the rich. Theoretically, it is possible to offset this by varying the rates of tax on different varieties of the final product. However, in practice it would be extremely difficult to calibrate the rates on final products to get a desired pattern of incidence.

4.5.   The second major defect of the extended system of cascading type of excises, such as that which existed before MODVAT was introduced in 1986, is that the taxes on inputs levied at different rates lead to unintended changes in the relative prices of inputs and hence to changes in the proportions in which different inputs are used. This result violates the rule that producers should not be unnecessarily made to change their decisions in regard to choice of inputs. Such interference could lead to serious economic distortions which the tax authorities or the Government cannot afford to ignore. Widespread taxation of inputs leads ultimately to an economically irrational tax structure, leading to inefficient use of resources.

4.6.   The third major defect of an extended system of cascading type of excises is that it leads to avoidable increases in costs and the prices of inputs as well as of final products. Since the intention is to tax the final users, obviously, a system which can reach them without raising costs in the economy is to be preferred. But the cascading type of tax implies that the tax paid at earlier stages of production forms part of the cost of production at subsequent stages. Until the tax levied at the different stages are collected from the consumers/final users, it is borne by the producers and costs in the economy are increased thereby. Also, the final increase in price will be greater than the yield of the tax to the Government. This is because, when an input is subjected to excise and/or sales tax, the manufacturer who uses it needs a larger amount of working capital to maintain the necessary stock of inputs; hence the interest cost goes up. This happens at every stage and the increase in the price of the final product must compensate for that. Besides, a manufacturer works out his own profit margin as a percentage of his costs which include taxes, and arrives at a price by adding a higher quantum of profit. On this price, the excise on the finished product is worked out. Then comes the sales tax which is levied on the price

147

inclusive of excise duty. Thereafter, the product goes to the wholesaler and then the retailer, each of whom once again, has to find a larger amount of finance which raises his costs and profit expectations. At each stage, the markup by producers and traders get inflated because the profits they seek to earn are related to the total capital which they employ, i.e., they would like to earn a certain rate of return on the capital employed, and the amount of capital employed, as explained above, invariably increases, if the costs of inputs are raised on account of indirect taxes levied on them. This snowballing or pyramiding effect, which is also referred to as 'cascading', raises the price of the final product to consumers by more than sum total of the different taxes levied at intermediate stages. In other words, the increase in consumer prices due to cascading is not limited to what accrues to the exchequer by way of revenue. The same amount of revenue may be raised with a smaller rise in the price of the final product and, therefore, a lower burden on the consumer, if a non-cumulative type of tax was imposed at the final stage of production, that is, on the finished product.

4.7. It is sometimes argued by tax administrators in developing countries that for administrative reasons, the government will have to content itself with taxing only inputs and a few selected final products. Taxing only inputs, such as raw materials and intermediate products and exempting final products because they are produced by a large number of undertakings has all the drawbacks mentioned above, that is, fortuitious and uncontrolled incidence on final products and hence on consumers in different income groups, distortions in producers' choices and escalation in costs and cascading. And, of course, there is the further disadvantage that value added at the final stages of production will be left out and the rates have to be higher, which could induce greater evasion. Administrative convenience must no doubt be given due weight, but all other — quite important — social and economic considerations cannot be ignored. After all, the object is not to raise revenue at any cost or in the easiest way possible.

4.8. As in the case of income tax, so also in the case of excises and sales taxes, small "taxable units" will have to be exempt. In respect of Central Excise, producers and manufacturers whose annual turnover is less than Rs.20 lakhs are exempt. This rule has to be applied to all industries, possibly with a few exceptions. And there is no need or justification to hike up the tax on the raw material or inputs when the final product is not taxed because there are too many small producers. The tax burden in respect of such commodities may be low or lower than in respect of the commodities. That is only a necessary consequence of favouring small producers. As pointed out earlier, heavy taxes on inputs make the tax system regressive.

4.9. The fourth major defect of the extended excise tax system without setoff for tax paid on inputs is that the burden of all the input taxes and the cost increases due to cascading will be carried by exports out of India, whereas most other countries are sending their exports free of all indirect taxes. It is well recognized in the realm of international trade that exports could and should be freed of all domestic indirect taxes. In order to try achieving this under the excise tax system on the gross value basis, a system of duty drawback has to be set up. But the accurate amount of duty to be given back is almost impossible to calculate. Apart from that and the large staff that would be called for, there could be appreciation that the cascading types of excise taxation combined with a similar type of sales taxes super-imposed on it would, and does, act as a great hindrance to our export effort. One of the main reasons for France inventing and adopting the VAT was to boost exports.

4.10. If exports are to be completely freed of excises, then the tax burden on the final export product arising from the taxation of all inputs and from that of machinery must be removed through setoff. (The VAT will thus become a purely consumption tax). As far as internal consumers are concerned, the tax on machinery, if not remitted, will like the tax on current inputs, lead to uncontrolled and regressive incidence, distortions of producers' choices and cascading. It is, therefore, necessary to grant VAT credit also to the tax on machinery.

4.11. Thus credit for tax paid on inputs, meaning all materials and services used in production, is a necessary concomitant of an extended excise tax system. It is given in the interests of the economy, to ensure efficient use of resources, minimize costs and to augment or preserve competitiveness in the export markets. Our discussions with many officials gave us the impression that the purpose of granting MODVAT credit was not generally understood and that it was often considered to be a relief to the producers. Since the economic justification for granting MODVAT credit is not understood, the grant of credit is looked upon as a relief which could be denied at the officer's discretion. That perhaps explains why duty credit was denied to inputs in several cases on the ground that "this input is really not intended to be given credit" (eg., "whitener" used in the manufacture of sugar) or that the input concerned is not fully incorporated into the product (eg., a battery fitted inside a clock even when the tax base of the clock includes the cost of the battery plus the tax on it).

4.12. As we had indicated in the Interim Report, in addition to the VAT at the manufacturing stage, there should be excises on a gross value basis on a few commodities, such as petroleum products, tobacco products and certain luxury goods. The rate structure for these goods has already been indicated. These excises would serve to achieve the objectives of sumptuary taxation as well as achieving a degree of progression in the taxation of consumption.

4.13. There would be some cases where taxes cannot be collected from the producers of final product for administrative reasons. In such special cases, the final products may be exempted, but the producers may be given option to come voluntarily and pay the tax if that would be beneficial for them. The fact that some final products would have to be exempted from the VAT does not invalidate the case for VAT.

TRANSITION TO VAT AT THE CENTRAL LEVEL

4.14. We urge that the following steps be taken simultaneously, over the next three to four years, in a phased manner:

(a) Extension of excises to cover most manufactured goods at present exempted and some select services mentioned in the interim report.

(b) Reduction in the level of rates on some commodities which are unduly high, such as plastic and synthetic resins, paints and dyes, glass and glassware, manmade filament yarn, tyres and tubes, motor vehicles, cosmetics and air-conditioning and refrigerating devices.

(c) Gradual reduction in the number of rates moving them towards three rates between 10 and 20 percent for all goods that would be covered by the VAT system.

(d) Extension of MODVAT credit to all inputs that are used in the production of, or incorporated in, taxable commodities except for office equipment, accessories and furniture, building materials and a few others.

(e) Extension of MODVAT credit for machinery not fully at the time of purchase but in installments during a subsequent period of years which could be laid down in the law and

(f) Extension of VAT to the more important services used by productive enterprises.

All these changes that we have suggested would transform the present mixed system of MODVAT and excise on gross value basis into a VAT at the manufacturing level.

4.15. We are of the view that within the next five years all products other than petroleum and tobacco products and matches should be brought within the ambit of VAT, even if the producers at the last manufacturing stage cannot be taxed in all cases.

4.16. Although the extension of MODVAT credit to inputs and machinery at present not eligible for such credit would lead to some loss of potential revenue, the extension of coverage to goods now exempted and to services would increase revenue considerably. For instance, a considerable amount of revenue could be derived from cycle tubes and tyres and other components because the larger part of the sales of those commodities are for replacement purposes. Similarly, taxation of services mostly used by households, such as residential telephone services would yield a large and increasing amount of revenue from the urban as well as the rural sector.

4.17. We believe that it is safe to proceed on the assumption that the growth of the economy will pick up from the next year or so and long with it industry will start growing at 8 to 9 per cent per annum as during the later half of the 1980s. Such a fast growth of industry would automatically lead to buoyancy in the revenue from the VAT and that should make possible adjustments in the rates and the extension of MODVAT credit. The final aim is not just to raise revenue anyhow, but to design and enforce a tax system which would facilitate and promote growth of output and exports which in turn would provide increasing amounts of revenue.

4.18. As indicated in the interim report, to begin with, the taxation of select services should be kept outside the system of the present MODVAT on commodities. However, when revenue considerations permit, the taxation of services could be extended to cover those which enter into production as inputs and taxes paid on them could also be made eligible for VAT credit.

4.19. At present, the four major sectors where the MODVAT system does not apply are petroleum products, tobacco products, textile and matches. The Committee is of the opinion that, since in any case petroleum and tobacco have to be subjected to high rates and their use discouraged, they need not be brought under the proposed VAT system. In principle, matches should be brought under VT, but given the nature of the industry, its relative significance and the fact that matches are more of a consumer product, the existing system of taxation may be allowed to constitute an important sector and enter significantly into all household budgets. They also form a significant proportion of our exports. IT is highly important that the taxation of textiles should be on a rational basis.

EXTENSION OF VAT TO THE WHOLESALE STAGE

4.20. It is generally agreed that there are disadvantages in imposing a sales tax or a VAT confined to the manufacturing stage, for one thing, the value added at the subsequent stages is left out of taxation, which creates discrimination among products. But what is more important, if a tax falls only at the manufacturing stage, there is an advantage in undervaluing taxable products at that stage because that would reduce tax liability. As we have seen, valuation of products for ad valorem levies is an important problem under excises and is the cause of many disputes. We deal with this problem later in the report with a view to suggesting a consistent method of valuation that would be fair and would also minimise disputes. However, it may be pointed out that if the VAT system (i.e., the reformed Central Excise) could be extended to the "wholesale stage", there would result a more rational system and the attempts at undervaluation would be considerably reduced and hence it would be possible to accept the invoice value in most cases.

4.21. By "wholesale" stage, we mean traders who buy from manufacturers and sell to other manufacturers or to traders. In practice, it will not be possible to identify traders by these characteristics. Also, even small traders might be buying from manufacturers and the intention is not to bring them under the extended VAT. Therefore, in practice, for purposes of this tax, we must define wholesalers to mean those with total turnover above a certain level, say, Rs.50 lakhs or Rs.1 crore. They should be subjected to VAT is addition to the manufacturers. This would be another advantage. The total burden on commodities need not increase, since there would simultaneously take place a reduction in the level of rates.

4.22. The above proposal for the extension of VAT to the "wholesale" stage has to face two problems, however. The first is that the inclusion of "wholesalers" will considerably increase the number of VAT assessees and the Excise Department cannot cope with such an increase. The VAT at the wholesale stage will, therefore, have to be collected by the officers of the Sales Tax Departments of the States concerned. This could be done in close cooperation with the officers of the Central Excise Department. The amount of VAT collected at the wholesale stage can be allowed to be retained by the State where it is collected.

4.23. The States will thus have an additional source of revenue, distributed on the basis of origin and in collecting that revenue, their own officers will play the major role. Nevertheless, the State Governments might not agree to the extension of the Central Excise to the "wholesale" stage because the power to levy a tax on the sale of goods lies within the Constitutional jurisdiction of the States. This is the second problem and it can be overcome only with the cooperation of the States. The States could be persuaded to accept the levy of central VAT upto the wholesale stage, because their own right to levy the sales tax on goods will in no way get the entire revenue from the VAT at the wholesale stage.

4.24. The stages in general have preferred to levy the first-point sales tax on most goods. This tax could be converted into a form of state VAT within the manufacturing sector, if the taxable manufacturers are given the benefit of setoff for tax paid on all inputs including machinery. If concessions and most exemptions under the sales tax are eliminated, as has been recommended for the excise tax, the tax could be levied at moderate rates. There may be no need for levying sales tax at more than two rates, since the distributional and other non-revenue objectives could be left to be performed by the central taxes which apply uniformly throughout the country.

4.25. The thorough going reform of the domestic indirect taxes levied by the centre and the states that we have recommended above would give the country a far more rational tax system that what exists today. The changes in the conditions of levy of the central sales tax that we have suggested in the interim report would further improve the equity and rationality of the system and prevent the fragmentation of the national economy. The ideal solution, from the economic point of view, would be to have a single VAT at the central level, reaching down to the retail stage in replacement of most indirect taxes other than protective duties and sumptuary excise duties - the central excise the state sales taxes, the municipal octroi, the goods and passengers tax and the electricity duty. The proceeds of the VAT will be shared among the three levels of government. Having only two major taxes, the income tax and the VAT, would also mean greatly reduced cost of compliance to business and industry as well as lesser obstacles to the fast growth of the economy. For the smaller businesses in particular, the elimination of the obligation to deal with municipal tax departments would be a great boon.

4.26. While the reluctance of the State Governments to give up or delegate their tax powers is understandable, it will give legitimate for trade and industry and the people in general to insist that the economic distortions caused by the sales tax structures should be removed. Given the imperative need to increase economic efficiency and to improve export competitiveness, the country cannot afford to let the central and state governments continue with the complicated and distortionary tax structures that have grown up. Therefore, even if a single VAT extending to the retail stage is not feasible at the moment, it is imperative to carry out the second-best reforms which we have advocated.

❏❏

ANNEXURE V

EXTRACTS FROM THE REPORT OF THE CENTRAL EXCISE (SELF REMOVAL PROCEDURE) REVIEW COMMITTEE, 1973.

9.   From 1956 onwards excise duties have been increasingly extended to raw materials and intermediate products primarily with the object of raising additional resources for financing development. In quite a few cases, it has also been found to be administratively more convenient to tax inputs in preference to the finished products. The latter, it appears to have been felt, tend to get diffused over several points in the system and are not readily amenable to effective control. One important consequence of such expansion in coverage has been to impart to excise tariff its present multi-point character. This has been criticized on the ground of undue cumulative incidence on the final product and the resultant effect on prices.

10.   Prior to 1962, the normal practice followed to mitigate the effect of multi-point levies was to issue an exempting notification by which duty on the final product was exempted to the extent specified in lieu of the duty paid on components or raw materials used in the manufacture of the final product. These notifications took several forms depending upon the needs and exigencies of different situations. With certain exceptions, eg., where the final product was completely exempted from duty, a detailed procedure was laid down for the generality of cases. This required, inter alia, that,

   (i) a prior notice would be given to the factory officer before such duty paid materials (including importing materials on which countervailing duty had been paid) were received in the licensed premises so that the factory officer could be present at the time of their receipt;

(ii) the duty paid materials would be brought in their original packing and produced before the factory officer for identification along with the original A.R.I/ Bill of entry etc., on which excise or countervailing customs duty has been paid;

(iii) proper account of such duty paid materials would be maintained indicating the quantity issued and used for manufacture of the finished product and a pro rata deduction made from the duty payable on the finished product on account of the excise or countervailing duty already paid, such deduction being made at the point of the clearance of the finished product from the factory and

(iv) all handling and storage losses of duty paid raw materials would be borne by the factory.

11. There also obtained, in addition to the setoff procedure indicated in the preceding paragraph the facility, on a selective basis, of in-bond movement of goods, ie., transport without payment of duty of materials and components required for use in the finished excisable goods. In such cases no abatement of the duty payable on the finished product was involved. At the same time, an account had to be maintained of the receipt and issue of such materials and components and producers were held to account for any shortages or losses which were not satisfactorily accounted for. This facility of in-bond movement was, however, allowed in very few cases. It was largely by way of an extra legal concession, the normal in-bond movement being confined to cases involving transport of goods to different points for purposes of storage for distribution as, for example, in the case of mineral oils.

12. Both the setoff procedure and the procedure for in-bond movement were considered unsatisfactory in some ways. The former was said to give to an integrated unit, producing both the components and the final product, an unfair advantage vis-à-vis isolated units which received duty paid components from elsewhere and got only a setoff on the finished product. This was because the setoff was related mostly to the weight of the finished product and not to the duty initially paid on the total weight of the material used for such manufacture. Similarly, the procedure for in-bond movement of goods was said to present some practical difficulties as the duty paid raw material received had to be accounted for and related to the quantity of the final product manufactured.

13. In November 1962, the government introduced what came to be known as the Proforma Credit procedure which envisaged that in respect of excisable commodities notified by the government, manufacturers will be permitted to obtain duty paid material or components and would be granted straight away proforma credit of duty paid on such material or components and that this credit could be utilized by the manufacturer for payment of duty on the final product. At the time of the introduction of this procedure, it was clarified that it was not the intention that "debit in the proforma account should be made only of the excise duty on the quantity of material/parts used in the manufacture of finished goods", and that "the manufacturer would be permitted credit of the entire amount of duty available in the proforma account even though some materials/parts received by him may continue to lie in the factory". This enunciation of the scope of the scheme of proforma credit seems to have undergone a modification some time ago when a view was taken by the government that proforma credit could be drawn upon only to the extent of the duty paid on materials and components actually used in the manufacture of notified goods. It has been repeatedly put to us by the industry that this has neutralized all the advantages of the scheme of proforma

159

credit. Another point made was that proforma credits remained un-utilised and could not be drawn upon, whenever the relevant goods i.e., those manufactured out of materials and components in respect of which proforma credit had been given, were exported under bond. We are glad to observe that both these difficulties have since removed through the Department's instruction issued in August 1993, which provides that "the credit of duty allowed in respect of any material or component part can be utilized towards payment of duty on any finished excisable goods for the manufacture of which such material or component parts were permitted to be brought into the factory..." and that "it should now be possible to allow utilization of proforma credit obtained on raw materials/components used in the manufacture of goods exported under bond towards payment of duty on other finished excisable goods for the manufacture of which such raw materials were brought in the factory".

14. Apart from the setoff, in-bond and proforma credit procedures, the central excise rules also contain a procedure commonly known as Chapter X procedure, under which duty leviable on goods used for special industrial purposes can be remitted. Here the intention is not to mitigate the effect of multi-point levies but to afford relief for certain industrial purposes. In effect, the procedure laid down amounts to in-bond movement of goods, and in certain cases, to obtain relief from double taxation.

15. We consider that, in so far as they concern the multi-point character of he levies there is scope for considerable simplification and rationalization of the existing procedure. The Central Excise Re-organisation Committee which went into this question observed that there was neither uniformity in the pattern of relief afforded nor was there any evident or expressly stated principle in these reliefs. In regard to the procedure of proforma credit they said that, apart from additional documentation and checks, the

procedure led to distortion of revenue statistics. The demand of the industry, they pointed out, was not so much for a single point levy as for a single point collection. Where goods are delivered to another factory for use as components for manufacture of articles, which are themselves subject to duty, they recommend that the duty liability should as a general rule be transferred to the latter and collected as and when the final product is charged to duty. In short, they recommended the in-bond movements of such goods.

16. We have carefully considered the procedural aspects of multipoint levy from the point of view of the system of selective control envisaged by us. We are of the view that having decided which excisable materials or components have to be exempted from duty, and to what extent, when they are used in the manufacture of other excisable goods, government should quantify the extent of exemption in concrete terms and notify that where such finished excisable goods are produced out of duty-paid components, the effective rate of duty for such goods will be rebated to that extent. Where the number and description of components going into the manufacture of a unit of the finished product are known, this will not present any difficulty. Where, however, the quantity of raw materials, to which duty exemptions is related required for manufacture of a unit of the finished product differs from factory to factory according to the technological process employed or the composition and quality of the raw material itself or for any other reasons, some sort of an average quantum of duty can be worked out on the basis of the chemical composition of the final product or with reference to other relevant data and notified. Where duty rates are ad valorem, the extent of exemption can be worked out on the basis of the average price prevailing over a point of time for the raw material/component used and then expressed as proportion or percentage of the average price of the finished product. It is true that in the case of commodities, subject to frequent price fluctuations,

this may lead to some distortions, but it would make a great deal of simplification and impart the necessary uniformity to procedures of assessment all over the country. The quantum of exemption notified may be kept under constant review and varied as and when required (though not too frequently, having regard to changes in duty structure of either the components/materials used or the end product or fluctuations in price or on account of policy decisions calling for a change in the extent of exemption already notified. The suggestion made by us is not unknown to the Government. Under the Central Excise and Customs Drawback Rules, where duty paid components/raw materials are utilised in a product which is exported, an exercise to determine the average incidence of duty is undertaken for fixing the amount to be rebated and a periodical review of these rates in done to see if ay change is required either because of changes in process of manufacture or changes in quantum or rates of duty on raw materials and components.

7.   We would recommend consideration of the feasibility of applying the procedure outlined above to all cases of multi-point levies in which duty relief is decided upon as a matter of policy including some of those which are presently covered by Chapter X procedure. Thereafter Chapter X procedure should, in our view, be confined to the purpose intended, namely, remission of duty leviable on goods used for special industrial purpose.

18.   In the matter of exports, several points have been made by the industry. Broadly recapitulated they are that,

   (i) physical examination whether by (or, at an earlier stage, on behalf) the Customs should be waived altogether since such examination is inconsistent with basic concept of SRP: duty rebates or credits in the running bond account should be allowed on the basis of shipping bills filed by the exporters;

(ii) supervision charges should not be levied because examination and sealing are jobs performed in government interest and,

(iii) where no physical examination and sealing of goods are asked for or provided, considerable simplification should be effected of the present procedure which requires that a 24 hour's advance notice of the extended removal of goods should be furnished to the department and a number of documents got certified or attested before removal of goods.

19. In support of their demand that physical examination of goods should be waived altogether, the industry has pointed out that in several fields, particularly textiles, there already exist statutory regulations for pre-shipment inspection of goods and that the Customs authorities should have no hesitation in accepting certification of inspection issued by component officers of the Textile Committee or the Export Inspection Council.

20. We note that pre-shipment inspection of goods is primarily a function of the Customs authorities, and that physical examination and sealing of goods carried out by excise authorities are, in a way, agency functions performed.

□□

ANNEXURE VI

EXTRACTS FROM THE REPORT OF THE INDIRECT TAXATION ENQUIRY COMMITTEE, 1977.

10.3.   The evaluation of indirect taxes in India is in many respects similar to the course it has taken in most other industrialized and developing countries. The emergence of an extended system of excise taxation or the overlapping between an excise tax system and a multi-point general sales tax, the problems of distortions and cascading that these give rise to, the attempts to deal with such problems all these developments have manifested themselves in different developed and developing countries as their economies grew complex and the burden of their fiscal system steadily increased. It was then realized that in order to avoid distortions, promote exports and to make intervention beneficial, selective and purposeful, it was necessary to think of a different system embodying a principle which would eliminate the above mentioned problems even under an extended commodity tax system. In pursuance of this objective, today, almost the whole of Western Europe (including the United Kingdom) as well as a number of developing countries such as, Brazil, Argentina and Ivory Coast, have gone on to the Value Added Tax (VAT) system. The question naturally arises whether India too, faced with similar problems could and should adopt VAT. In fact, our terms of reference require us specifically to examine the feasibility of adopting some form of VAT in the field of indirect taxation. If the answer is in the affirmative, we have further been asked to indicate what would be the appropriate stage at which the principle of VAT should be applied. When we elicited the views of trade and industry on the subject, we found that although there were several who expressed doubts and reservations about the administrative feasibility of adopting VAT in India, there was an impressive measure of support for such a change - one important source of such support being the Federation of Indian Chambers of Commerce and Industry.

10.4.   A detailed exposition of the VAT system is given later in the Report. Essentially, VAT in its comprehensive form is a tax on all goods and services (except exports and government services), its special characteristic being that it falls on the value added at each stage from the state of production to the retail stage. However, in practice, no attempt is made to ascertain the amount of value added, but instead each tax payer is allowed to deduct from the tax payable on his output the taxes he has paid on his inputs. Administratively, this is a simpler way of reaching the value added. It is also clear that the producers are in effect freed from the taxation of inputs at every stage. Thus, a distinctive merit of the VAT is that it enables a country to have an extended system of commodity taxation and yet avoid the problems of cascading and escalation of costs that are concomitants of general sales and excise taxes. It is also relatively easy under the VAT system to completely free exports of internal commodity taxation.

10.5.   In European countries that we have adopted the full fledged VAT system, VAT is applied to internal production as well as imports while exports are exempt. Individual imported commodities may be, and are, in addition subject to protective duties. This means, that apart from affording a certain degree of needed protection, imports are placed on the same footing as domestic products for the purpose of taxation.

10.6.   The VAT in its comprehensive form extends from the mining and manufacturing stages to the retail stage. It can replace all other forms of internal indirect taxes. Thereby, the maximum benefit can be derived from

VAT. However, such a total or near total replacement is, for obvious reasons, more easily done under a unitary system of Government than under a federal system, for in the latter, the State Governments need to be given certain independent powers of taxation.

10.7.   The first question we need to consider is whether we should take as our long term objective the replacement of the existing systems of excises, sales taxation and action by a comprehensive VAT. This would have several economic advantages. It would also be consistent with the oft-expressed desire of trade and industry to deal with a single tax authority in the indirect tax field, which in turn is at the root of the demand for the merger of sales taxes with excises.

10.8.   However, there is a more important problem to be faced, namely, the administrative problem of enforcing VAT at the wholesale and retail stages, because, firstly, the number of taxpayers to be dealt with gets larger as we move further down the line in the chain of transactions; and secondly, the smaller dealers in a developing country, and even in developed countries, maintain only a primitive form of accounting and may find it extremely difficult to cope with the accounting requirements of VAT. There is also the further consideration that wholesalers, and even more retailers, are likely to be dealing in a variety of commodities so that the matching output and input taxes becomes difficult.

Value Added Tax at Manufacturer's Stage (MANVAT)

10.9.   For these reasons, we consider that it would be premature now to think in terms of a comprehensive system of VAT extending down to the retail level. But in order to put Central taxation on a rational basis, we would urge that serious consideration be given for moving over to a VAT system at the manufacturing level

- the so-called MANVAT. It is our view that in the ultimate analysis a satisfactory solution to the various distortions and problems that arise from an extended system of excise taxation lies in the adoption of MANVAT. The main advantage of MANVAT would be that it would altogether eliminate cascading on account of taxation of raw materials and other inputs. The tax levied on a final product would be the total tax on it and the tax on inputs at earlier stages will not affect its cost or price. The consequent reduction in interest charges and in successive mark-ups would also be favourable factors as far as prices of final products are concerned. The community would know the real tax burden on each product and it would also facilitate the gradation of different products under lower or higher rates in order to achieve the desired degree of progression. MANVAT may also minimize the requirement of physical checks to ensure that there is not much evasion. Besides, the competitiveness of our products in the export markets will get a major thrust.

10.10. From the administrative angle, MANVAT should not present insurmountable difficulties. From the point of view of accounting, the larger manufacturers would not find it too difficult to cope with the requirements of VAT and the number of taxpayers to be dealt with would be manageable.

10.11. Theoretically, VAT can be applied in two ways: either a given rate of tax can be applied to a base which is equal to the value of output minus the cost of inputs, or the producer may be allowed to deduct from the tax payable on output, the tax he has paid on inputs. The latter is referred to as the tax credit method. This is the method that we would recommend for adoption in India for MANVAT. This method would ensure that the actual rate of tax paid on a final product would be equal to the nominal rate of tax on it. Moreover, this method would enable us to tax value added at stages before the

167

manufacturing stage where MANAT may not be made applicable for some reasons.

10.12. Under the VAT system, relief is provided in respect of taxation of inputs. One question that arises in this connection is whether the capital goods purchased by a producer should be considered as inputs for this purpose. In most of the European VAT systems relief is provided also for the tax paid on capital goods. However, under Indian conditions, it would not be prudent to provide such tax relief not only on revenue considerations but also in order not to give encouragement to capital-intensive methods of production. Our aim should be to provide relief in respect of taxes on all inputs including physical ingredients, consumable stores and packaging material.

10.13. We have pointed out earlier that present excise tax system contains a provision under Rule 56-A for set-off tax paid on inputs against the tax payable on the output, under certain conditions. The tax credit available under the VAT is exactly of the same kind. The extension of the scope for relief under Rule 56-A, which we have recommended, would in fact be one of the preparatory steps for the introduction of MANVAT. The main difference between an extended system of application of Rule 56-A and the MANVAT is that the former is based on procedures involving physical checks, whereas the latter would be mainly based on the invoice or the accounts method. We have heard that a number of cumbersome regulations have to be complied with in order that a producer may avail himself of the benefit of Rule 56-A; for example, the information about the receipt in the factory of the input concerned has to be communicated to the tax authorities within a specified period. Obviously, such a stipulation would create complications if the application of this provision were to be made general.

10.14. If the excise tax system only were to be put on a value added basis, relief would be given only for excise tax paid on inputs. Such a relief cannot be given either in respect of sales taxes or customs duties. Hence, if sales taxes continue in roughly the present form, they would impinge on inputs and much of the advantage of MANVAT would be lost. Therefore, simultaneously with the introduction of MANVAT, or even preparatory to it, the existing system of sales taxation would have to be reformed. Since the implementation of our recommendations would nearly eliminate sales taxation of inputs sole to taxable manufacturers, if MANVAT also were to be introduced, we would in fact be reaping one of the main advantages that flow from a comprehensive VAT. However, just as a conversion of the excise tax system into MANVAT would not have much significance unless the sales tax system is also reformed, it would be equally true that there would not be much force in our insisting on the states to refrain from taxation of inputs if Central Excises continue to fall on them irrespective of economic considerations.

10.15. As regards import duties, they cannot immediately be brought within the ambit of MANVAT. One of the main reasons for this is that at present fairly stiff rates on imported raw and intermediates are levied to bring in sizable amount of revenue. Import levies on inputs will have to be reduced first to such levels as are necessary for purely economic considerations, namely to protect industry and to introduce an element of discouragement for the use of imported products. There would be no case for refunding the levies imposed for the above reasons, which should not be looked upon primarily as sources of revenue but are deliberately intended to raise the landed cost of the concerned imports. In addition to these, the equivalent of MANVAT on the same domestic products should be levied as countervailing duties. In course of time, after such rationalization has taken place, when revenue needs permit it, relief under

MANVAT could be made admissible in respect of such countervailing duties.

10.16. The advantages of the system that we are recommending are not simply theoretical. If a system of MANVAT were to be adopted and sales taxation on inputs were also to be eliminated, substantial benefits would accrue to the economy. In order to gain an idea of the major benefits that will be derived from the application of VAT, we have had carried out a study of the impact of the present system of taxation on cists and prices in an important industry. The study shows that in the case of truck and bus chassis there would be a saving in costs to the tune of Rs.3000/- (about 5 per cent of the tax exclusive price), through the reduction of interest charges on working capital and the reduction in mark-up at different stages of production. The saving will still be sizable even if VAT were to replace the existing excise alone. Additionally, a considerable amount of scarce working capital which is locked up as the tax component in inventories would be released for productive purposes.

10.17. In European countries as well as in certain developing countries, such as Brazil, which have adopted VAT, while the system is made applicable to all industries, some products, such as petroleum, tobacco and liquor, are in addition subjected to non-refundable excise duties. In Germany, a few more commodities are added to this list and all of them are subjected to what are called consumption taxes. Under Indian conditions, it would be preferable to keep quite a number of industries outside the scope of MANVAT and continue on them the present system of excises. These would include industries in whose final products not much cascading of tax is involved as well as those whose products have to be taxed at special or at high rates for economic or sumptuary reasons. Taxation of such products has to follow its own logic and cannot be fitted into the general system. The kind of industries that we have in mind are petroleum products, tobacco and tobacco products, sugar, coffee, tea, and matches. Together they yielded in 1976-77 Rs.2081 crores which formed 46.4 per cent of the total excise revenue. Incidentally, keeping them out of the system of MANVAT would correspondingly reduce the administrative burden of running the new system.

10.18. We would not suggest, however that an attempt should be made to apply MANVAT to all the rest of the industries at one stroke. It would be prudent to make a start with 3 or 4 industries at one stroke which reduce final products (such as automobiles and diesel engines) in respect of which cascading and other ill effects arising from widespread input taxation are pronounces. Such a pilot project would enable tax administration to test out procedures and study the reaction of tax payers. An industry itself may have a wide range of products. If the experiment is to be made on a somewhat wider scale one could consider, say, the entire range of products. If the experiment is to be made on a somewhat wider scale one consider, say, the entire range of products falling under the automobile industry. On the other hand, if the experiment is to be pinpointed, one could think of products like trucks, tractors and diesel engines for launching a pilot project, because in the interests of safeguarding revenue it is necessary to establish its workability before a widespread application of the system is contemplated.

10.19. As has been amply demonstrated by experience of other countries, it would not be possible to work the VAT system with a plethora of rates of tax on different inputs and finished products. While theorists who advocate complete neutrality in indirect taxation argue in favour of a single rate of VAT, even most of the developed countries have found it necessary to have more than one rate to tax and also to impose additional higher levies on a range of luxury products. Before embarking upon MANVAT, it would be necessary, as one of the preparatory steps, to rationalize the excise duty structure so as to have only 4 to 5 rates. As we have argued earlier, in the rationalized duty structure, the same rate of tax should apply to final products which could be identified as belonging to the same group of necessaries for life, conventional necessities or luxuries, depending upon the income group which predominantly consume them. Also, there should be non-discriminatory taxation as between competing raw materials or other inputs unless there are special economic reasons for a contrary treatment.

10.20. Another preparatory step for the introduction of MANVAT would be the extension of the scope for relief under Rule 56-A. We have also argued that the average rate on raw materials should be brought down. Once the number of rates on final products has been cut down, the burden of taxation on raw materials is reduced and relief under Rule 56-A has been sufficiently liberalized, the divergence between the cumulative levies and the nominal rates on the final products would be considerably narrowed down. The stage would then be set for the introduction of MANVAT.

10.21. In applying the MANVAT system, some practical problems may have to be faced. A point often made is that the system would mean maintaining detailed books of accounts, casting, as a result, a much heavier burden of tax compliance on the small and medium scale manufacturers that at present. To assess the magnitude of this problem, the Committees Secretariat undertook a small sample study of the purchase and sales pattern as well as the accounting system of manufacturers with different out-turn ranging from less than Rs.2 lakhs per annum to that exceeding Rs.1 crore per annum. All the manufacturing units covered under the study were found to be issuing invoices with comprehensive details. It was noticed that manufacturers whose turnover exceeds

172

Rs.15 to Rs.20 lakhs per annum do, by and large, get most of their inputs under cover of regular invoices which are maintained properly. These invoices show detailed particulars, but excise duty is not shown where the purchases are from dealers. Such manufacturers keep detailed accounts of their purchases, production, sales and stocks in balance, of inputs as well as of finished goods. Though, in several cases, the bulk of the purchases of inputs was direct from other manufacturers, there were also purchases from local dealers and those situated outside. In the case of manufacturers whose turnover is less than Rs.15 lakhs, accounts maintained for purchases, production and sales gave reasonable details tough the system was not sophisticated enough. In their case, the larger portion of their purchases was from dealers (and even retailers sometimes) and the corresponding invoices (which were generally obtained) did not mention the excise duty particulars. Thus it could be assumed that manufacturers whose turnover exceeds Rs.16 lakhs could be reasonably expected to conform to VAT documentation without much difficulty. As for manufacturers with smaller outturn (who incidentally contribute not even 5 per cent of the total excise tax revenue as per our study), it is possible when in 1954 VAT was initially experimented with at the manufacturing stage and special schemes were devised for this purpose. Based on the experience of other countries, it should not, therefore, be difficult to find an appropriate solution to this problem in the Indian context. One of the possibilities which could be explored would be suitable liberalization of the existing provisions of Rule 56-A which already allows tax credit if there is one dealer in between two manufacturers. The other possibility could be to allow the dealers to register voluntarily and to empower them to issue tax vouchers. Perhaps a better method may be to allow tax credit on a notional basis after deducting from the invoice prices a gross margin for the wholesale sector. Under this scheme, tax credits would be granted at notified rates, which would be related to the relevant rates of tax on inputs as also the pattern of production of the inputs in the organized and small sectors. In fact, a critical study of the schemes operating in other countries would be of great help in devising appropriate solutions in the Indian context. The introduction of VAT for selected industries in the first instance, as recommended by us, would enable Government and Tax Administration to obtain a clear idea of the special problems of the kind we have indicated above. On the basis of the experience gained, suitable schemes could be devised before extending MANVAT to other industries.

❑❑

ANNEXURE VII

EXTRACTS OF THE REPORT OF THE TECHNICAL STUDY GROUP ON CENTRAL EXCISE TARIFF, 1985.

7.1. The cascading effect in indirect taxes has been the subject matter of considerable debate in recent years. Considering the fact that the total duty burden imposed on the country by the major indirect taxes, ie., customs, excises and sales tax is of the order of Rs.28,000/- crores per annum and that each of these has a wide tax base, the snowballing effect of multi-stage taxation as also the interaction of individual taxes between them cannot but be large. In order to reduce or minimize the cascading effect what is needed is an integrated approach, which would cover all these major duties as well as other indirect taxes like octroi.

7.2. One solution could be to have a unified Value Added Tax system, which would operate as a transaction tax stretching from the production or manufacturing stage to the retail stage. Such a system would mean a major change in the taxing power of the Union and States, requiring a constitutional amendment. The observations of the Jha Committee on this point sum up the arguments against the introduction of a comprehensive VAT:

"There could be, however, two major arguments against the introduction of a comprehensive VAT in India: one is a political and the other is administrative. The political argument is the obvious one that the loss of power to levy sales taxes would seriously erode the fiscal autonomy of the State Governments and weaken the federal principle that each subordinate level of government should have the discretion to raise more or less revenue as the people of the state concerned, desire. Without taking any side on this issue, we simply draw

175

attention to the political judgement involved. The second argument points to the administrative problem of enforcing VAT at the wholesale and retail stages. Enforcement of VAT in relation to wholesalers and retailers is likely to create serious problems because, firstly, the number of tax payers to deal with gets larger as we move further down the line in the chain of transaction; and secondly, the smaller dealers in a developing country, and even in developed countries, maintain only a primitive form of accounting and may find it extremely difficult to cope with the accounting requirement of VAT. Besides, the wholesalers, and more so the retailers, are likely to be dealing in a variety of commodities so that the matching of output and input taxes becomes more difficult in their case".

7.3. The second best alternative would be to rationalize each one of these duty systems and build into them suitable corrective measures so that the adverse effects of the interaction of these duties are minimized. With this objective in view, the group looked into the existing input duty credit schemes under Central Excise law.

7.4. Existing input duty relief schemes - the proforma credit procedure.

The three important input duty relief schemes in this sphere are in the "Proforma Credit Procedure", the "Set-off Procedure", and "In-bond Movement Procedure", commonly known as the "Chapter X Procedure". Of these, the most extensively applied input relief scheme is the proforma credit procedure. The coverage of this procedure is selective; more often it has been extended to dutiable final products whose inputs falls under the same Tariff Item as the final product. The procedure extends similar benefits in respect of 'countervailing duty' paid on imported inputs, except where such inputs if made in India fall under Tariff Item 68. The procedure has not so far been extended to packing materials and consumable

176

stores. Further, the prescribed procedure provides for physical checks at various stages which tends to impede at times the smooth flow of the manufacturing process.

7.5. Set-off procedure
The set-off procedure under which the relief in respect of input taxation is provided by a notification exempting the final product to the extent of excise paid on the specified inputs used in its manufacture, operates on the 'physical ingredient' principle and is somewhat stricter than the proforma credit procedure in terms of compliance requirements. Further, under this procedure, availing of the credit is at the point of actual clearance of the finished product manufactured from input and restricted to the extent of the duty paid on the quantum of input contained in the finished products. This procedure is generally extended to excise duty paid on inputs and not to countervailing duty paid on imported inputs.

7.6. Chapter X procedure
The other procedure meant to relieve input duty tax burden is the one laid down in Chapter X of the Central Excise Rules. This procedure permits removal under bond and for use in specified industrial processes dutiable raw materials or intermediate products with full or partial exemption from duty. The basic distinction between the provisions discussed earlier and this procedure is that in case of former full duty is collected on the inputs at the first instance and allowed to be set off or used as proforma credit eventually, in the case of the latter the intended duty concession on the inputs, whether fill or partial is allowed ab initio at the time of their clearance, and further movements is under bond to safeguard against diversion and abuse. The procedure has not been extended to imported inputs.

7.7. Other methods
For achieving similar objectives, certain methods are also adopted. In some cases, inputs are completely exempted

from duty, if used for certain specified purposes, keeping in view the fact that the duty is leviable on final product also. In some other cases, finished products are exempted from duty or are subject to intermediates are used in their manufacture. In the context of these exemption, goods purchased from the market are deemed to be duty-paid. These methods have generally been applied as measures of administrative convenience.

7.8.   Comparative merits of the various procedures
Of the three main procedures, the proforma credit procedure has been more extensively used for relieving the cumulative duty burden on account of input duties. In comparison with the set-off procedure, the requirement under the proforma credit procedure is less rigorous and provides the manufacturer with greater flexibility in using the duty credit. Unlike the position under set-off procedure, in the scheme of proforma credit, the benefit of duty credit is not denied in respect of the inputs which might be lost in the process and do not actually get ingrained in the product. Where duty credit has to be provided in a chain, the proforma credit procedure is better suited. In comparison with the Chapter X procedure, the proforma credit is more desirable and appropriate as a measure for giving duty credit on a wider basis since it ensures payment of duty on the input at the first stage thereby reducing the risk of revenue to a considerable extent. On the other hand, the Chapter X procedure, which requires a stricter vigil, is more beneficial to the manufacturer since he would be in a position to save on working capital and sales tax on excise duty component of the cost of the inputs.

7.9.   VAT Versus Proforma Credit procedure
The group also considered the merits of "Value added tax at the manufacturer's stage" (MANVAT) in lieu of central excises, a plea for which has been made by some organizations which replied to the group's questionnaire. A comparative study of the VAT procedure and the

proforma credit procedure reveals that if the latter is given a general coverage and procedural requirements like filing an intimation of receipts, routine physical checks before they are taken into use and other such constraints are removed, then the main difference between the two is basically in the time and manner of payment of duty to the exchequer. The Jha Committee, which had recommended the adoption of MANVAT as a long-term reform, had itself observed thus in this regard:

"In fact, if the application of Rule 56A is generalised, it would amount to a virtual adoption of VAT at the manufacturing stage".

Under the standard VAT procedures in the countries where VAT is in force, while the assessee collects the VAT from his customers on every sale, he is required to remit it to Government in consolidated sums at prescribed intervals of time, making available to him during such intervals interest free funds; and he can considerably defer this liability by suitable inventory management. In the Indian context, collection of duty at the point of removal of goods from the factory, which is the core feature of the Central Excise levy, has its own merit and justification. Further the VAT system lays great store on an "invoice culture" whereunder all purchase and sale transactions are duly and correctly documented. But such an invoice culture, essential for successful implementation of VAT, has yet to take roots in the country. Incidentally, the cost of tax compliance under VAT even in developed countries is substantial particularly in the case of small assessees. On the positive side, the proforma credit procedure too has its disadvantages. Since under this procedure, the credit is available for utilization soon after the receipt of inputs in the factory and such credit can be used for paying duty on final products which do not physically contain the inputs, the working capital cost incident on input duty is relieved almost immediately. The burden of paying duty on removal of final products is, thus, effectively lightened. A general extension of the proforma credit procedure - along with the rate categorisation as suggested earlier - should achieve the objective of minimising the 'cascading effect' of excise duties nearly as effectively as a MANVAT system would, with the added advantage of prompter revenue realization and less risk to revenue.

7.10.   Thus, in the circumstances at percent obtaining both from the administrative and tax compliance angles, the group would recommend as of general application proforma credit procedure, in preference even to MANVAT for extending duty credit under Central Excise law with a view to mitigating the cascading effect of input duties. The group is also of the view that where the final products are 'zero rated', or manufactured by the exempted sector, these should atleast bear the input duty. IT follows that the set-off procedure need no longer be in vogue for it can be wholly replaced by the proforma credit procedure. Nor should the Chapter X procedure which envisages movement in bond also be generally necessary.

7.11.   General application of the proforma credit procedure
Next comes the issue of application of the proforma credit procedure. Presently the coverage under this procedure is somewhat selective. In the case of countervailing duty on inputs falling under Tariff Item 68, it is even discriminating. In the recent past, the benefit of duty credit has been extended in substantial measures to a wide range of products, in particular, products of the engineering industry where the inputs used bear relatively high rates of duty. In some areas where set-off or proforma credit is not allowed, the objective of reducing the cumulative duty burden has been sought to be achieved through adjustment of duty rates on inputs of finished products. The approach adopted could have its own justification but the fact remains that the efforts at minimising the cascading effect of input duties leaves still much to be desired.

7.12. General application of the proforma credit procedure

The group therefore, recommended a general extension of the proforma credit procedure to all excisable goods including packing materials and consumables, with very few exceptions. Further, the benefit of duty credit should be available in respect of countervailing duty paid on imported inputs, including those classifiable in the present Tariff Item 68 if produced in India. These duties are meant to equate the purchase price of the inputs and any denial of credit would discriminate against users of imported inputs. If revenue considerations intervene it will be more appropriate to make necessary adjustments in the basic duty of Customs keeping the principle of duty credit intact. The commodities which may have to be kept out of the proforma credit network would be:

(a) petroleum products in respect of which a new system of collection based on crude throughout has been suggested;

(b) cigarettes, where shifting a part of the duty incidence on final product to the inputs has been suggested and

(c) matches which are manufactured in the decentralized sector and the system of collection of duty is through banderoles.

It may not also be possible to extend credit of yarn duty since at the fabric stage unprocessed fabrics are fully exempted from duty.

7.13. With these exceptions, the extension of duty credit would touch a revenue net of about Rs.6000 crores which, in terms of the annual budget, is about 50per cent of the excise revenues. Its revenue implications could not be completed due to paucity of data. During 1983-84, revenue implications of the existing duty credit schemes were estimated to be of the order of Rs.443 crores. With the suggested general extension of the scheme, the

181

revenue implication would be significantly larger. The question is whether the country can afford it. The Group feels that the general extension of duty credit, by itself, is so salutary that ways should be found to raise the required revenues without giving up or diluting it. In the long terms perspective of higher yield from lower rates, it is conceivable' that with the growth of industry and increase in production, a time may come when revenue targets can be achieved without too much botheration and without much cost to revenues of such general extension. Till such time that is not feasible, the Group feels that while refixing the duty rates on final products note can be taken of the input duty incidence, and the entire exercise of extending duty could be so evolved as to be incidence, and the entire exercise of extending duty could be so evolved as to be neutral in terms of revenue. It may not be out of place to mention that with such adjustments the rates of duty on final products are likely to be very high increasing in its wake, the risk of evasion which would need to be administratively tackled.

7.14. In the sphere in which it would operate, the general extension of the proforma credit procedure could minimize the cascading effect on account of excise duties on inputs. Further, since in this scheme the cumulative duty burden on various products would be more clearly discernible, the task of imparting the requisite degree of progression to the tax structure would be easier. There would be greater neutrality as regards producers, "choice of inputs and consumers" choice of final products. Besides, the nominal duties applicable to the products themselves could be rebated fully when exported, without having to fix drawback in an extensive manner.

7.15. At the same time, it must be realized that the proposed scheme cannot be a total panacea for cascading or high cost economy. Nor could it be, by itself, be expected to reduce the overall burden of indirect taxes on the country's economy. Apart from the cascading effect of other indirect taxes, factors like economies of scale, heavy inventories, technological obsolescence, low productivity, long credits, high cost of money, all add up to higher cost of production. It is beyond the terms of this Group to opine whether 'octroi' should continue or some other ways should be found for generating resources for the civic bodies. Nor the impending consignment tax, whether the industrial inputs could not be exempted from sales tax. What the suggested extension would achieve in a limited sphere is outlay of working capital which should enable producers to reduce the prices by adopting lower mark-ups (in absolute terms) on duty, as the input duty element, in such systems, should not enter the cost stream.

7.16. The economic benefit of the proposed scheme would stand to increase if it is found possible to think of certain other measures, which are not entirely within the sphere of Central taxation, such as providing credit of the sales tax paid on the 'inputs', adjusting the duty rate on the final products with appropriate alteration in the sharing ratio of excise duties. If this is not favoured, an alternative, simpler but inadequate, could be to persuade the State Governments to exclude from the value for the purpose of sales tax, the element of Central excise duty on inputs used for further manufacture in their own states.

7.17. Problems and suggestions
While recommending a general extension of the proforma credit procedure, the Group has taken note of the problems which are likely to come into sharp focus in the light of such an extension. The more important of these are:

(a) In the case of purchases on inputs from the open market by manufacturers, there could arise difficulties in extension of tax credit without 'duty paying' documents.

(b) Where the purchase of inputs are made from small manufacturers, who avail of full duty exemption, the downstream manufacturers may not be able to get the benefit of duty credit, on account of a break in chain of duty credit.

7.18. In regard to the first problem, two approaches are possible.

One approach could be to deem all goods bought from the market to be duty-paid. This approach lays store on the presumption that all goods finding their way into the market ought to have discharged the duty liability and a purchase accounted for in the books, would be legitimate one. Ex facie attractive, this approach carries a serious risk to revenue. Besides, the goods in the market could have borne different duty incidence and it would not be always easy to determine with precision, the credit that ought to be allowed. An alternative approach would be to disallow duty where the purchase is not covered by a document evidencing payment duty. In broad terms, this would be conducive to brining about a desirable and healthy discipline in the industry. But medium-scale units who buy their requirements in small lots and middlemen are likely to be affected by such an approach.

7.19. The Group would commend, for the present, the following approach in this regard

(1) In cases where the duty paid character of the input is established directly or indirectly (eg., on back-to-back basis), through verification of invoices, full duty credit could be allowed.

(2) In all other cases, an ad hoc duty credit, equivalent to say 25per cent of the normal duty on the input can be given. Where the input is subject to an ad volorem rate, the assessable value could be derived by allowing specified standard deduction from the purchase price of the input and applying the normal duty applicable to the input. The amount of duty

credit could thereafter be worked out as 25per cent of duty on the derived assessable value.

(3) In the long term, a move towards accepting all purchases under a clear invoice as duty paid will have to be explored.

7.20. As regards the second problem, one way of tackling it could be consider the ancillary unit to be 'an extended factory' of the manufacturer buying the inputs. The other way could be to allow credit on the same footing as purchases from the market. In any case, suitable methods would have to be devised so that the small manufacturer is not placed at a disadvantage vis-à-vis the bigger manufacturer who may be able to pass on the duty credit in full.

7.21. Another issue which is presently posing some problems in the lack of a suitable system to ensure adjustment of duty credit in case the duty on the input is varied subsequently. In this regard, it is felt that in the context of the assessment procedure envisaged by the Group such problems should not arise. Where a manufacturer proves that the product in respect of which differential duty is required to be recovered, has been utilized for further manufacturer and duty credit thereon has been availed of by another manufacturer, different duty need not be recovered at all. The procedure of granting refund after ensuring reversal of the credit entry is inane and cumbrous without any material advantage to anyone. Once the credit is taken by the second stage manufacturer on the inputs purchased by him there should be no refund of excise duty to the manufacturers of such inputs.

7.22. Procedural changes
Along with a general extension of the proforma credit procedure, the Group would also like to suggest the following procedural changes:

(a) Prior approval for availing of the proforma credit procedure can be dispensed with. In its place, manufacturers intending to take the benefit of the procedure should file a declaration with the jurisdictional officer, indicating the input-output norm for major raw materials/inputs.

(b) The filing of intimation of receipts of inputs (in form D3) can also be dispensed with. Accordingly, users of inputs can utilised the inputs straightaway on their receipt.

(c) Manufacturers availing of the benefit of duty credit may be required to file as part of the RT12, a material balance statement every month, indicating the stock position in relation to the major inputs.

7.23. In sum, the group would suggest that the proforma credit procedure should be generally extended in respect of Central Excise duty or countervailing duty, paid on all inputs, including raw materials, consumables and packaging materials. To enable this scheme to succeed, 'zero-rating' of inputs should be kept to the minimum since by doing so the chain of duty credit is likely to be broken and as far as possible, ad valorem rates should be adopted effectively to recover the duty on the value addition.

7.24. In preferring the general extension of proforma credit scheme to VAT, the Group has been largely influenced by the prevailing industrial culture and circumstances. Needless to add that the working of the scheme would require to be closely watched and problems encountered in the implementation resolved in a pragmatic manner. Whereas comprehensive VAT, as obtaining in other countries, may be out of question in India given the present constitutional setup, the general extension of the proforma credit could, in course of time prepare the grounds and conditions for a shift to MANVAT.

While it could be claimed that, in practical terms, the suggested extension of proforma credit scheme would achieve the substance of MANVAT, the votaries of VAT, keen on its introduction, may not be fully satisfied with the proforma credit scheme. For one thing, the scheme would provide for credit only of the excise paid on the industrial input. Apart from indirect taxes like octroi and sales tax recovered on such inputs, the other elements going into the cost of such inputs, would not get recovered. The hesitation to introduction of MANVAT is not so much on account of any reservation as to its underlying principle or concept but more due to apprehensions with regard to its implementation in Indian conditions. If one were to test on the ground whether such apprehensions are unfounded, a beginning could be made as an experiment with respect to a selected product group considered most suitable for VAT. The Group feels that having regard, interalia, to the narrow range of the extent of duty rates applicable, ease of developing the norms of input output ration, and of existence of substantial organized sector in the industry, chemical products as a group would be most suitable for MANVAT experiment. Its introduction could be considered after the general proforma credit scheme has been in force for some time and industry gets accustomed to the requisite documentation. Operating the MANVAT with respect to this group of products simultaneously when the proforma credit scheme covers the other excisable goods, would help in ironing out the difficulties and making the necessary adjustments and eventually assist in making a long term choice.

⊓⊔

ANNEXURE VIII

REQUIREMENTS OF VAT COMPUTER SYSTEM

I. REGISTRATION

1. Create a file of potential taxpayers from every available source, such as paper records and computer business files of business income, excise and sales tax payers who may qualify for the VAT requirements, as well as importers and exporters from customs records and files.

2. Pre address registration forms with instructions and send to all potential VAT taxpayers. Invite all others (who did not receive forms) to register.

3. Add a VAT prefix to each existing (if reliable) income tax identification number for each approved applicant, put a VAT indicator in their tax account record, or create a new VAT file, but cross reference both numbers in both files.

4. Add a VAT section to each VAT taxpayer's master file account or create a new VAT master file.

5. Send a certificate to each VAT taxpayer.

6. Print a register reflecting historical data about registration, returns filed, and payments made, as well as the current compliance status of each taxpayer. This data can also be accessed via terminals. The first register would, of course, show limited data.

II. TAX RETURNS AND PAYMENTS

7. Preaddress VAT return forms with several payment vouchers or labels (for customs forms), with instructions to taxpayers.

188

8. Post payment voucher data and customs accounting transactions to the master file account.

9. Process tax return fully, including mathematical verification of computations, computer generation of late filing and paying penalties and interest, and identification of errors.

10. Post tax returns data to master file accounts, referring invalid transactions, such as those with invalid TINs and differences between total taxes paid and total remittances received for research.

11. Print payment demand notices and refund checks and send them to officials for quality review and distribution to taxpayers.

12. Print and issue follow up demand notices and notices of levy and lien as necessary for arrears.

13. Post payments, adjustments and write-offs to arrears accounts.

14. Print lists of average accounts for action by supervisors.

III. RETURNS FOR AUDIT

15. Based on audit selection criteria developed through auditing procedures and the master file's historical and tax returns data, print lists of potential audit cases and audit assignment control forms and distribute them to audit supervisors.

16. Record the results of the audits and revise the criteria as necessary. Also, post additional or reduced assessment figures to taxpayer's accounts, as well as subsequent payments received or refunds issued.

17. Computer match sales and purchases data from income and excise tax returns with VAT returns data for leads for audits and investigation.

18. Cross-check by computer, buyers and sellers invoices for discrepancies requiring investigation or audit.

IV. MANAGEMENT INFORMATION

19. Provide complete accounting summaries by type of VAT taxpayers and by location, including returns received, amounts collected, number and amount of notices and refund checks issued, and arrears accounts. Calculate the number and amount of audit assessments and penalties and interest assessed.

20. Generate statistical data such as VAT sales, purchases and exemptions, number of registered VAT taxpayers by type and location, number of returns received by tax period and sales ranges.

21. Prepare management analysis, such as comparative data about amounts collected for several tax periods, as well as various, such as the ratio of penalties assessed to total collections, ratio of audit assessments to voluntarily filed return assessments, and ratio of arrears and write-offs to collections.

V. RESOURCE REQUIREMENTS

1. Computer equipment (computers, printers, terminals, modems and telecommunication lines):

   Depends mainly on the number of VAT taxpayers, the location of data entry and conversion stations, the method of transmitting data and the number of central computers already available and with extra capacity to share with the new VAT processing.

2. Software (systems design and programming):

    Depends mostly on the skills and the availability of internal computer staff, external consultants, or a combination of the two. Also depends on the availability and adaptability of software, such as accounting packages.

3. Operating staff:

    Depends mostly on skills level and availability of present data processing managers, data conversion, computer room operators, disk and tape libraries as well as the number of additional tax returns, terminals, processing sites, computers, error rates and quality and security control measures that are required. Also, such supporting services as paper forms and file maintenance, research and taxpayer assistance.

    ▢▢

ANNEXURE IX

EXPANSION OF SERVICE TAX BASE

1. Imposed for the first time in 1994 for 3 services namely, Stock Brokers, Telephone and Insurance (other than Life Insurance).

2. 1996-97 : Advertising, Courier and Radio Paging services added.

3. Thereafter, more and more services were added and as on date, in all there are 51 services attracting Service Tax. (Please see next page for year).

4. In 2001, self-assessment facility introduced.

5. In 2002, set-off facility (like CENVAT Credit Scheme) introduced.

6. In 2004, rate of service tax raised from 8% to 10% and service tax credit and excise duty credit integrated and extended across goods and services. Thirteen new services were brought under tax net and some were redefined.

LIST OF SERVICE WITH EFFECTIVE DATES

Sr. No.	NAME OF THE SERVICE	S. TAX LEVIED FROM
1.	GENERAL INSURANCE SERVICES	01.07.1994
2.	STOCK BROKERS	01.07.1994
3.	TELEPHONE SERVICES	01.07.1994
4.	ADVERTISING AGENCY	01.11.1996
5.	COURIER SERVICES	01.11.1996

Sr. No.	NAME OF THE SERVICE	S. TAX LEVIED FROM
6.	PAGER SERVICES	01.11.1996
7.	AIR TRAVEL AGENTS	01.07.1997
8.	MANDAP KEEPERS	01.07.1997
9.	CUSTOM HOUSE AGENTS	16.06.1997
10.	STEAMER AGENTS	15.06.1997
11.	CONSULTING ENGINEERS	07.07.1997
12.	MANPOWER RECRUITMENT AGENCIES	07.07.1997
13.	CLEARING & FORWARDING AGENTS	16.07.1997
14.	GOODS TRANSPORT OPERATORS	16.11.1997
15.	ARCHITECTS	16.10.1998
16.	CHARTERED ACCOUNTANTS	16.10.1998
17.	COMPANY SECRETARIES	16.10.1998
18.	COST ACCOUNTANTS	16.10.1998
19.	CREDIT RATING AGENCIES	16.10.1998
20.	INTERIOR DECORATORS	16.10.1998
21.	MANAGEMENT CONSULTANTS	16.10.1998
22.	MARKET RESEARCH AGENCIES	16.10.1998
23.	REAL ESTATE AGENTS	16.10.1998
24.	SECURITY AGENCIES	16.10.1998
25.	UNDERWRITERS	16.10.1998
26.	RENT A CAB SCHEME OPERATORS	01.04.2000
27.	TOUR OPERATORS	01.04.2000

Sr. No.	NAME OF THE SERVICE	S. TAX LEVIED FROM
28.	SCIENTIFIC OR TECHNICAL CONSULTANCY	16.07.2001
29.	PHOTOGRAPHY	16.07.2001
30.	HOLDING OF CONVENTION	16.07.2001
31.	LEASING OF CIRCUITS BY TELEGRAPH AUTHORITY	16.07.2001
32.	COMMUNICATION THROUGH TELEGRAPH	16.07.2001
33.	COMMUNICATION THROUGH TELEX	16.07.2001
34.	FASCIMILE COMMUNICATION	16.07.2001
35.	ONLINE INFORMATION & DATABASE ACCESS AND RETRIEVAL	16.07.2001
36.	VIDEO TAPE PRODUCTION	16.07.2001
37.	SOUND RECORDING	16.07.2001
38.	BROADCASTING	16.07.2001
39.	INSURANCE AUXILIARY SERVICES	16.07.2001
40.	BANKING & OTHER FINANCIAL SERVICES	16.07.2001
41.	PORT SERVICES	16.07.2001
42.	AUTHORISED SERVICE STATIONS FOR AUTOMOBILES	16.07.2001
43.	LIFE INSURANCE AUXILIARY	16.08.2002
44.	CARGO HANDLING	16.08.2002
45.	STORAGE & WAREHOUSING	16.08.2002
46.	EVENT MANAGEMENT	16.08.2002

Sr. No.	NAME OF THE SERVICE	S. TAX LEVIED FROM
47.	RAIL TRAVEL AGENTS	16.08.2002
48.	HEALTH CLUBS & FITNESS CENTRES	16.08.2002
49.	BEAUTY PARLOURS	16.08.2002
50.	CABLE OPERATORS	16.08.2002
51.	DRY CLEANING SERVICES	16.08.2002
52.	COMMERCIAL VOCATIONAL INSTITUTES, COACHING CENTERS AND PRIVATE TUTORIALS	Date & year to be Notified
53.	TECHNICAL TESTING, ANALYSIS AND INSPECTION SERVICES	"
54.	MAINTENANCE AND REPAIR SERVICES	"
55.	COMMISSIONING AND INSTALLATION SERVICES	"
56.	BUSINESS PROMOTERS AND SUPPORT SERVICES	"
57.	INTERNET CAFÉ	"
58.	FRANCHISE SERVICES	"
59.	MINOR PORTS	"
60.	MAXI CAB SERVICES	"
61.	FOREIGN EXCHANGE BROKING SERVICE	"
62.	BUSINESS EXHIBITION SERVICES	Finance Bill 2004
63.	AIRPORT SERVICES	"
64.	TRANSPORT OF GOODS (applicable to an agency issuing consignment note)	"

Sr. No.	NAME OF THE SERVICE	S. TAX LEVIED FROM
65.	TRANSPORT OF GOODS BY AIR	Finance Bill 2004
66.	SURVEY AND EXPLORATION OF MINERALS	"
67.	OPINION POLL SERVICES	"
68.	INTELLECTUAL PROPERTY SERVICES OTHER THAN COPYRIGHT	"
69.	FORWARD CONTRACT SERVICES	"
70.	PANDAL OR SHAMIANA SERVICES	"
71.	OUTDOOR CATERING	"
72.	TV or RADIO PROGRAMME PRODUCTION	"
73.	CONSTRUCTION SERVICES IN RESPECT OF COMMERCIAL OR INDUSTRIAL BUILDINGS AND CIVIL STRUCTURES	"
74.	TRAVEL AGENTS (other than Air/Rail travel agents)	"

Source: Budgets and notifications of the Central Government.

❑❑

ANNEXURE X

EXTRACTS OF THE BUDGET SPEECHES (2003-04 and 2004-05) RELATED TO TAX REFORMS

X. TAX REFORM, REVISED ESTIMATES AND BUDGET ESTIMATES

I now come to taxes, tax reforms, and the book-keeping of the current year, as also 2003-04. Mr. Speaker, I want to emphasize six important aspects in this regard. First, the coming year will be historic with the States switching over to a Value Added Tax (VAT). The Central Government has been a partner with the States, in the highest tradition of cooperative federalism, in this path-breaking reform. This will also involve an amendment to the Additional Excise Duty Act. Second, it is proposed to make 2003-04 the year when a long-overdue Constitutional amendment to integrate services into the tax net in a comprehensive manner is enacted and implemented. This will give a boost to revenues, and help implement VAT. Third, there will be major improvements in tax administration through greater application of IT, and a discretion-free, impersonal system. Fourth, excise duties are being rationalized further. Fifth, the momentum of reducing customs duty is being maintained so as to improve the competitiveness of Indian industry in international markets. And, sixth, Government shall continue to strive towards fiscal consolidation through expenditure reprioritization, and revenue augmentation.

State-level Value Added Tax (VAT)

The Conference of State Chief Ministers, presided over by the Prime Minister, held on October 18, 2002 confirmed the final decision that all States and Union Territories would introduce VAT from April 2003. The Empowered Committee of State Finance Ministers, on February 8, 2003, has again endorsed the suggestion that all State legislations on VAT should have a minimum set of common features. Apart from avoiding cascading of taxes, the introduction of VAT is expected to increase revenues as the coverage expands to value addition at all stages of sale in the production and distribution chain. However, in view of the apprehensions expressed by a large number of States, about possible revenue loss, in the initial years of introduction of VAT, the Central Government has agreed to compensate 100 per cent of the loss in the first year, 75 per cent of the loss in second year and 50 per cent of the loss in the third year of the introduction of VAT; this loss being computed on the basis of an agreed formula.

Additional excise duty (AED) in lieu of sales tax

While continuing to give States the additional 1.5 per cent of all shareable taxes and duties, in order to enable them to generate more revenues, the Additional Duties of Excise (Goods of Special Importance) Act, 1957 is being amended, from a date to be notified. This will allow the States to levy sales tax on textiles, sugar and tobacco products at a rate not exceeding 4 per cent. This will also enable the States to integrate these three important products in the VAT chain.

Service tax: a proposed Constitutional amendment

To enable levy of tax on services as a specific and important source of revenue, an amendment to the Constitution is proposed. This Constitutional amendment, and the consequent legislation would give the Central Government the power to levy the tax and both the Central and the State Governments sufficient powers to collect the proceeds.

Central Sales Tax

With the introduction of VAT, there is need to now phase, out the CST, and move to a completely destination-based system. This can not be done in one step. We must let VAT stabilize; but also recognize that these two - VAT and CST - cannot remain in tandem, in perpetuity. Therefore, in the first instance, the ceiling rate of CST for inter-State sale between registered dealers will be reduced to 2 per cent during 2003-04, with effect from a date to be notified. The Government of India will compensate the States for loss of revenue from this reduction of the CST. This will be done, as all these steps have been undertaken, only after arriving at a consensus with the Empowered Committee of State Finance Ministers.

By opening up the budget-making process, the Kelkar Committee Reports have more than fulfilled my basic purpose of involving, as far as practical, our citizens, in the annual budgetary exercise. I have personally benefited very greatly from these Reports, as also from this open debate. I take this opportunity to express my sincere gratitude to the two Chairmen and all members of the Task Forces, as also members of the public for their valuable comments and suggestions.

The basic philosophy of these reports is sound. For a modern, forward-looking and in the long run, revenue-beneficial taxation system the proposals that have been mooted may be the most appropriate. There is need to, eventually, move away from an exemption and discretion based system to a different, more current order. That is the ideal that the Task Forces, particularly in respect of direct taxes have suggested; a radically new approach to taxation.

This ideal is difficult to achieve in one leap, and I can scarcely cross the existing conceptual chasm in two. We cannot ignore the commitments made, or wish them away. That is why I choose to bridge the divide. We will, therefore, stay with the basics of the present system of taxation, but we will, indeed have already accepted, most of the suggestions made by the Task Forces designed to eliminate procedural complexities, reduce paper work, simplify tax administration and to enhance efficiency, also integrate such tax proposals as the system can, at present, absorb, with one overriding thought: Mr. Speaker, Sir, this will be a move away from a suspicion-ridden, harassment generating, coercion-inclined regime to a trust-based, 'green channel' system. I do this entirely on the basis of my faith in my countrymen and women.

Administrative reform

In the area of tax administration, Government has initiated a whole basket of reforms, mainly on the basis of the recommendations of the Kelkar Committee. Some of the principal ones are:

(a) outsourcing of non-core activities of Income Tax Department, namely allotment of PAN, and creation of data bank of high value transactions through tax information network;

(b) immediate abolition of present discretion-based system for selection of returns for scrutiny; this will be replaced by a computer generated, intelligent, random selection of only 2 per cent of the returns, annually;

(c) expanding the scope of taxpayer services, including extension of interactive voice response system to more cities and software for preparation of returns;

(d) direct crediting of all refunds to the bank account of the taxpayer, through electronic clearance system; but obviously only if the taxpayer furnishes a bank account number;

(e) reduce the compliance cost of the taxpayer, through halving the number of forms presently used in furnishing of applications, returns, etc., for the purposes of tax deduction and tax collection at source, from the present 42 to just 22. Hon'ble Members, if in only one attempt I could halve this headache, please reflect upon the immense possibilities that lie on this route;

(f) immediate introduction of a one-page only return form for individual tax payers, having income from salary, house property and interest, etc. This has already been devised, and will come into operation from April 1 onwards;

(g) the Income Tax Act is being amended to enable electronic filing of returns;

(h) abolition of tax-clearance certificates currently needed by a person leaving India, or any person submitting a tender for a government contract. Henceforth, only expatriates who come to India in connection with business, profession or employment, would have to furnish a guarantee from their employer, etc. in respect of the tax payable before they leave India. An Indian citizen, before leaving India, will only have to give his/her permanent account number, and the period of his/her intended visit abroad to the emigration authorities; and

(i) simplifying the procedure and methods employed during search and seizure, and during survey by the Income Tax department. First, hereafter, stocks found during the course of a search and seizure operation will not be seized under any circumstances. Second, no confession shall be obtained during such search and seizure operations. Third, no survey operation will be authorized by an officer below the rank of Joint Commissioner of Income Tax. Finally, books of account impounded during survey will not be retained beyond ten days, without the prior approval of the Chief Commissioner.

Indirect taxes: excise

Rationalisation and relief

Rationalisation of excise rate structure and reduction of the multiplicity of rates are integral to the total tax reform process. In this regard, I propose to prescribe a 3-tier excise duty structure of 8 per cent, 16 per cent and 24 per cent. These rates would, however, not apply in the case of petroleum and tobacco products, pan masala, and items attracting specific duty rates. I have already announced a separate package for textiles, and some changes in the duty structure relevant for some other key sectors while dealing with those sectors. I will now refer to the changes proposed in various other commodities.

Trade facilitation measures

For trade facilitation, I propose to take the following measures,-

(a)   The present system of fortnightly payment of excise duty will be liberalized to permit payment of duty at the end of the month. Further, the excise duty will be considered to have been paid on the date the cheque is presented to the bank subject to realisation.

(b)   Deduction from the transaction value is allowed on actual freight incurred, provided that is clearly shown in the invoice. This facility will now be extended to cases where freight is worked out on an equalized basis also.

(c)   Over the years, the Maximum Retail Price (MRP) based excise levy has proved to be an effective measure of simplification by reducing valuation disputes. I propose to extend the MRP-based excise levy to chewing tobacco and insecticides.

Service tax

I propose to enhance the general service tax rate from 5 per cent to 8 per cent, and also impose service tax on 10 new services. While the increase in the tax rates will come into effect on enactment of the Finance Bill, the levy of tax on the new services will take effect from a date to be notified.

Last year credit of service tax on input services were extended for payment of service tax, provided the input and the final services fell within the same category. I propose to extend this facility across all services. Thus, the credit will now be available even if the input and the final services fall under different categories.

Indirect taxes: customs

External liberalisation

Rate rationalisation and reduction of peak rates of customs duties has been an integral part of economic reform in the country. The economy has not only 'weathered' the removal of quantitative restrictions on imports and the reduction in customs duty rates, but has responded by improving its competitiveness and demonstrating the inherent strength of its external balance of payments. As a part of this continuous process, and in line with the pronouncements made by several of my predecessors, I now propose to reduce the peak rate of customs duty from 30 per cent to 25 per cent, excluding agriculture and dairy products.

Trade facilitation

I assure Hon'ble Members of faster clearance hereafter of cargo and fewer procedures, by reducing the transaction cost, thus facilitating exports and imports. For this, a number of measures have been taken to simplify and modernize the customs clearance procedures, with the main emphasis being on cutting down contact of trade with the officers, to the extent possible, and introducing computerization in customs clearances. While these efforts will continue, as a further trade facilitation measure, I propose to increase the interest-free period for warehoused goods from 30 to 90 days and to reduce the rate of interest for the period beyond 90 days to reflect the market rate of interest.

To bring our customs clearance procedures at par with best international practices, I propose to introduce, this year itself, a self-assessment scheme for importers and exporters. Briefly stated, under the self-assessment scheme, the importer himself/herself will determine the classification of goods, including claim for any exemption benefit, and the system will calculate the duty based on his/her declaration. Physical inspection of imported goods will be done by using risk-assessment and management techniques on a computer-based system and not on the orders of customs examining staff. Further, the existing system of concurrent audit of import documents will be replaced by post-clearance audit, as prevalent in developed countries.

Budget – (2004-2005)

Value added tax is a tax that has been tested and tried, and found beneficial throughout the world. The country needs a modern and efficient trade tax system that incorporates the

VAT WORKING MODEL
(Chain of Transactions in Rupees)

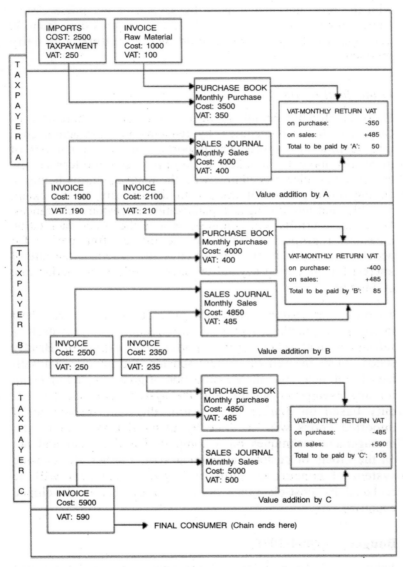

Figure 5

Source: Adapted from IMF

international best practices. At the June 18, 2004, meeting of the Empowered Committee of State Finance ministers, to which all finance ministers were invited, and chaired by my distinguished friend Dr. Asim Das Gupta, there was a broad consensus among the States to implement VAT. April 1, 2005 has been set as the date for implementation. I welcome the decision and warmly congratulate the State Governments. I urge all States that have not yet passed the relevant VAT legislation to do so before the end of 2004. International experience, as well as the experience of the state of Haryana, suggests that VAT will lead to an increase in revenue and not a loss in revenue. Nevertheless, in order to give comfort to the States, I propose to evolve a formula for determining the compensation for the loss of revenue, if any. I have offered the States, the services of a Technical Experts Committee. The Committee will work with the States closely, and help them move steadily towards the stage of implementation.

Source: Budget (2003-2004 & 2004-05) of the Central Government.

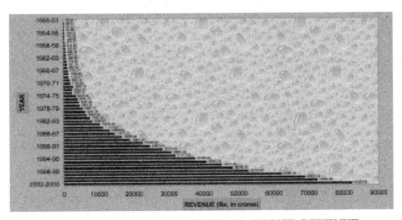

Figure 6 : GROWTH OF CENTRAL EXCISE REVENUE
(Rs. in crores)

Source: Budgets of the Central Government

205

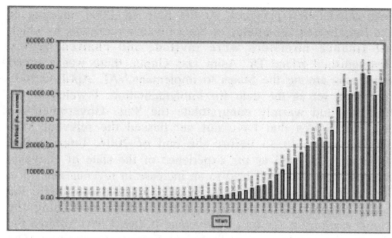

Figure 7 : GROWTH OF CUSTOMS REVENUE: 1950-51 TO 2002-03
(Rs. in crores)
Source: Budgets of the Central Government

Table III : A DECADE OF PROGRESS IN CENTRAL EXCISE REFORMS

YEAR	PROGRESS	AUTHORITY
1986	▪ Removal of Bonds/Securities	▪ Notfn. 111A-111F all dt.27.2.1986
	▪ Restriction of visits to SSI units	▪ CBEC F.No.223/17/86-CX.6 dt10.3.86
1994	▪ Abolition of Price Lists	▪ Notfn.No:4/94-CE (NT) dt. 1.3.1994
	▪ Simplification of Export Procedure	▪ Notfn.No.40/94(NT)-58/94 (NT) all dt 22.9.1994 & CBEC F.No:209/18/93-CX.6 dt.26.9.94
	▪ Replacement of gate-pass with Invoice	▪ Notfn.No.4/94-CE(NT) dt.1.3.94
1995	▪ Abolition of Classification Lists	▪ Notfn.No.11/95-CE(NT) dt.16.3.95
1996	▪ Simplified Export procedure for Exempted Units	▪ Cir No.212/46/96-CX dt.20.5.96
1997	▪ Simplification of EOU Procedures	▪ FTT Cir. No.19/97 dt 12.6.97
	▪ Simplification of Exemption for SSI Units	▪ Notfn.No. 16/67 CE dt.01.04.97

YEAR	PROGRESS	AUTHORITY
2001	■ Further simplification of Export Procedures	■ Notfn.No.40/01-CE (NT) to 47/01-CE(NT) all dt. 26.06.01 & Cir. No.579/16/2001-CX dt.26.6.2001 & 581/18/2001 CX dt.29.6.01
	■ 234 C. Excise rules omitted & replaced with 5 sets of Rules w.e.f. 1.07.01; they are:- – C. Excise Rules – CENVAT Credit Rules – C. Excise (Appeals) Rules – C. Excise (Settlement of Cases) Rules – C. Excise (Removal of goods at Concessional Rates of Duty for Manufacture of goods) Rules..	■ Notfn.No. 30/2001-CE (NT) to 34/2001-CE (NT) all dt. 21.6.01
2004	■ Integration of services tax credit and excise duty credit across goods and services	Finance Bill 2004

MAJOR CHANGES IN EXCISE LAW

YEAR	PROGRESS	AUTHORITY
1992	■ Licence replaced with "Registration"	■ Notfn. No. 11/92-CE(NT) dt. 14.5.92
	■ Consumer Welfare Fund Rules, 1992 introduced.	■ Notfn. No.29/92-CE(NT) Dt.25.11.92
1994	■ Number of exemptions withdrawn.	■ Notfn.No. 64/94-CE dt.1.3.94
	■ Invoice replaces gate-pass.	■ Notfn.No. 4/94-CE (NT) dt. 1.3.94
	■ Requirement of obtaining Registration Certificate from Directorate of Industries to avail SSI Notification done away with	■ Notfn.No.59/94-CE dt.1.3.94

YEAR	PROGRESS	AUTHORITY
	• Brand Name concept in SSI Notification modified to deny concession for goods bearing brand name of another person (even if the other person is an SSI)	• Notfn.No.59/94-CE dt.1.3.94
1995	• Nomenclature changed from "Collector" to "Commissioner".	• Notfn.No.26/95-CE(NT) dt.6.6.95
	• Sec. 11AA introduced (Interest on delayed payment) w.e.f. 26.5.2001	• Section 73 of Finance Act, 1995
	• Sec. 11BB introduced (interest on delayedrefund) w.e.f. 26.5.2001	• Section 73 of Finance Act, 1995
	• Sec.14A (Special Azudit) introduced.	• Section 76 of Finance Act, 1995
1996	• The word "Salt" omitted from the title of the Act.	• Section 71 of Finance Act, 1996
	• Place of removal extended to depot w.e.f 28.9.96	• Section 74 of Finance Act, 1996
	• Sec 11AB introduced (interest) w.e.f. 28.9.96	• Section 76 of Finance Act, 1996
	• Sec 11AC introduced (penalty) w.e.f. 28.9.96	• Section 76 of Finance Act, 1996
	• Self-assessment introduced	• Notfn.No. 36/96-CE(NT) dt.21.11.96.read with Cir.No.249/83/96-CX dt.11.10.96 & 273/107/96-CX dt.21.11.96
	• Filing of invoices with monthly returns abolished	• Cir.No>249/83/96-CX dt.11.10.96
	• Selective Audit based on revenue payment introduced	• Cir.No.267/101/96-CX dt.13.11.96
1997	• Sec 4A (MRP based valuation) introduced w.e.f. 14.5.97	• Sec 82 of Finance Act, 1997
	• Sec 14AA (for Cost Audit) introduced w.e.f. 14.05.97.	• Sec 83 of Finance Act, 1997

YEAR	PROGRESS	AUTHORITY
	▪ Pre-authentification of job work challans dispensed with.	▪ Notfn. No. 6/97-CE (NT) dt.1.3.97
	▪ Compounded Levy Scheme for induction Furnaces and Re-Rolling Mills introduced w.e.f. 1.9.97	▪ Notfn.No.30/97-CE(NT) dt.1.8.97.amended by Notfn.No.43/97 CE(NT) dt.30.08.97
1998	▪ In case of refunds arising because of finalisation of Provisional Assessments, time-limit to start from date of finalisation w.e.f. 1.8.98	▪ Sec 108 of Finance Act, 1998.
	▪ Compounded Levy under Sec 3A introduced for independent Textile Processors.	▪ Notfn. No. 41/98-CE (NT) dt.10.12.98
	▪ KAR VIVAD SAMADHAN Scheme introduced w.e.f. 1.9.98 valid upto 31.3.99	▪ Sec 98 of Finance Act, 1998
	▪ Settlement Commission Rules introduced w.e.f. 1.8.98	▪ Sec 110 of Finance Act, 1998
1999	▪ Advance Ruling Authority - Provisions introduced.	▪ Section 124 of Finance Act, 1999
2000	▪ Fortnightly payment of duty introduced w.e.f.1.4.2000	▪ Notfn. No. 11/2000-CE(NT) dt.1.3.2000
	▪ Statutory records except PLA and RG-1 abolished (w.e.f.1.07.2000)	▪ Notfn. No. 44/2000-CE(NT) dt.30.6..2000
	▪ Special Audit under Sec 14A and 14AA to be on Government cost instead of assessee's w.e.f. 12.5.2000	▪ Sec 104, 105 of Finance Act, 2000
	▪ Prior approval of Commissioner / Chief commissioner is required to issue Show Cause Notice w.e.f.12.5.2000	▪ Sec 97 of Finance Act, 2000
	▪ Retrospective legislation to reopen approved classification list.	▪ Sec 97 of Finance Act, 2000

YEAR	PROGRESS	AUTHORITY
	▪ Compounded Levy on independent Textile Processors modified w.e.f. 1.4.2000	▪ Notfn. No. 11/2000-CE(NT) dt. 1.3.2000
	▪ Compounded Levy for Induction Furnaces & Re-rolling units abolished (w.e.f. 01.04.2000); 16 per cent advelorem introduced	▪ Notfn.No. 16/2000-CE dt.1.3.2000
	▪ Time-limit under Sec 11A increased from 6 months to 1 year w.e.f.12.5.2000	▪ Sec 97 of Finance Act, 2000
	▪ Time-limit under Sec 11B increased from 6 months to 1 year w.e.f.12.5.2000	▪ Sec 101 of Finance Act, 2000
	▪ If demand is paid within 30 days, penalty will be 25per cent and not 100per cent under Sec 11AC w.e.f. 12.5.2000	▪ Sec 100 of Finance Act, 2000
	▪ Machinery provision given for Sec 11D..	▪ Sec 103 of Finance Act, 2000
2001	▪ Compilation of all Central Excise Procedures, Circulars, Instructions has been done & issued as a Manual by the CBEC on 01.09.2001.	▪ Under Rule 31 of C. Excise Rules, 2001
	▪ Merchant-exporter required to furnish bond; block transfer of credit replaced with CT1 certificate; CT1 certificate valid for 1 year.	▪ Ch 7, part-I, para 1.2.2, 3.8, 3.9, 3.10, 5.8, Annexure 17 of CBEC Manual
	▪ Document called 'Proof of Export' to be given by Assistant Commissioner to the exporter abolished.	▪ Ch 7, Part-II, para 13.4 & 13.5 of CBEC Manual
	▪ Provision of self-sealing and self-certification extended to all exporters.	▪ Ch 7, Part-II, PARA 10 of CBEC Manual

YEAR	PROGRESS	AUTHORITY
	▪ Concepts of PBC and RBC not in vogue.	▪ By abolition of C. Excise Rules, 1944
	▪ Ch. X Procedure replaced by new set of rules called 'C. Excise (Removal of Goods at Concessional Rate of Duty for Manufacture of excisable Goods) Rules, 2001; broadly, the new procedure is the same.	▪ Notfn.No.34/2001-CE(NT) dt.21.6.2001
	▪ Defacement of Modvat Credit availed documents abolished	▪ By abolition of C. Excise Rules, 1944
	▪ Tariff rate @ 60per cent MRP introduced for garments (Ch. 62)	▪ Rule 4 of Finance Act, 2001
	▪ Merchant-Manufacturer of garments made liable for duty payment, instead of actual manufacturer of garments.	▪ Sec 35 of Finance Act, 2001
	▪ Time-limit for filing appeal with Commissioner (Appeals) reduced from 3 months to 60 days w.e.f.11.5.2001.	▪ Sec 128 of Finance Act, 2001
	▪ Power of Commissioner (appeals) to remand cases withdrawn w.e.f. 11.5.2001	▪ Sec 128 of Finance Act, 2001
	▪ Commissioner (appeals) to decide cases with in 6 months w.e.f. 11.5.2001	▪ Sec 128 of Finance Act, 2001
	▪ Departmental adjudication to be done within 6 months and within 1 year for cases involving suppression w.e.f.11.5.2001.	▪ Sec 123 of Finance Act, 2001
	New Sec 38 A(saving clause) for all previous amendments omissions introduced w.e.f. 11.5.2001.	▪ Sec 131 of Finance Act, 2001

YEAR	PROGRESS	AUTHORITY
2002	▪ Administrative Price Mechanism for Petrol & Diesel dismantled	▪ F.No:354/55/2002-TRU dt. 23.4.2002 addressed to all CCs.
	▪ Optional Compounded Levy Scheme for independent Textile Processors abolished	▪ Notfn.No. 16/2002-CE dt 1.3.2002
	Advance Ruling Authority for NRI associated ventures created.	▪ Notfn.No. 28/2002-CE (NT) dt.23.8.2002 & Cir No. 16/6/ 2002 of Advance Ruling Authority
	▪ Government can clarify scope of examination Notfn.; Such clarification has retrospective effect. (w.e.f. 11.5.2002)	▪ Sec 134 of Finance Act, 2002
	▪ CEGAT to dispose appeal within 3 years w.e.f. 11.5.2002	▪ Sec 140 of Finance Act, 2002
	▪ CEGAT to decide main case within 180 days of stay order; otherwise stay stands vacated w.e.f. 11.5.2002	▪ Sec 140 of Finance Act, 2002
	▪ Central Government can specify by way of Notification any process as amounting to manufacture w.e.f. 11.5.2002	▪ Sec 132 of Finance Act, 2002
2004	▪ Chief Commissioners empowered to compound offence cases — amendment to Section 9	▪ Finance Bill 2004
	▪ Dues can be collected from the transferee of assets of a defaulter — amendment to Section 11	▪ Finance Bill 2004
	▪ Not more than 3 adjournments by adjudicating and appellate authority — amendment to Section 33 & 35	▪ Finance Bill 2004

Source: Budgets and Notifications of the Central Government.

Table IV : CHANGES IN RATES OF EXCISE DUTIES

- Gradual reduction in peak rates of duty.
- Switchover to Advalorem
- Removal of end-use based Notifications.

YEAR	CHANGE
1991	■ SED increased from 5per cent to 10per cent
1992	■ Special Excise Duty increased from 10per cent to 15per cent
1993	■ SED merged with BED.
1994	■ Many of the specific rates changed to advolorem rates.
1996	■ Reduction in various Tariff Rates
1997	■ Rates of duty structure of 8per cent, 13per cent and 18per cent introduced. ■ Effective rates given in the Tariff Schedule itself to reduce the size of Exemption Notification. ■Tariff Value imposed for 'Pan Masala'. ■ SSI Exemption slabs restructured.
1999	■ Special Duty of Excise (Second Schedule) introduced. ■ New Duty structure introduced - 8per cent, 16per cent & 24per cent.
2000	■ Single rate of duty 16per cent introduced; this single rate is called 'CENVAT'.
2001	■ Both BED and SED changed to 16per cent. ■ SSI Exemption withdrawn for ball-bearings, cotton yarn, and arms & ammunition. ■ National Calamity Contingent Duty imposed on select commodities.
2002	■ Special Duty of Excise abolished on 6 items namely, Cosmetics, Cement, Travel Kits, Boards, Arms & Fur. ■ Duty reduced on petrol, diesel; Administrative Price mechanism abolished. ■ Duty on fabrics and garments reduced from 16per cent to 12per cent; 12per cent remain till 28.02.2005 ■ Prevailing Rates of Duties are 4per cent, 8per cent, 12per cent, 16per cent & 16per cent + 16per cent.

YEAR	CHANGE
	▪ The rates of 4per cent & 8per cent are on Escalator to reach 16per cent
2004	▪ Education Cess @2% on aggregate duties of excise paid/payable on the goods cleared with effect from 9.7.2004

Source: Budgets and Notifications of the Central Government.

Table V : CHANGES IN RULES OF VALUATION

YEAR	CHANGE	AUTHORITY
1994	▪ Filing of Price List done away (w.e.f. 01.04.94).	▪ Notfn No. 4/94-CE(NT) Dt. 1.3.94
1996	▪ Place of removal extended to Depots (w.e.f. 28.9.96).	▪ Section 74 of Finance (No.2) Act, 1996
1997	▪ Sec. 4A introduced w.e.f. 14.5.97	▪ Section 82 of Finance Act, 1997
1999	▪ Confiscation prescribed under Sec.4A in case MRP is not affixed w.e.f. 11.5.99	▪ Section 122 of Finance Act, 1999
2000	▪ New Sec. 4 replacing normal price with Transaction Value came into effect from 01.7.2000.	▪ Section 94 of Finance Act, 2000
	▪ New Valuation Rules, 2000 introduced in place of old Valuation Rules, 1975.	▪ Notfn No. 45/2000-CE (NT) Dt. 30.06.2000
	▪ Abatement allowed only for actual Cost of Transportation and not, equated cost of production as was done under old Sec.4.	▪ F.No.354/81/2000-TRU Dt. 30.06.2000 (para no.18)
	▪ Valuation on comparable goods concept done away with for Captive Consumption.	▪ Para no. 21 of F.No.354/81/ 2000-TRU Dt. 30.06.2000
	▪ Fixed Margin of Profit @ 15per cent introduced for captively consumed goods.	▪ Rule 8 of C.Ex. Valuation Rules, 2000; para no.21 of F.No.354/81/2000-TRU

YEAR	CHANGE	AUTHORITY
	▪ A new concept called 'Normal Transaction Value' introduced for sales through Deports and through related persons.	▪ Rule 7 & 9 of C.Ex. Valuation Rules, 2000; Rule 2(b) of C.Ex. Valuation Rules, 2000.
	▪ Under Sec. 4A (MRP Valuation), different MRP for different packages for different areas allowed.	▪ Cir.No. 531/27/2000 Dt. 24.5.2000
2001	▪ Declaration of Marketing Pattern abolished w.e.f. 01.7.01.	▪ Rule 173 C(3A) of C.Ex. Rules, 1944 supreseded by New Central Excise (No.2) Rules, 2001
2002	▪ First clarification on new Sec. 4 issued given by CBEC.	▪ Cir No.643/34/2002-CX dt. 01.7.2002

Source:- Budgets and Notifications of the Central Government.

Table VI : TRANSITION FROM MODVAT TO CENVAT

YEAR	EVENT	AUTHORITY
1986	▪ Introduction; Scheme did not include Machines & Packing Materials.	▪ Notfn 176/86-CE (NT) Dt. 1.3.86
1994	▪ Capital Goods Credit introduced.	▪ Notfn 4/94-CE (NT) Dt. 1.3.94
1997	▪ Modvat Credit Rules re-written in simple language.	▪ Notfn 6/97-CE (NT) Dt. 1.3.97
	▪ Invoices issued by depot, consignment agent of an importer are made eligible invoices to avail Modvat Credit.	▪ Notfn 6/97-CE (NT) Dt. 1.3.97
2000	▪ Modvat Credit Rules replaced with CENVAT Credit Rules.	▪ Notfn No.27/2000-CE (NT) Dt. 31.3.2000
	▪ Input Credit and Capital Goods merged into single set of Rules.	▪ Notfn No.27/2000-CE (NT) Dt. 31.3.2000

YEAR	EVENT	AUTHORITY
	▪ Special Duty of Excise non-modvatable w.e.f. 1.4.2000	▪ Rule 57AB of Central Excise Rules,1944
	▪ Capital Goods Credit allowed in two installments w.e.f. 1.4.2000	▪ Rule 57AC of Central Excise Rules,1944
	▪ Modvat scheme to be called CENVAT Credit scheme	▪ F.No.334/1/2000-TRU Dt. 29.2.2000
	▪ New and separate set of simplified CENVAT Credit Rules introduced w.e.f 01.4.2000.	▪ Notfn No.27/2000-CE (NT) Dt. 31.3.2000
	▪ CENVAT Credit Scheme not available for Matches.	▪ Notfn No.27/2000-CE (NT) Dt. 31.3.2000
	▪ Restriction on credit (75per cent) for project import removed	▪ Notfn No.27/2000-CE (NT) Dt. 31.3.2000
2001	▪ Special Duty of Excise allowed as credit.	▪ Notfn No.6/2001-CE (NT) Dt. 1.3.2001
	▪ National Calamity Contingent Duty allowed as credit.	▪ Notfn No.6/2001-CE (NT) Dt. 1.3.2001
	▪ Jigs & Fixtures can also be sent to job worker, apart from Moulds, after availment of credit.	▪ Notfn No.6/2001-CE (NT) Dt. 1.3.2001
	▪ General permission to clear product direct from job worker end to ultimate buyer.	▪ Notfn No.6/2001-CE (NT) Dt. 1.3.2001
	▪ Procedures under Modvat Rules relating to Dealers continue as such under CENVAT Credit Rules also; w.e.f. 01.09.2001	▪ Chapter 5 Para 3.11 of CBEC Manual
2004	▪ Service tax credit and excise duty credit integrated and extended across goods and services	▪ Finance Bill 2004
	▪ AED Credit is made available for CENVAT duty on final goods	▪ Amendment to Rule 6 of CENVAT Credit Rules

Source: Budgets and Notifications of the Central Government.

216

Table VII : CENTRAL EXCISE REVENUE FROM TOP 20 COMMODITIES

(2002-2003)

TARIFF HEADING	DESCRIPTION OF COMMODITY	REVENUE (Rs. in crores) (2002-2003)
2710.30	R.D.Oil	10255.79
2710.10	Motor Spirit	11562.82
24.03	Cigarettes	5139.97
72	Iron & Steel	5885.88
25.02	Cement	3441.14
27 (others)	All others goods of C 27	3482.52
	Cess on crude oil	4501.42
87.03	Motor vehicles for transport of persons	2451.37
84 (others)	All other goods of C 84	1911.85
39	Plastics	1858.58
27.11	Petroleum gases, other gaseous hydrocarbons	2445.36
87(others)	All other goods of C 87	1738.44
30	Pharmaceutical products	1421.00
29	Organic chemicals	1609.13
54.01	Synthetic filament yarn & thread	1304.60
2710.40	Other Diesel Oil	1351.85
2710.20	Kerosene	1390.39
17.01	Sugar	1276.52
40.11	Tyres and tubes	1123.75
48	Paper & paper board	1154.78
	Total :	**65307.16**
	Remaining Commodities :	**21795.28**
	Grand total :	**87102.44**

Source: Budgets and Notifications of the Central Government.

217

Table VIII : COMMODITIES GIVING REVENUE OF MORE THAN Rs. 500 CRORES BUT LESS THAN Rs. 1000 CRORES

Sr. No.	TARIFF HEADING	DESCRIPTION	REVENUE REALISED
1.	17	Miscellaneous Chemical Products	816.60
2.	19	Rubber and articles thereof	612.70
3.	10	Inorganic chemicals	641.35
4.	32	Articles of Iron & Steel	645.65
5.	9	Other mineral fuels, oils, waxes and bituminous substances	859.11
6.	50	Project imports	775.28
7.	6	Ores Slag and Ash	634.32
8.	28	Primary materials of Iron and Steel	560.39
		Total of these commodities :	**5545.40**
		Total of all Commodities (Gross) :	**47013.16**
		Percentage of the total revenue :	**11.80**

Source: Budgets and Notifications of the Central Government.

Table IX : CUSTOMS REVENUE FROM MAJOR ITEMS OF IMPORT

(Rs. in Crores)

Sr. No.	ITEMS	2000-01	2001-02	2002-03
1.	Petroleum Oils (Ch 27)	11249.07	6766.8	9165.91
2.	Machinery including machine tools, & electrical machinery (Ch. 84 & 85)	11070.71	10084.74	12083.61
3.	Chemicals (Ch 28 & 29)	3063.39	2793.58	3111.05
4.	Animal or Vegetable Fats & Oils & their product (Ch 15)	2324.11	4216.12	3916.85
5.	Project Imports & Baggage (Ch 98.01 & 98.03)	1674.19	1105.89	899.29
6.	Iron & Steel & articles	1851.8	1584.12	1750.23
7.	Plastics & articles (Ch 39)	1450.76	1318.86	1444.71
8.	Motor Vehicles & Parts (Ch 87)	1429.38	965.6	1227.80
9.	Optical, Photographic, Cinematographic, Medical & Surgical Instruments	981.64	1064.48	1285.63
10.	Miscellaneous Chemical Products (Ch 38)	800.85	825.25	816.60
11.	Rubber	673.41	585.07	612.70
12.	Dyes, colours, paints & varnishes	424.78	403.82	480.03
13.	Copper (Ch 74)	362.66	294.94	282.55
14.	Pulp paper, Paper Board & Articles thereof (Ch 47 & 48)	339.8	296.42	326.67
15.	Photographic & Cinematographic goods (Ch 37)	288.05	267.32	240.49
16.	Minerals (Ch 25)	222.94		210.12
17.	Ores	427.01	489.60	634.32
18.	Fruits, dried and fresh	308.1	244.71	201.74
19.	Tools & other Misc Articles	376.8	315.86	308.57
	TOTAL	**39319.45**	**33623.18**	**38998.87**

Source: Budgets and Notifications of the Central Government.

Table X : TOP TEN CUSTOMS COMMISSIONERATES

COMMISSIONERATES	REVENUE (Rs. In crores) (2002-2003)
MUMBAI (CUS)	5323.62
NHAVA SHEVA	4861.24
CHENNAI (SEA)	4566.34
SAHAR (AIR) (CARGO)	3536.28
DELHI (ICD)	3096.39
KOLKATA (CUS)	3035.48
DELHI (CARGO)	2511.20
NEW KANDLA	2347.72
RAJKOT	1947.38
AHMEDABAD (P)	1725.08

Source: Budgets of the Central Government.

Table XI : COMMODITIES GIVING CUSTOMS REVENUE OF Rs. 1000 CRORES AND MORE

Sr. No.	TARIFF HEADING	DESCRIPTION	REVENUE REALISED
1.	7	Petroleum oils (crude)	6819.50
2.	41	Machinery excluding machine tools and their parts and accessories	6094.96
3.	44	Electrical machinery	5381.13
4.	11	Organic chemicals	2469.70
5.	3	Animal or vegetable fats & oils and their products	3916.85
6.	8	Petroleum oils other than crude	1487.30
7.	18	Plastics and articles thereof	1444.71
8.	48	Optical, Photographic, Cinematographic, Medical & Surgical Instruments	1285.63
9.	46	Motor vehicles and parts thereof	1227.80
10.	52	All other articles	5193.27
		Total of these commodities :	35320.85
		Total of all commodities (Gross) :	47013.16
		Percentage of the total revenue :	75.13

Source: Budgets of the Central Government.

TABLE XII : GROWTH OF PERSONAL INCOME TAX BASE

Financial year	Number of tax payers (as on 1st April of the year)	Exemption limit (at current prices)	Financial year	Number of tax payers (as on 1st April of the year)	Exemption limit (at current prices)
1965-66	2126398	3000	1984-85	4932094	15000
1966-67	N. A.	3500	1985-86	4937657	18000
1967-68	2696407	3500	1986-87	5502142	18000
1968-69	2708464	3500	1987-88	6261465	18000
1969-70	N. A.	3500	1988-89	7883247	18000
1970-71	3230000	5000	1989-90	8583690	18000
1971-72	3012570	5000	1990-91	8934442	22000
1972-73	3208516	5000	1991-92	9391172	22000
1973-74	3388259	5000	1992-93	9671289	28000
1974-75	3460843	6000	1993-94	10450677	30000
1975-76	3637434	6000	1994-95	11668075	35000
1976-77	3796258	8000	1995-96	13208781	40000
1977-78	3778724	10000	1996-97	14094644	40000
1978-79	3955244	10000	1997-98	15979205	40000
1979-80	3969965	10000	1998-99	17578326	50000
1980-81	4175615	12000	1999-2000	21744508	50000
1981-82	4594425	15000	2000-01	25052380	50000
1982-83	4660865	15000	2001-02	28681380	50000
1983-84	4797260	15000	2002-03	34407380	50000

Source: Kelkar Committee report.

222

TABLE XIII : COST OF COLLECTION OF CUSTOMS & CENTRAL EXCISE REVENUE

(Rs. in Crore)

CUSTOMS			CENTRAL EXCISE			CUSTOMS+C.EX		
YEAR	TOTAL REVE-NUE	COST OF COLLE-CTION	COST AS %OF RE-VENUE	TOTAL REVE-NUE	COST OF COLLE-CTION	COST AS %OF	TOTAL REVE-NUE	COST OF COLL-ECTION	COST AS % OF REVENUE
1	2	3	4	5	6	7	8	9	10
1989-90	17908	148	0.82	22489	134	0.59	40397	282	0.70
1990-91	20568	168	0.81	24355	144	0.59	44923	312	0.69
1991-92	21302	205	0.95	28042	198	0.70	49344	403	0.79
1992-93	23993	235	0.98	30512	219	0.71	54505	454	0.83
1993-94	22058	204	0.93	31592	256	0.78	53650	450	0.83
1994-95	26777	295	1.10	37372	275	0.73	64145	570	0.89
1995-96	35502	335	0.94	41659	286	0.69	77161	622	0.81
1996-97	42834	388	0.91	46916	359	0.77	89750	747	0.83
1997-98	40537	461	1.14	48137	471	0.98	88674	932	1.05
1998-99	41278	505	1.22	52724	511	0.97	94002	1011	1.07
1999-00	48334	510	1.06	61981	551	0.89	110315	1061	0.96
2000-01	47565	598	1.26	68903	590	0.86	116468	1188	1.02
2001-02	40096	640	1.60	72384	610	0.84	112480	1250	1.11
2002-03	44912	425	0.95	82253	679	0.83	127165	1104	1.78

Source: Budgets of the Central Government.

TABLE XIV : INDIA'S EXPORT OF PRINCIPAL COMMODITIES

Sr. No.	COMMODITY	US$ MILLION
1.	Textiles	4800
2.	Gem & Jewellery	3400
3.	Chemicals	3000
4.	Engineering Goods	2700
5.	Agri. & Allied Products	1775
6.	Machinery	1300
7.	Leather	1000
8.	Engineering Items	1000
9.	Petroleum Products	1000
10.	Marine Products	640
11.	Electronic Goods	600
12.	Ores & Minerals	540
13.	Iron & Steel	440
14.	Plantations	320
15.	Handicrafts	275
16.	Carpets	250
17.	Sports Goods	34

Source: Economic Survey and Import Export Policy Announcements.

TABLE XV : INCOME TAX RATE FOR UPPER MIDDLE CLASS IN SOME ASIAN COUNTRIES (INCOME AT RS.5 LAKHS PER ANNUM)

COUNTRY	TAX RATE
Hong Kong	17.0
Singapore	15.0
Taiwan	13.0
Indonesia	15.0
Thailand	20.0
Japan	20.0
Pakistan	25.0
India	30.0
Philippines	30.0
Bangladesh	25.0

Source: Compiled by the author.

TABLE XVI : ESTIMATED EXCISE EVASION DURING PAST 10 YEARS

Year	No. of cases	Duty evasion (Rs. in crores)	% Increase/Decrease (+/-) No. of Cases	Duty Evasion (Rs. in crores)
1991-1992	5639	562.64		
1992-1993	5376	721.24	- 4.66	28.19
1993-1994	5286	911.36	- 1.67	26.36
1994-1995	7606	1386.03	43.89	52.08
1995-1996	7326	1345.58	- 3.68	- 2.92
1996-1997	7053	1421.42	- 3.73	5.64
1997-1998	6312	1558.23	- 10.51	9.62
1998-1999	7345	2365.87	16.37	51.83
1999-2000	5827	2812.44	- 20.67	18.88
2000-2001	5616	3618.25	- 3.62	8.65

Source:- Budgets of the Central Government.

TABLE XVII

SERVICE TAX : REVENUE & NUMBER OF ASSESSEES

Year	Services Taxed	Assessees	Revenue in Crores
94-95	3	3943	410
95-96	3	4866	846
96-97	6	13982	1022
97-98	18	45991	1515
98-99	30	107479	1787
99-00	27	115495	2072
00-01	26	122326	2540
01-02	41	187577	3305
02-03	51	224452	4125
03-04	58	—	8000 (B.E)

Source : Budgets of the Central Government.

SELECTED BIBLIOGRAPHY

Adams, D.W., 1980. "The Distributive Effect of VAT in the UK, Ireland, Belgium and Germany" Three Banks Review No. 128, December.

Ahamad, S EHTISHAM and Nicholas Stern., 1986. "An Alternative Structure of Indirect Taxation for Pakistan, The VAT", Provisional Papers in Public Economics 3 PE-86-13, World Bank Development Research Department, Washington D.C.

Ahamad, S EHTISHAM and Nicholas Stern., 1984. "The Theory of Reform and Indian indirect Taxes". Journal of Public Economics 25(December)

Alverson, Teree.,1986. "Does the Value Tax Contribute to Increase Government Spending and Taxation"?, Economic Outlook, Chambers of Commerce of the US, April/May.

Angrish, A. C., 1970. "Agriculture and Non-agriculture Taxation: An Estimate of their burden in Rajasthan", Economic and political Weekly Vol.5(Jan).

Anjanaiah, M., 1971."Do excise duties aggravate inflation?", Economic and Political Weekly (Feb.18)

Atkinson, A.B. & Stiglitz, J.E., 1972. "The Structure of Indirect Taxation and Economic Efficiency", jouranl of Public Economics.

Atkinson, A.B. & Stiglitz, J.E., 1990. "Lectures on Public Economics, McGraw Hill, New York.

Ballard, Charles L. John Kari Scholz and John, B. Shoven., 1986. "The Value Added Tax, A General Equilibrium Look at its Efficiency and Incidence", A paper presented at

National Bureau of Economic Research Conference on the effects of Taxation on Capital Formation, Palm Beach, Florida, February.

Bhagwati Jagdish, N., 1984. "Why are Services Cheaper in the poor Countries?", Economic Journal 94,No.374(June).

Birch, Melissa H. and John F. Due., 1985. "Paraguay, The Retail Sales Tax", Bulletin for International Fiscal Documentation 39, No 3 (March)

Bird, Richard M. & Malcolm Gillis., 1971. "Sales Tax Reform", In R. Musgrave and M. Gillis eds., Fiscal Reform for Colombia, Final Report and Staff Papers for the Colombian Commission on Tax Reform, Cambridge, Mass, Harvard Law School, International Tax Program.

Bird, Richard M. & Luc DeWulf., 1973. "Taxation and Income distribution in Latin America A Critical Review of Empirical Studies", IMF Staff papers 10 (November)

Bird, Richard M. & Sijibren Cnossen., 1984. "Foreign Experience with National Sales Taxes". Paper presented at 77th Annual Conference of the National Tax Association, Tax Institute of America, Nashville.

Bradford, David & other., 1984. "Blueprints of Basic Tax Reform", 2nd Ed. Arington, Va, Tax Analysis.

Brecher, S. M & Others. 1982. "The Economic Impact of the Introduction of VAT", New Jersey, Financial Executive Research Foundation.

Browning, Edgar K., 1985. "Tax Incidence, Indirect Taxes and Transfers", National Tax Journal 38, No.4(December)

Buckett, Alan,1992. "VAT in the European Community", London Butterworths.

Carver, Thomas W., 1896. "The Shifting of Taxes", Yale Review, Vol.5(Nov)

Casanegra de Jantscher M., 1987, "Problems in Administering a Value Asses Tax in Development Countries: An Overview", DRD 246, Washington D.C., World Bank.

Chelliah, R.J., 1960. "Fiscal Policy in Under-developed Countries", London, George Allen and Unwin.

Choi, Kurang., 1984. "Value Added Taxation: Experiences and lessons of Korea", Working paper, 84-06, Seoul Korea Development Institute.

Cnossen, Sijbren. 1982. "What Rate Structure for a Value Added Tax", Finanzarchiv 39, No2.

Cnossen, Sijbren., 1983a. "Harmonization of Indirect Taxes in the EEC". In Charles E. McLure, Jr.ed. Tax assignment in Federal Countries, Canberra, ANU Press, reprinted in British Tax Review N.4.

Cnossen, Sijbren., 1985. "The Netherlands", in Herry J Aaron Eds " The Value Added Tax: Lesson from Europe", Washington D.C. Brookings Institution.

Commission of the European Communities., 1983. "Competing the Internal Market", White Paper from the commission to the European Council, Brissels.

Cook, S.T., & Jackson, P.M., 1979. "Current issue in Fiscal Policy" Oxford, Martin Robertson.

DeWulf, Luc., 1975. "Fiscal Incidence Studies in Developing Countries : Survey and Critique", IMF Staff papers 22(March)

Due, John F. & JohnMikesell., 1983. "Sales Taxation : State and Local Structure and Administration" , Baltimore, Md. John Hopkins University Press.

Due, John F.,1970. "Indirect Taxation in Developing Economies" , Baltimore, Md. John Hopkins University Press.

Due, John F.,1984. "The Exclusion of Small Firms from Sales and Related Taxes", Public Finance 39, No.2,

Due, John F.,1985b. "The Retail Sales Tax: The United States Experience", in Sijbren Cnossen, Ed. Comparative Tax Studies, Essays in Honour of Richard Goode, Amsterdam, North Holland.

European Communities., (1985). "Harmonization of VAT"

European Economic Community., 1963. The EEC Reports on Tax Harmonization The Report of the Fiscal and Financial Committee and the Report of the Sub-Groups A, B and C, Unofficial Translation by H. Thurston, Amsterdam International Bureau of Fiscal Documentation.

Gillis, Malcolm S., 1985. "Summary of EEC VAT Treatment of Various Transactions", Report prepared for the Government of Canada, Tax Analysis and Commodity Tax Division, Ottawa.

Gillis, Malcolm S., 1986. "Worldwide Experience in Sales Taxation, Lessons from North America:, Policy Sciences 19, 125-42.

Godwin M.R., 1976. "VAT - the Compliance Cost to the Independent Retailer", Accountancy 87, No. 997 (September), 48-60.

Government of India (1991)., Interim Report of Tax Reforms Committee, Department of Revenue, Ministry of Finance, New Delhi.

Government of India, Incidence of Indirect Taxation 1958-59, New Delhi, Ministry of Finance, 1960.

Government of India, Report of the Central Excise (Self-removal procedure (Review) Committee., 1971. New Delhi, Ministry of Finance, 71.

Government of India, Report of the Finance Commissions, (1st to 6th) New Delhi, Ministry of Finance, (for different periods)

Government of India, Report of the Taxation Enquiry Commission (1924-25) New Delhi, 1926.

Government of India., 1992. Tax Reforms Committee, Final Report, Part I, Department of Revenue, Ministry of Finance, New Delhi.

Government of India., Economic Survey (for various years upto 1994-95) New Delhi, Ministry of Finance.

Government of India., Explanatory Memorandum to the General Budget (for various years upto 1984-85) New Delhi, Ministry of Finance.

Government of India., Final Report on Rationalisation and Simplification of the Tax Structure (Prepared by S.Bhoothalingam), New Delhi, Ministry of Finance, 1968.

Government of India., Incidence of Indirect Taxation, 1963-64, New Delhi, Ministry of Finance, 1969.

Government of India., Report of the Central Excise Re-organisation Committee, New Delhi, Ministry of Finance, 1963.

Government of India., Report of the Indirect Taxation Enquiry Committee, New Delhi, Ministry of Finance, January, 1978.

Government of India., Report of the Taxation Enquiry Commission (1953-54) New Delhi, Vol I to IV, Deptt. of Economic Affairs, Ministry of Finance, 195.

Han, Seung Soo., 1982. "The Tax Burden Distribution and Optimal Tax Rates (in Korean), Seoul, Korea Economic Research Institute.

Heian, Betty C and Terry Monson., 1987. The Value Added Tax in the Dote D'Ivoire, DRD 227, Washington D C World Bank.

Hill T.P., 1977. "On Goods and Services", Review of Income and Wealth 23 (Dec), 315-38.

Holland J C., 1987. "The Nature of VAT", Bulletin for International Bureau of Fiscal Documentation, Vol.41, January pp 23-28.

International Monetary fund., 1992. BrazilL Issues for Fundamental Tax Reforms Fiscal Affairs Department, Washington DC.

James, J.C., 1987. "Japanese Tax Policy in the Wake of the Shoup Mission", Dissertation for Part Two of the Tripos in Oriental Studies, Cambridge University Kings Colleges.

Jhaveri N.J., 1971. "Agenda for Tax base Reform, A Comment", Economic and Political Weekly, (17 July).

Khadka, Rup Bahadur, "VAT in Asia and the Pacific Region", (Amsterdam: International Bureau of Fiscal Documentation, 1989).

King, Mervyn and Don Fullerton eds., 1984. "The Taxation of Income From Capital Chicago", University of Chicago Press.

Korea, Republic of., 1975. "Theory and Practice of Value Added Tax (in Korean) Seoul.

Korea, Republic of., 1977. "The VAT : What kind of tax is it?", (in Korean) Seoul.

233

Korea, Republic of., 1980. "The Survey Report on the Practice of Value Added Tax (in Korean) Seoul.

Krugman, Paul and Martin Feldstein, "International Trade Effects of Value Added Taxation", NBER Working Paper No. 3163 (Cambridge, Massachusetts: National Bureau of Economic Research, November 1989).

Kwang Choi., 1983. "Value Added Taxation in the Republic of Korea", Economic Bulletin for Asia and the Pacific (December) 15-40.

Lane, Malcolm G and H Hutabarat., 1986. Computerisation of VAT in Indonesia, DRD-19 Washington, D C World Bank.

Levin J., 1968. "The Effects of Economic Development on the Base of a Sales Tax, A Case study of Colombia IMF Staff Papers (March).

Longo Carlos., 1986. Lessons From the Brazilian Experience with the VAT, DRD, 222, Washington DC Bank.

Marsden, Keith., 1983. "Taxes and Growth", Finance and Development, 12, PP 6 to 10.

Mirrlees J.A., 1975. "Optimal Commodity Taxation in a Two Class Economy", Jounral of Public Economics, 4, pp 27-33.

Musgrave R.A. Case, Karl E and Herman, Leonard., 1974. "The Distribution of Fiscal Burdens and Benefits", Public Finance Quarterly, Vol 2 (July) pp 259-311.

Musgrave R.A., 1983. "International Trends in the Distribution of Tax Burdens : Implications for Tax Policy", Institute for Fiscal Studies, (London, October).

Musgrave Richard & Malcom Gillis., 1971. "Fiscal Reform for Colombia" Cambridge, International Tax Programme.

National Council of Applied Economic Research, Incidence of

Taxation in Mysore State, New Delhi, 1972.

National Council of Applied Economic Research, Sales Tax Systems in Andhra Pradesh: A Review, New Delhi, 1973.

National Institute of Public Finance and Policy (1989), The Operation of MODVAT, New Delhi, NIPFP.

Nayak, P.B. & Nayak Atri, KK, 1977. "Trends, Composition and Elasticity of Union Excise and Import Duties", National Institute of Public Finance and Policy, New Delhi, August, 1977.

Nellore, David., 1987. "The Effect of the Value Added Tax Ratio", International Monetary Fund Working Paper WP/87/47 (unpublished) Washington D.C.

Peacock, Alan T. & Shaw, G.K., 1976. "The Economic Theory of Fiscal Policy", London, George Allen and Unwin, (2nd Edition).

Pechman, Joseph A. and Benjamin, A Okner., 1974. "Who Bears the Tax Burden?", Washington D.C., Brookings Institution.

Pillai, G.K., 1994. "Value Added Tax - A Model for Indian Tax Reform",Alwaye, Personal Services Sales.

Poddar S., 1987. Value-Added Tax at the State Level DRD 247, Washington, DC World Bank.

Price Waterhouse Co. 1979. Information Guide to Value Added Tax, Washington DC.

Purohit, Mahesh C., 1993. "Principles and Practices of Value Added Tax Lessons for Developing Countries", Delhi, Gayatri Publications.

Raj Hemalata., 1971. "Tax Incidence on Agricultural Sector in Uttar Pradesh", Economic and Political Weekly, Vol 6, (Sept.11) pp 1961-68.

Rao V. Ganapati & Hanumanta K.S., 1971. "The Incidence of the Corporate Income Tax in the Short run : The Case of Indian Corporation Public Finance, Vol 26 (No.4) pp 586-600.

Recktenwald, Horst, Clause., 1971. "Tax Incidence and Income Redistribution : An Introduction", Detroit, Wayne State University Press.

Report of the Royal Commissions on Taxation in Canada, Vol.I - VI, Queens Printer, Ottawa, 1966.

Sand Ford, C and Others., 1981. "Costs and Benefits of VAT", London, Heinemann Educational Books.

Sandford, Cedric., 1984b. "Irish Commission Seeks Overhaul of Indirect Taxes", Accountancy 95 (September) 83-84.

Sandmo, A., 1976. "Optimal Taxation : An introduction to the Literature", Journal of Public Economics, 6, pp 37-54.

Sarma, K.S.R.N. & Thevaraj, M.J.K., 1971. "Estimation of Tax Incidence in India", Economic and Political Weekly, Vol 6 (may 8) pp 1625-32.

Schenk, Alan, Reporter, "Value Added Tax : A Model Statute and Commentary", A Report of the Committee on Value Added Tax of the American Bar Association Section of Taxation (Chicago : American Bar Association, 1989).

Schenone Osvaldo Haracio., 1987. "The Argentinean Experience with the Value-Added Tax, DRD 235, Washington DC World Bank.

Schuyler, Michael A., 1984. Consumption Taxes : Promises and Problems Fiscal Issues 4, Washington DEC, Institute for Research on the Economics of Taxation.

Scott, Claudia., "The VAT and Tax Reform", Provisional Papers in Papers Economics 3 PE-86-20, The World Bank Development Research Department, Washington DC.

Shalizi, Z.V. Gandhi and Squire, L., 1986. "Tax Policy for Sub-Saharan Africa", World Bank, Country Policy Department, Washington DC.

Shaw, Edward., 1973. "Financial Deepening and Economic Development", Washington DC Brookings Institution.

Shoup, Carl S., 1969B. Public Finance, Chicago, Aldine.

Sicat, Gerardo P., 1987. "Adopting a Value Added Tax in a Developing Country, DRD 240, Washington DC World Bank.

Singh, Verinderjeet., 1992. Malaysia Administrative Aspects and Implications of the Introduction of VAT, APTRC Bulletin, March pp 103-111.

Slemrod, J. and N.Sorum., 1984. "Compliance costs of the United States, Individual Tax System", National Tax Journal 37, No.4, 461-74.

Smith, Dan Throop and Others., 1972. "The Value Added Tax", London; Mc Graw Hill.

Smith, Dan Throop, and Others, 1973. "What you should know about the Value Added Tax", Homewood, III, Dow Jones Irwin.

Stiglitz J.E. and Dasgupta, P.S., 1971. "Differential Taxation Public Goods and Economic Efficiency", Review of Economic Studies 38, pp 151-174.

Stockfisch J.A., 1985. "Value Added Tax and the Size of Government", National Tax Journal 38, No 4, 549.

Sullivan, Clara K., 1967. "Indirect Taxation and Goals of the

European Economic Community", In Carl S. Shoup, ed. Fiscal Harmonization in common markets, 2 Vols., New York, Colombia University Press.

Tait, Alan A. and Others., 1979. "Korea, Taxes in the 1980s", Study prepared for the Korean Ministry of France, Seoul.

Tait, Alan A., 1972. "Value Added Tax", London Mc Graw Hill.

Tait, Alan A., 1976. "Report on the Proposed Korean Value Added Tax with Special Reference to the Effects on the Retail Price Index and Household Expenditure", International Monetary Fund, Washington DC.

Tait, Alan A., 1985. "The Value Added Tax, Why and How", In 1984, Conference Report of the Thirty · Sixth Tax Conference, Canadian Tax Foundation, Toronto, pp 488-89.

Tabzi, Vito., 1983. "Quantitative Characteristics of the Tax Systems of Developing Countries", Report IMF/FAD DM/ 83/79 International Monetary Fund, Washington DC.

Tax Council (1983)Sixth Report to the President of the Republic on Value Added Tax, Paris.

Taxation Enquiry Committee Report Vol.I, Government of Pakistan Press, Karachi, 1963.

The Economist., 1984. "No VAT on Loud Barkers", October 27.

Thimmaiah, G., 1965. "The Sensitivity of the Taxes of the Mysore State", Indian Economic Journal (Jan-March).

Thon, Dominique., 1985. "Alternative Petroleum Taxation Systems : Comparisons under Uncertainty", Paper presented at American Economic Association Meetings, December.

Timmermans, Jean-paul and Joseph Ghislain., 1980. "Value Added Tax: National Modifications to comply with the Sixty

Directive of the Council of the European Communities, European Taxation 20.

Turnier, William J., 1984. "Designing an Efficient Value Added Tax", Tax Law Review, Vol 32, pp 435-472.

Turro, John., 1992. "European Community Finance Ministers Reach Consensus of VAT Rates", Tax News International, November 2, pp 911-913.

United Kingdom, 1978b. Review of Value Added Tax, Cmnd 7415. London: Her Majesty's Stationery Office.

United Kingdom, Department of Trade and Industry, 1985. . Burdens on Business. London: Her Majesty's Stationery Office.

United Nations Department of Economic and Social Affairs: 1976. Sales Tax Administration: Major Structural and Practical Issues with Special Reference to the Needs of Developing Countries, New Yord.

United States, Department of the Treasury, Office of the Secretary 1977. Blueprints for Basic Tax Reform, Washington DC.

Virmani, Arvind., 1986. "Implications of a VAT in India: The Deductability System", Discussion Paper DRD 165. World Bank, Development Research Department, Washington DC.

Vlachapapa-dopoulos, George T., 1971. "The Tax System in Greece", Studies in Tax Reform Planning, United Nations, Deptt. of Economic and Social Affairs, ESA/ECOSOC/ LI.MISC.2/ADD.4.

Walsh, Damian, "Vat in Australia? A Study of the Asian Pacific Region", International VAT Monitor (Amsterdam), No.4 (April 1990), pp 2-7.

239

Weiscoff R., 1970. "Income Distribution and Economic growth in Puerto Rico, Argentina and Mexico", Review of Income and Wealth Series 16 (Dec), pp 303-332.

Whalley, John, and Deborah Fretz, "The Economics of the Goods and Services Tax (Toronto: Canadian Tax Foundation, 1990.

Whalley, John., 1981. "Border Adjustments and Tax Harmonization : Comment or Berglas", Journal of Public Economics 16, Wisecarver, D.1980", "Sobre la Regresividad delos Impuestos al consumo", Cuadernos de Economia 17, No. 52 (December).

Whalley, John., 1979. "Uniform Domestic Tax Rates", "Trade Distortions and Economic Integration", Journal of Public Economics 11, No.2.

Wise J., 1962. "The effect of Specific Excise Taxes on the output of the individual multi-product", RE St XXIX, pp 324-326.

Youngoco, Angel & Trinidad, Ruben F., 1968. "Fiscal Systems and Practices in Asian Countries", New York, Frederick A Praeger.

❏❏

FAQs & AS ON VAT

Question 1 : What is VAT?

Answer   : It is actually a tax on the value addition made by a firm or individual on goods and services purchased from others. VAT taxes only the economic activity performed by the taxpayer as it allows full credit for the taxes paid on the inputs and intermediates and even on capital goods.

Question 2 : Is it a direct or indirect tax?

Answer   : VAT is an indirect tax as its incidence is invariably passed on to the next point in the chain of transactions. Direct taxes mean that the tax incidence is borne by the taxpayer. It cannot be shifted to the consumer. Income tax is an example of a direct tax.

Question 3 : Is VAT registration compulsory for all dealers?

Answer   : The existing dealers paying Sales Tax will be automatically registered under the VAT Act. It will be compulsory for dealers having turnover above the threshold limit to be decided by the state concerned.

Under the scheme proposed by the Empowered Committee, small dealers with a gross turnover upto Rs.5 lakhs per annum may not come under VAT. Further, for small firms and retailers, an option is available for a composition scheme, which will discharge their tax liability by paying a small percentage of gross turnover as tax. It will be applicable upto the turnover of Rs.25 lakhs as decided by the states.

Question 4 : Will the dealers below the threshold and those who opt for composition scheme be allowed to issue tax invoices?

Answer   : They will not be eligible to issue tax invoices as they are not bearing the full tax liability.

Question 5 : Is there any requirement of security deposit for registration?

Answer   : Presently, there is no proposal for security deposit, but the states are free to insist upon it if they apprehend large scale tax evasion.

Question 6 : Who will be the registering authority for VAT?

Answer   : The registering authority will be the same that currently administers Sales Tax in the state.

Question 7 : Will I be able to access the registering authority on line for registration?

Answer   : The Empowered Committee has suggested simultaneous restructuring and computerization of all Sales Tax directorates. Within a reasonable period of time after the introduction of VAT, it may be possible to register on line and also submit electronically the self-assessment returns and other related papers.

Question 8 : Which authority will administer VAT?

Answer   : VAT will be administered by the Sales Tax

directorates of every state. Those who are already registered for sales tax payment will automatically be re-registered by VAT administration.

Question 9 : **If a dealer has a number of branch offices, can he register with the administration at the Head Office and obtain branch certificate for others?**

Answer : VAT registration number of each dealer will be a ten digit unique code for the entire country. The ten-digit code will contain the state code, office code, proper number, statute code and a check code. The branch offices can function using the code allotted to the dealer.

Question 10: Is there any separate registration required for different kinds of business activities like manufacturing, trading, job work, works contract and so on?

Answer : A dealer once registered under the VAT Act will be assigned a ten digit code for payment of all taxes under that act. If taxable activities like services are rendered separately under different statutes, different registrations will be required under each Act. Otherwise, same registration number will suffice.

Question 11: What is input tax and will I get the full benefit of all my previous tax payments?

Answer : Input tax is the tax already paid on inputs, intermediates and so on. VAT is being adopted for replacing the Sales Tax system, which has tremendous cascading effect. A set off of the taxes already paid earlier will be available at every transaction point. It will give a lesser tax

243

liability with full transparency to all transactions. According to the proposed scheme, VAT has to be paid by a registered dealer only on the value addition of the goods sold by him. The tax liability will be calculated after deducting input tax credit from the tax collected by the dealer during the payment period.

Question 12: What is tax credit?

Answer   : Taxes paid on the purchase of inputs from within the state will be given the credit within the same month. The credit is available if the purchased inputs are utilized or sold during the same period.

Question 13: Can you give a simple example of tax credit and set off assuming the tax rate is 10%?

Answer   : The following table gives a simple example of tax credit:

A — Input purchased from within the state in a given month : Rs.10,000/-

B — Goods sold in the same month : Rs.20,000/-

C — Input tax paid @ 4% : Rs.400/-

D — Tax collected @ 10% : Rs.2000/-

E — VAT payable during the month (Rs.2000 – Rs.400) : Rs.1600/-

Question 14: Can the tax credit be carried over if it exceeds the sale value in a month?

Answer   : The excess credit can be carried over to the next month and even upto the end of the financial year. If there is any excess VAT after the end of the financial year it will be refunded.

Question 15: What about tax credit on capital goods?

Answer   : As in the case of input tax, credit is also available for taxes paid on capital goods. It will be adjusted over a maximum period of 36 equal monthly installments.

Question 16: Can you give an example for the set off available for tax on capital goods?

Answer   : The following table gives the adjustment of taxes paid on capital goods.

(1) Inputs bought from the state in a month	: Rs.10,000/-
(2) Value of capital goods bought from the state	: 9,00,000/-
(3) Value of goods sold in the month	: Rs.20,000/-
(4) VAT payable on Sales (10%)	: Rs.2,000/-
(5) Input tax paid @ 4%	: Rs.400/-
(6) Total capital goods tax paid @ 4%	: Rs.36,000/-
(7) Tax credit available on capital goods (36000/36)	: Rs.1,000/-
(8) Total tax credit available (5 + 7)	: Rs.1,400/-
(9) VAT payable during the month (2000-1400)	: Rs.600/-

Question 17: What is the VAT liability of the goods exported from a state?

Answer   : Taxes paid within the state will be refunded in full for all exports immediately after the end of the financial year. The exporter will have to give proof of export and proof of tax payment for claiming the refund.

Question 18: **Will input tax credit be available on inter-state purchases?**

Answer   : Ideally, tax credit should be available on all inter-state and intra-state transactions. It will be possible if VAT is the only tax applicable all over the country and the CST will be totally replaced by the new VAT system. But so long as CST continues, no credit will be available for its payment. It is a pity that the government is still not conceding this legitimate demand of the trade.

Question 19: **What about stock transfer?**

Answer   : For stock transfer, input tax paid in excess of 4% will get tax credit as the inter-state sales carries CST of 4%. This excess payment will be VATable in the importing state. If CST is abolished, tax paid on stock transfer would become fully VATable at the destination. In the present scenario, tax paid on inputs procured from other states through stock transfer or intra-state sale will not be eligible for credit.

Question 20: **Is it necessary to have the original sale invoice for claiming input tax credit?**

Answer   : The exact mechanism for availing tax credit may differ from state to state. But the original sale invoice or similar duty paying evidences will be an essential requirement for claiming tax credit.

Question 21: **Will the dealer receive credit on the transitional stock?**

Answer : The dealer will get input tax credit on the transitional stock subject to production of details regarding goods purchased on or after the prescribed cut off date. The dealer will have to produce proof of payment of the tax and the resellers holding tax paid goods will also be eligible for tax credit. Some conditions of verifications may have to be complied with for the acceptance of such claims.

Question 22: **Will I get any input credit on purchases from unregistered dealers?**

Answer : Unregistered dealers falling below the threshold limit cannot issue taxable invoices. The dealers opting for composition scheme also cannot issue VATable invoices.

Question 23: **Can input credit be claimed for imports from overseas?**

Answer : Presently the VAT scheme does not envisage extending the benefit of tax credit for the duty paid for purchase of material from abroad.

Question 24: **Can the dealer use the invoices currently being issued under the Sales Tax Act for VAT transactions?**

Answer : Since there are changes in tax rates and other details, a different form will be prescribed by each state depending on its requirements.

Question 25: **Can a dealer make as many number of copies of the invoices as he wants?**

Answer : The states may put some restrictions on the

number of copies of invoices that can be made for VATable transactions. Presently, the number is not finalized.

Question 26: Why should VAT replace Sales Tax? Don't you feel that a known devil is better than an unknown one?

Answer : Our sales tax system is an archaic one which leads to lot of evasion. VAT is the most modern tax system, which is fully amenable to automation. Sales tax does not have an automatic tax credit mechanism.

VAT is functioning well in about 120 countries and even different sovereign nations in European Union worked well under the single umbrella of VAT. It satisfies all requirements of transparency, accountability and reduced levels of tax evasion. Such multi-faceted capabilities are not available with the outdated sales tax administration. If we want to truly globalize, we have to change our outdated systems with modern substitutes.

Question 27: Will the introduction of VAT improve the tax ratios in our country?

Answer : The present tax ratio is about 14% of the GDP which is much less than the average ratio of 20% found in US, Canada and even Brazil. UK has the highest ratio of 35% and even Turkey and Australia have 22% each. In spite of the fact that our tax incidence is one of the highest in the world, the tax ratios are lower due to the massive evasion of sales tax. The evasion, according to the Chairman of the Empowered Committee, is about Rs. one lakh crore per annum. If we can salvage about 50% of the tax evaded, our fiscal deficit can be totally controlled, and the tax ratio would be around 20%.

Question 28: How can VAT neutralize the cascading effect of a tax?

Answer   : The main advantage of VAT is that the tax paid on the inputs and intermediates are given automatic credit before one pays the final liability. In conventional taxes, input tax credit is not automatic and physical mechanisms will have to be used for reducing the cascading effect. But VAT will be payable only after deducting all the earlier tax payments. In that way, VAT is a tax only on the actual value addition made by the taxpayer. Not only that, it also allows credit on the taxes paid on capital goods albeit in an installment manner.

Question 29: Is it true that the introduction of VAT will increase the prices of all commodities across the board?

Answer   : It is a misapprehension. Unless the VAT rate is much higher than the existing conventional tax rates, there is no question of an inflationary impact at the time of introduction of VAT. The Empowered Committee has proposed 1%, 4% and 10-12.5% as the tax rates for replacing the prevailing sales tax. Since they are all comparable with the existing rates, no adverse price effect is expected. Even the 20% rate proposed for liquor is consistent with the present tax level.

Question 30: What are the major hurdles in adopting VAT?

Answer   : All the major procedural hurdles have already been resolved by reaching a consensus on rate structure and other allied matters by the Empowered Committee. The basic features of VAT now evolved by the Committee will make tax rates and administration uniform throughout the country. It will be a tremendous achievement that augurs well for the fiscal health of the country. VAT is actually the best medicine for both the citizen and the states.

There are several other hurdles like apprehension of revenue loss, misplaced anxieties of the trade, etc. that possibly delay the implementation. Lack of awareness of the positive features of VAT is perhaps one main reason for the inordinate delay in the implementation. Now there is a national consensus on the implementation of VAT as it figures in the manifestos of both major political parties. Let us hope that the advent of VAT will not be delayed further in view of the promise given in the Common Minimum Programme of the United Progressive Alliance.

INDEX

ad valorem 34, 35, 184
African 27, 70
Argentina 90, 108, 239
Asia 51
Atkinson 227

Basic Customs Duties 44
Brazil 87, 99, 170

Carl Shoup 236
cascading effect 14, 38, 45, 49, 71, 83, 100
Central Board of Excise and Customs 64
Central Excise (Self-Removal Procedure Review Committee) 157
Central Sales Tax (CST) 46-47, 89, 198
Chapter X Procedure 79-80, 177
Chellaiah Committee Report (see also Tax Reforms Committee) 82
Chile 73, 94, 106
China 53, 66, 125
closed economy 20
Columbia 73, 95
compatible 28
concurrent list 31
Constitution of India 31, 39, 46
cross-checking 72, 112

deficiencies 33, 52, 71
Denmark 90
Destination Principle 19, 23, 29, 96, 98, 107
Direct tax 33, 65
dynamic economy 20

economic efficiency 21, 29, 75-76
elasticity coefficient 35
European Union 28, 96
exemption 24, 109
expenditure 118

Finance Commission 31, 99, 101
France 90

GDP 31-34, 50
General Sales Tax (GST) 46, 89
Germany 90, 170
Gross National Product (GNP) 72, 92
Harmonized System of Classification of Commodities 69

Indirect Taxation Enquiry Committee 39, 164
Indonesia 43, 72-73, 93

Korea 43, 72-75, 91, 99, 108

Latin America 51, 70

Management Information
    System 190
Manufacturer's VAT 26, 73,
    178
Mexico 108, 239
MODVAT 45, 78-86
Musgrave Commission 95

National Development Council
    (NDC) 99
National Institute of Public
    Finance and Policy
    (NIPFP) 42, 234
National Council of Applied
    Economic Research
    (NCAER) 233
Netherlands 90
New Zealand 72

open economy 20
Optimal Tax Theory 75-76
Optimal tax rates 232
Origin Principle 19, 23

Portugal 72
price effect 35, 74
production effect 36
proforma credit 79, 176

rates inclusive or exclusive of
    Tax 26
regressive 39-40, 69

Republic of Korea 41, 91
Reserve Bank of India 10,
    102
Retail VAT 27
Rule 57A 79

set-off procedure 79, 177
SRP Review Committee 42
SSI 58-59
Stigligz 236
sumptuary levies 102

tax credit 22, 29, 36, 51, 72,
    99
taxpayer 21, 65-66, 71-73, 115
Tax Reforms Committee
    (TRC) 99, 103, 145
tax relief 74
tax threshold 59, 69
T.D.S. 16
TIN 15-16, 18

under valuation 40
United Kingdom (UK) 75
United States (USA) 14
Universal VAT 14
varieties of VAT 19
VAT rates 25

wholesale VAT 27, 153

Zero-rating 24, 96

❑❑